Poetic
WONDERS

Poetic WONDERS

LEO DSOUZA

PARTRIDGE
A Penguin Random House Company

To order additional copies of this book, contact
Partridge India
000 800 10062 62
www.partridgepublishing.com/india
orders.india@partridgepublishing.com

CONTENTS

Dedication

This book is dedicated to

My Parents, and all deceased members

Of our Family.

2014/2/22 21:40

1. Lorraine Gail Marie (Sister),
2. Tony & Gertie My Parents)
3. Charles Anthony (Brother)

Acknowledgements

As an Author I wish to extend my boundless thanks to my family especially my Wife Audrey for being my Critic and for the encouragement extended to me during the writing of these Poems. During their life time, My Parents (Anthony Michael & Gertrude DSouza) who, read and whose face glowed with each completed poem.

During my School days, to my English Teacher the Late Edmund DSouza, who always had faith in me and encouraged me. In my College, to my Relative cum Professor Miss Denise Lobo, who stood by me and was always ready to lend a helping hand, guiding me and inculcating in me the love for Poetry.
I also wish to Thank the Publishers starting with Mr Gian Reaves, Ms Ann Minoza for their valuable guidance in helping me in the Process of Publishing and last but not the least all those at Partridge' for fine tuning it and making it marketable.

Foreword

Since my School days, I had been fond of poetry and often tried my hand at composing verses of my own. What started off as something fanciful, soon got into my veins, so much so that at every opportunity I got, I would scribble small verses.

Most of them were tucked away into copybooks, Diaries or put into paper envelopes. No specific intention then, just a childish satisfaction of achievement perhaps. Sadly only some of these survived. Others, perhaps like most old papers thought to be of no intrinsic value, may have found their way into trash cans.

Little did I know then, that some day like today, I would have decided to get my verses published into a book. Like I always believed, No use crying over spilt milk. As long as the grey cells were working and capable of churning out newer poetic wonders. The verses just continued. Thoughts would come at most inappropriate time and places., often when Pen and paper were not available, some of these vanished before they could be scribbled down.

I Thank the Lord for blessing me with the ability to write verses in rhyme and to convert feelings and emotions in a manner that touched those that read them. Many a time, being invited to a party unaware of the occasion for the celebration, often found me empty handed. On such occasions, a hurried verse about the Hosts and occasion would find its way scribbled on a serviette and made an impromptu gift, appreciated and treasured by some.

My Topics have never been planned, neither the contents. Just thoughts flowing as the writing progresses. Words interchanged only to rhyme.

From my School and College days, I loved to attend Elocution Contests, perhaps harbouring a secret thought that someday, some elocutionist would be standing on a stage somewhere, eloquently elocuting my creations. Composing Sagas is what I love, and putting life into simple everyday things is what I always imagine.. My verses helped me to do just that.

My intention and hope is that my readers everywhere, find my Poetry inculcating in them, the love for Nature and animals besides finding inanimate things as interesting as I did. That Children take to reading poetry and perhaps, they themselves try their hand at composing verses better than what I have done. Using plain simple language, instead of flowery words or language, I feel, touches and is enjoyed by more people instead of only enjoying a Status symbol in Libraries, Book-Stores and bookcases in homes but, forgotten after a read.

I hope that after traversing through the pages of my book "Poetic Wonders', many will enjoy my humble writings. Teachers will find ample material for their Elocution Contests and general Poetry lovers will enjoy reading these over and over again. It will be this that will be my greatest reward, and impetus to encourage me to keep writing again and again.

Chapter I

Prayerful Notes

This chapter is devoted to Poems composed

On Religious Topics in generality, in a lighter vein

without hurting the sentiments

Knowingly or unknowingly, of any religious

Order and/or Community.

(1.1)

THANK YOU LORD . . . for another Year.
By Leo DSouza on Sunday, January 1, 2012 at 11:12pm
(Dedicated to all the Old People and specially those in **PREM DAAN**-Nagpur)

All around outside my room I hear quite a din
Unable to move, I peep outside and Thank God for a year that's bin
Good to me in so many ways . . . in spite of me being tied down in bed
I Thank Him more for everything . . . specially keeping me alive not Dead.

Day after day I gazed outside and saw the people pass
Sometimes Alfred, Mrs. Smith and good old Mr. Dass.
They waved at me and threw me a smile
Knowing I too wanted to but, haven't been able for quite a while.

Little Rodger cycles by squealing with utmost joy,
Pointing to his bicycle . . . his present his toy.
A tear rolls down my cheek as I too recall
Running down the same road with Sue and all.

I Thank Him for the stories being read to me, cos now my eyes are weak
But, never once do I curse Him or think that my days are bleak
I'm grateful for Shanti holding my hand and making me walk
a bit, while Mary makes it a point daily, to sit by me and talk.

I Thank Him for my Dentures that fell but did not break
Also for moving my bowels and making me make.
I Praise him when I see across the street beyond
Little street kids enjoying their day by the pond.

My food is now very Bland but I think it's grand
What can I expect at this old age when I cannot Digest or Stand
Spicy delicacies and the like. For me Life now is a scoop
With Porridge, boiled food and evening soup.

Outside my window Revelers' sing and dance away the passing year
While I sit and think of all the good things to me that were so dear.
As a teenager I joined my group, dancing away the nights
Today the world passing below my window are my only' sights'

I enjoy this age as much as I did when I was young
Though I don't have' Glories' about me that need to be sung
I don't pity myself as often others say.. 'Poor thing'
Cannot move now and, offer something they could bring.

Why, think I, in the twilight of my days
Should I not still enjoy the sun and its rays
Marvel at the beautiful clouds floating by the silver oak tree
Changing shapes, I didn't bother, in my youth to see.

Why must I be sad . . . . God gave me so Much that wasn't bad
And I enjoyed much more of whatever I had
Our days we had no TV, Computer or gadgets of today
But we had peace and calm, coming home from a long work day

We sat around in the hall, just sharing our lives
With Fathers, mothers, brothers, sisters and wives.
I thank God Today for the year that has passed
Knowing that this year has 365 days too and won't, forever last.

I thank him for the tumor he gave me, cos I realize now,
He had a purpose that's why he doesn't tell us Why, When What or How.
I thank him for all the lovely blue, yellow, and red Pills
That have kept me to praise him . . . in spite of my ills.

When he beckons me..I know I won't feel bad or cry
Because everyone born, someday . . . has to die.
I'll just reach out my hand, in my mind and say
Lord your work I've done . . . I'm coming home to stay.

(1.2)

The 14 Stations on the way to a Fathers Love
Composed by: Leo DSouza on Good Friday 6th Aril 2012

At Gethsemane it had all begun,
Asking His Father to give Him strength and not run
When suddenly surrounded by Soldiers was he
He knew the Time had come for what had to be.

Chained and Shackled before Pilot he was alone and forlorn,
His followers now turned foes . . . one by one.
Peter too denied him Thrice, round a fire to keep from a shiver
While Judas sold him for 16 pieces of Silver.

1st Station: Before Pilot, standing, He heard the Allegations
Slapped & Abused by soldiers & Congregation
He humbly took upon him all . . . . for love of us
Without grumbling, defending or..Making a fuss.
The Mob and Pilot, then condemned Him to Death
But, from that..Did we learn our Lesson yet?

2nd Station:; Dejected and Broken, to carry his Cross He was made
Upon his shoulders, with our sins, it was laid.
His end He knew . . . but not the others
He did it for us . . . His sisters & Brothers.

3rd Station: Weight of our Sins, Bruised body, bleeding gashes and all
It was telling on him as a man..And he had his 1st fall.
He didn't mind as he was doing it for us all

4th Station: In this state . . . in the crowd He did behold
His weeping mother Mary with . . . a heart of Gold.
Longing to stretch his arms out . . . for comfort from her
He was forced to plod on, which He did without Fear.

4

5th Station: *Weak and worn now, the soldiers didn't want him on the streets to die*
They got Simon of Cyrene, carry the cross and Help him to try.
Pushed and goaded on, they were together
The soldiers not realizing, it was a Heavy Cross not a feather

6th Station: *Disturbed and Filled with pity seeing Jesus in this state*
Veronica wiped with a towel his face..And like a slate
His imprint on the towel . . . did make
He was bearing all this misery . . . for our sake.

7th Station: *Badly bruised, bleeding and now so weak*
He dragged the Cross . . . very humbly and meek
But Human that he was..He fell the 2nd time
From the road . . . his face covered in blood and grime.

8th Station: *The women of Jerusalem he consoled on the way*
They cried and lamented for him, listening to what he had to say
'weep not for me, but for your children, he said
For he knew in a short time from now He'll be . . . Dead.

9th Station: *Weak and Torn with the sufferings he Bore*
Added to the weight of the Cross, the 3rd time he fell to the Floor
Still no mercy to him the soldiers did show
Whipping him, they made him get up and onward go.

10th Station: *To humiliate him further, his garments off they stripped*
Unmindful of his bleeding body.. Which they had whipped.
Casting lots amongst them..His clothes they took
With just a loin cloth..So dejected and alone.. he did look.

11th Station: *Having reached Golgotha they decided Him to Crucify*
Spread eagling him on the cross. His hands they did tie
Then nailed . . . followed thereafter with his feet.
A pitiful sight for everyone's eyes to meet.

12th Station: *With the excruciating pain in the scorching sun.. he did hang*
While they secured the Cross & into the ground did it bang
On either side 2 thieves too they nailed and tied
It was thus.. Till the 9th hour.. he hung and Died.

13th Station: *With permission, His disciples, his body down they took*
Laying his Lifeless body in Mary's arms, for a last look
Her son whom she bore at God's will
Now lying before her.. so dead and still.

14th Station: *They took his body covered in a shroud*
to the Tomb, wove their way.. Through a small crowd
Then gently laying him down, they wept and left,
Sealing the Tomb with a huge boulder they kept.
The Romans, not trusting them, on guard 2 soldiers they left.

These 14 stations traversed, brought freedom for all of us
By a man who undertook the journey . . . without a fuss
He did it, mile by mile.. to keep us from SIN
so one day in His Heavenly Fathers house.. We may Dwell in.

(1.3)

The Bible—in verse—

by Leo DSouza Thursday, December 9, 2010 at 11:19am

The Bible—our Holy Book is divided in two
Testaments they are called—old and new.
You'll not find a Book of such a kind
The more you read—you get 'Peace of Mind'

The Bible mentions that man had far progressed
But, falling into sin often—from God's ways had transgressed.
So, to save man—His Son He decided to send
To teach man how—his ways to mend.

Angel Gabriel to Mary one day—did appear in prayer
Making her Jesus' mother—asking her for Him to care.
Joseph the Carpenter as her husband—her he would assist
Caring for them both & from Herod's threats to desist.

Then one day on a cold December morn
In a manger, since no Inns or rooms, Jesus was born.
At 12 yrs of age to the temple—Jesus they took
He got lost returning—worried & hurried everywhere they did look.

Finding him in the Temple—with High priests and elders
Answering questions & quizzing them with ease and splendour
At 32 He began seriously taking up his Public life.
Roaming and preaching, sorting petty problems/quarrels & strife.

To a wedding at Cana with Mary He went one day
The wine was over, the hosts, had no words to say.
Jesus called the servants, 12 pitchers of water, He asked to fill
Blessing these, to wine he changed—with Gods will.

Many more miracles during his life he performed
If you read the Bible—details you'll be informed.
His friend Lazarus, 3 days dead, he called out of the grave
Then calling Martha, her brother back to her, he gave.

7

He cured the sick—the blind—they could see
All men followed him—so adoringly.
The dead he raised—and asked them to walk
He soon became, of the town, the center of talk.

One day thousands followed to hear his Sermon on the Mount
No food was there—just 5 loaves & 2 fish, his men did count.
Non plussed, he bade to sit them down—one and all
He blessed and distributed—all getting their fill—both big and small.

12 baskets left—was what they gathered in awe!
Everyman believed in Him, after this miracle they saw.
Preaching the Kingdom of God & miracles kept Him in the news
He was soon proclaimed, 'Jesus—King of the Jews'

This troubled Pilot the then Roman Ruler's—peace of mind
Commanding his soldiers—for Jesus, to hunt and find.
Roman soldiers amongst the faithful—they did infiltrate
Trying undoing the good, slowly spreading against Jesus-'Hate'

Judas Iscariot to them did fall prey, we're told
Who for 30 silver pieces—Jesus—he sold!
During prayers, in the garden of Gethsemane—they arrested Him
yet, Pilot's cup was not filled to the brim.

A mock trial for him they conducted in open court
'Crucify Him, Crucify Him' the crowd began to shout.
Barnabas a thief was released & Jesus they condemned to die
Having his soldiers to scourge him, while his hands they did tie.

A crown of thorns they, on His head did place
Parading him through streets—to bring Him disgrace.
A heavy cross He was made to carry and walk
Falling thrice, with hardly any strength to talk.

Simon of Cyrene to his aid was given
While, along the way, He was whipped and driven.
Women comforted him along the way
Wiping his face, Veronica's towel, an impression she got they say.

When they reached the site at Golgotha Hill
to 'Crucify' Him was decided—Death overcomes Him—Till.
Two thieves on either side—were also nailed
While, with torments & abuses Him they assailed.

The criminals, at sunset, their legs the soldiers broke.
Jesus being dead—only his side they did poke.
His body was, to Mary and disciples, brought down and given
His disciples remained Humble, 'cos dying, his enemies were forgiven,

Into a sepulcher—his body—to rest was laid
A huge boulder, the entrance closed-and a soldier to guard was paid
Three days later—when Simon Peter, he came to check
No soldiers or boulder he saw and thought," what the heck?"

Entering he was shocked to see—only shroud—but no Jesus there
He ran in fright—wondering to tell others—should he dare?
His disciples recalled Him saying," I'll rise again on the 3rd day"
So they got down on knees and to God—to give Praise and Pray.

Others believed—after all they saw roundabout
Except Thomas—who wanted proof & had a doubt.
Our Bible tells us, Jesus to his disciples did again appear
Calling Thomas to put his finger in his wounds without fear.

Then blessings the apostles He sent them to spread his mission along
To bring, us, His children, to His father's Home—where we rightfully belong!!

(1.4)

Priestly Quest
(Composed by Leonard DSouza

One day he got down as usual to Pray
Asking GOD to show him the way,
And not on the wayside to fall
It was that day, I Think, He got his Call.

He went about his normal work
Seriously he toiled, not being one to shirk
But, one could see, he was very upset
Pensive in thought but, troubled yet.

Then next day he said, 'Mum & Dad,
Last night, A Revelation I've had
GOD I feel wants me as his Emissary
I've decided to go and join the Seminary.'

At first they were shocked and wild
For he was their only Child.
Slowly they both accepted the fact
That he, to serve GOD, had signed a pact.

Several years studies he had to undergo
Feeling blessed each passing day more and more.
With Graces from GOD, he was sustained
And then finally, 'A Priest' he was ordained.

Into the missions among the poor
He visited them daily, door to door.
He was their mentor, Doctor, Teacher rolled in one
To each home, he was from GOD a son.

Mission work of late has been taking its toll
People seeking materialistic things ruining their soul.
Political and Religious turmoil's Missionaries face.
As each Leader is in the Mileage race.

They face persecutions with each passing day
Just because they walk along 'CHRIST given way'
Sadly the youth are Career oriented more
Resulting in shortage of Priests, more and more.

Preachers & Teachers, good were, the older ones
Younger Priests, in different directions their Ideas run.
The Qualities they often lack, the youth, to inspire
Because theirs was not a 'Call' with Zeal and Fire.

With Retreats, we now hope, from youth, Priests to churn
Sadly though today's Incumbents, make it a Profession to earn
Stop and Think. How many Religious teach in Sunday school?
Giving the Laity this duty, is becoming a rule.

No 'Calls' can come when foundations are not strong
Only those making this a Profession will throng
To Parents this call goes out today
Make Daily Prayers & Rosary in each home to stay.
I'm sure God will then Bless us all
Giving us Priests with a genuine 'call'

(1.5)

"Callings": None for a Nun.
Composed by Leo DSouza

Religious Women Groups in early times there were none,
With missionary zeal, few got together, this to overcome.
Many Western devout Women gave their heart and soul,
Making Mission Work their only goal.

For the poor they cared, Lepers they attended
Broken homes and lives they mended.
Into the World, into remote corners of the Globe
A zestful Missionary garb was their Robe.

In India too many Anglo's and Goans joined
Each Congregation their own 'Habits' designed.
With their Western heads, they did gel together
Opening Schools too, illiteracy they began to weather.

Imparting Quality education was their aim it did seem
Bringing backward Indians into the main stream.
But soon times changed, there was a sudden crunch
Foreign Nuns went home, reducing the bunch.

Now local areas, they began to tap
Girls from economically weaker sections, they began to grab.
For these damsels, joining was 'an easy way out'
From the burdens of the 'dowry clout'

The ideals of missionary zeal soon took a back seat
A comfortable life they envisioned, and began to greet.
But when 'Dubai' and 'Call Centres' horizons, their attention kindled,
The influx suddenly began to dwindle.

Today the South paw is almost dry
So the focus shifted to the eastern Sky
From Odisha girls trooped in to join
Herds of them they came, for a better life, they began to, pine

Education and guaranteed meals was always there
They came with a thought; Why not give it a dare.
Soon many were on the run
Achieving the desired education, their mission done!

Convents in India, retreated back to square one
'Cos for joining a nunnery, it was 'None for Nun"
With this to Parents of Girls I appeal
Develop and encourage in them a missionary feel

Support them, if they really have a Zeal
But not to make it a 'Ticket for a free Meal'
If they have the 'Calling' of the Lord Divine
It'll help our Community to continue shine.

Not just to escape 'dowry demands' if they Marry
But if it's a "Call", then they must not Tarry.
Or find an escape because the family is economically poor
'Cos only if its Gods calling, they can do so much more..

Chapter II

Natures Delight

In this Chapter I have composed verses on Nature as I

have perceived things. Being an ardent Nature lover,

I see beauty in even the very ordinary happenings around me.

(2.1)

Bubbles
by Leo D'Souza

We experience Bubbles early in life,
As babies, we've blown it-, you, me . . . every one.
On infant's lips it comes, without any strife,
But makes the Mommies, to wipe it, run.

They are there inside me, I think
How else, do they appear on my lips?
They're always fresh—not stale or stink
Even in my feeding bottle, as I sip.

Mum too creates them, in my Bath tub
While I 'soak in', and splash around
Floating in it's froth, I resemble a 'sub'
My splashes creating them, small, big and round.

As we grow older, if blowing it, we dare
A Stern look from Dad, why we wonder and frown.
Why the Guests and Dad—at us did stare?
Did only their wrinkles cause that frown?

They're there in school—when friends of ours we play
But hiding, frightened of our Teacher, I guess
But here, No Mum or Dad at us to stare
So boldly we friends, blow in 'Recess'

They come into the swimming pool with us
Joining many others along the side.
Some burst, yet others come, without a fuss
I guess they too love the wavy surface ride.

I looked into my fish pot, just today
Saw even my fishes blew them around
Like Pearls, the Goldies tucked them away,
Beneath the leaves, each one sought and found.

(2.2)

Behavior of Trees . . .
Composed by Leonard DSouza

Have you heard of a tree speak?
It's True, so here, see How, I'll give you a peek.
Didn't you ever hear our leaves whistle?
Whether we are Bamboo, Pipal or Thistle.

Our Best friend is' wind, who hovers round
Dancing between us, without a sound.
You know, when man doesn't think of us first
We droop our leaves, telling him, we thirst.

We move our branches, as though by magic
But, not too vigorous, lest it turns for us, tragic.
When its warm we rustle our leaves
To give man & others around, some breeze.

We spread our leaves creating a shade
To protect our roots and to cool man's head
In our branches, birds seek to build their nests
So in the evenings, they can return and rest.

In return we ask them, our seeds to carry
To scatter around, 'cos we can't move to marry!
When Seasons change we are the first to tell.
We act and are looked upon, like a weather Bell.

In autumn, we shed our leaves, little by little
Not wanting our tender branches to get brittle.
With our fallen leaves, we carpet the floor
Our leaves of brown and yellow, add luster and glow.

In monsoons, our roots take up water to store
'Cos in winter, our saplings need moisture to grow.
Summer it's too hot for most of us too
The earth around our roots is crusted anew.
Just looking at us one can tell
It's changing Season, as sure as Heaven and Hell.
From Trees we get a lot to learn
The most Important . . . be satisfied, never Yearn.
Stand tall and always give
If, happy in this world, you have to live.
Like our branches spread love far and wide
Be very open, have nothing to hide.

Lastly live your life like a Tree
Give everything off you . . . Willingly.

(2.3)

Changing Seasons.
Composed by Leo D.Souza on Sunday, May 13, 2012 at 12:29am
(Dedicated to all Nature Lovers)

This Planet was created by God for us
Hoping we'd accept each change, without a fuss.
For us it's just Day passing into Night
To darkness from gradual, diminishing light.
We take these changes in our stride
Just like her Husband's home, does a bride.

Many of us just Love the winter cold
But, teeth chattering days, it's for the old.
We clad ourselves with thick winter wear
Yet, some to colder heights & winter sports..still dare.
The nights many enjoy . . . snugly clad in bed
for some others, it's shivering time . . . with noses red.
Higher regions wear, their coats of Snow
Though, not too pleasant either, are the plains below.
Winter is, December to February . . . generally
Though Global Warming's . . . changing this gradually.

SPRING when she moves in from March to May
It's here when we get equal Night and day
It's not too cold and not too hot
we Humans develop..a spring . . . in our trot
Some feathered friends this time, their nests, begin to build
Working in unison..Male and female..like a guild.
Some trees, not all, their leaves begin to shed
Creating a leafy blanket in colours of yellow, orange or red.

In Schools this time for Exams, up they gear
Kids heads buried in books, cramming, to pass this year
Knowing after this.. there's time to relax
'Cos there'll be no bags or books on their backs.

19

The days begin to warm as Earth moves towards the sun
While people towards shady trees . . . begin to run.
Days get longer . . . nights get short
Holidays are planned . . . at some or other Resort.
Beaches you find packed, all in a holiday mood
People's diet shifts to Juices and cooling food.
But, Nature for the plains, has a cruel joke to play
As water becomes scarce . . . from day to day.
Animals move and birds do fly
to suitable terrain, as water-holes go dry.
SUMMER's long spells, brings out our sweat,
Many this time they hate, others still adjusting..yet.

Like a Damsel AUTUMN comes, strolling in bold
When it's not too hot and not too cold
Remaining Nature spreads a multi-coloured carpet on the floor
Each tree lending it's leafy colours . . . more and more.
The rustle of leaves, sound, like a happy damsel's skirt
When she skips with joy and full of mirth.
Little pups enjoy among the brown golden leaves, to roll
Managing to sneak from their master's eye, reaching their goal.

Birds tweeting & chirping excitedly, knowing new foliage is near
As it happens . . . . year after year,
Now starts little raindrops from Mother Nature's eyes
As tiny little droplets falling from the skies
The MONSOONS herald damp and wet days ahead
Trees again turning green, which, till now looked dead.

Then the droplets heavier get and flow
Pit-patting on window panes and terrace floors.
Like a young dancing girls gentle steps
Coziness in bed and Romantic feelings it peps

At times it floods the roads and town
Clogging drains and bogging vehicles down
Children jumping in puddles they quite enjoy
Ecstasy written large on tiny faces all lit up with joy.
No fees or timings, for these GOD given Pools

Who cares-? If the Elite think of them as . . .fools.
Loud claps of thunder come which, not everyone likes
Preceded by sharp lightening when it strikes.
It's like the Skies too do grumble and bawl
Telling us, this Planet, has gone thru . . . . the Seasons all

Each Season brings and adds it's own charm
Picking your sagging feelings and adding, a touch of warm.
When 'one' is there, some may not like it completely so
But, when it's time, a sliver of feeling within us, hating it go.
Looking back we realize, these Changing seasons bring
Happiness, sadness, and a time to sing
The Natural beauty of each Changing Season
Gives us Hope on Earth, and to live, a very good reason.
So come spring, summer, Winter or Fall
We Love to live with you all.

(2.4)

My 'SUNBEAM'
by Leo DSouza. June 28,2013 at 3.02pm

I'll tell you a story of my Sunbeam,
As she peeps through my window pane,
Brightening my room and breaking my dream
Gently parting my curtains, an entry to gain.

A Misty white robe, is her dress
So pleasant early morning to see
Jumping from my window, tenderly my face she will caress
Shaking and cuddling, gently . . . . Me.

I climb out of bed groggily looking for her
But sadly, she slipped away.
I think, as my Milk I stir
Why does she come so, every day?

Then little Mary and Ruth in school too
Tell me, 'she' daily whispers in their ears
'Get up sweethearts' you've morning studies to do
B'fast to eat, while calling them 'sweet dears'.

Then, I knew why she doesn't wait
So many kiddies, she has to wake.
No wonder! She rushes out of my gate,
Just as Mommy brings, bread and cake.

God made 'A Sunbeam' for all of us
To brighten other's brand new days,
So we can spread Joy and Trust
By being 'Gentle and kind' always.

(2.5)

'Twilight'

Composed by Leo DSouza Saturday, December 1, 2012 at 11:10am

It's that part and time of the Day
When the Sun colours the Sky with a fading ray
Flashing vivid colours, as he dips to go
Kissing the Horizon, in a final show.

Contrasting with the twilight of our lives
Past holding 'Colours', the Present, mostly Sighs.
It's the time when, half our energy, is mostly gone
Leaving many thinking back, now, Lost and Forlorn.

Twilight to some, enthuses one last spurt
To achieve their ambitions, pulling up their girt.
Some look back, at days that had been
Of the good times, and the days they had seen.

With a contended heart, some pass the Mantle
To their Kith & Kin, for them now to handle.
They sit back enjoying, the riot of colours
That once had been, their Twilight years

Slowly they feel, time just passing by
For things 'undone', they sigh, but do not cry
With their maker, they now mentally unite
Passing in 'Prayer', their days and night

Thanking God, for their Lives & what HE did
'Cos soon, this world they know, 'farewell' they'll Bid.
Like the Sun, allowing the Moon, to hold sway
As she 'glimmers' in Hope, while He calls it a Day.

(2.6)

LYRICS to NATURE!!.
Composed by Leo DSouza Sept 4, 2013 at 13.46 hrs

Bursting thru the clouds, early in the morn,
Gently kissing hill tops, as she glides
An orange yellow dress, as she does adorn
The darkness with her sunbeams, she hides.

Welcoming the break of the new day
are insects, as they too leave their perch.
Some to early birds, just fall prey,
Others heading for food, to search.

Ruffling feathers, blinking beady eyes,
Birds early morn, the Silence break.
While lazy folks, stretch in bed and sigh,
Through windows, with mornings fresh breath intake.

Tree branches swing and wave carefree,
Exposing the mystery of the morning breeze.
Among flowers, come butterflies, and an occasional bee,
As Nature Lovers, these scenes, click and freeze.

White like cotton, clouds smoothly float,
Continuously changing patterns, against a plain blue sky.
If perchance, you're asked to vote
Unhesitatingly you'll do . . . . and not ask why.

By mid-day, on different times and seasons,
She causes and creates a new outlook.
becoming the focal of a reason,
Why the weather a change, it took.

Soothing situations, glides in Lady Moon,
Lending her translucent light to cover.
Shadows of sky's black dress, quite soon.
bringing mixed emotions, to many a lover!

To Natures Glory, down the years, many have sung,
Ballard's & Rhapsody's, in an emotional verse and voice.
Reminiscing for the old, day dreams for the young,
Poor Poets like me too, composing lyrics to her, our only choice.

Chapter III

Jingling Christmas

In this Chapter I have brought out the feeling of Christmas which touches every human being during this festive season.

(3.1)

"Gifts Santa Did Bring" . . .
Composed by Leo DSouza. Monday, December 31, 2012 at 12:25am

'Santa' was created eons ago
Ever since, he just went along with the flow.
An instant craze he is with the kids
Each year when he appears, Good tidings he bids.
His Big stuffed bag and gown of red
Is the Trademark to his name, that's wed?
I recall as a kid, he always came on 24th night
Leaving for us a packet of delight!

How exactly he knew, I wondered as a lad
Bringing the things, so confidentially told, to Mum n Dad
So familiar the sweets in our stockings we fond
Tasting like Mum's, matching even length and round.

His rotund figure had a very familiar gait
His features too matched that of Dad (A K Tate)
He brings the toys, balloons and sweets
To every young heart, that's a treat!

A Cycle for Rob, a Doll for Jane
Little Mario once got even a toy train.
Books for Sue, A guitar for Shane
How I wondered, he remembered everyone's name?

When young, so contented were we that
We never asked or expected a gift from Mum n Dad
How strange then, I thought and wondered more
That he always seemed to come to a Christian door.
Till one day, my friend Ramu said,' it just might',
That at Diwali,'he used the services of the 'God of Light'
Bringing gifts for us non Christians with his Love
And the Blessings from the God Above.

Sometimes he brought things we did not ask
'A Bottle' he gave Granny when, I asked for her a Flask.
As I grew, the familiarity I thought I knew
Sharing my thoughts & Observations, with friends only few

'Cos last Christmas, as a teen, I could not sleep
So up the Chimney & in the yard I did peep
I saw Santa and Mum in an embrace
Hoping dad hadn't seen, 'cos it would've been a disgrace!

Santa's coming always brought glee
To kids all around town and our vicinity.
He'd come with a stuffed bag, throwing sweets and crying Ho! Ho!
While kids, running behind, trying to gather more!

His real identity, in every home is a mystery
That takes him down to make History.
A days sojourn, but to everyone, himself he'd endear
Till his visit again . . . the following Year.

(3.2)

It was JINGLE BELLS Time again!!
Composed by Leo DSouza. Sunday, December 30, 2012 at 1:50am

The Air was cold and the right moods were the reason
To Herald in the Christmas Season.
Markets got geared for all the Xmas shopping
From the simplest pin to a sparkling Gold ring.

Groups of Carol Singers, good tidings they did sing
Into the Christmas mood, me and you to bring.
Christmas trees, they adorned each Hall
With buntings, hollies, balloons and all.

Santa unfolded his Red hooded suit
And polished his long black boot
His Bag of Surprises, got heavier, along the way
As he bought gifts, each new day.

His Reindeer he fed and Sledge he mended
Being alone, these things alone he tended.
Children got anxious to hear, that familiar Bell
As he approached, ringing . . . . Jingle Bell, Jingle Bell

No Church, No Pastor, ever had such swaying power
That Santa Claus has had on people, so far.
Revelers' planned and chalked things for the whole week
Fresh Avenues for outings, they did seek.

Clubs and Resorts, their Prices, up they jacked
'Cos it was the Best time they felt, to make a whack.
It was Jingle Bells time again, so smile
And Spread God's love, mile after mile.

(3.3)

'Meaning of Christmas'
Composed by Leo DSouza Wednesday, December 5, 2012 at 12:40am

When Herod decreed the death of all males 1st born
Mary & Joseph got perturbed and felt forlorn
They escaped that night, taking a Donkey with them
Till they reached, the town of Bethlehem

No Rooms they found at any Inn
So into an old disused Manger, they stepped in.
'Twas here Mary delivered her baby son Jesus
Whom GOD sent into the world, to deliver us.

The Birthday of Jesus, thus became Christmas Day
In no time, the world was in it's sway.
Xmas plans they start, well in advance
Housewives' wanting New Curtains, taking the chance.

Kids get writing to Santa, with the 'list of Toys'
A common feature with young 'Girls and Boys'.
Shops too bedeck themselves with Christmas Trees
While the weather changes, chilling the breeze.

Buntings and Twinkling Stars, hang out shimmering bright
Proclaiming to the world, Christmas is in sight.
Bakeries gear up, your orders to take
Christmas Cakes & Goodies, to order they make.

Church groups herald the Joy, as Carols they sing
Localities they roam, Good Cheer they bring.
Liturgically, it's known as 'time of Advent'
'Preparedness' is the Theme, your life to mend.

To be Pure & Clean of heart, all are advised
As 'Purity of hearts' is required, when Welcoming CHRIST.
It's the season when Friends and relatives, each other Greet
With Cards or Sweets, or each other meet.

Clubs & Hotels, plan Bonanza's of Fun
Special Menu's and events, for everyone.
On Christmas Eve, Carols in Church loudly proclaim
Joy of that Great Day, 2000 years ago in Bethlehem

The faithful, for Midnight Service, they do flock
To 'bring in' the Birth of Jesus, before they "ROCK"!!
Christmas now, has become, A Universal Feast
North to South, West to East

Christmas is all about, 'JOY' to spread
Making Jesus Christ, in all families . . . their HEAD!!

(3.4)

'Sights at Christmas Time'
Composed by Leo DSouza 17.12.13

Sometimes I walk and often run.
It's that time of the year
Heralding that Christmas is Near.

I see Painted and Spruced almost every house
Even neighbours forgetting their next door's grouse.
In the yard, little kids, their stockings dry
Their excitement, not to show, they try.

Mothers too busy with the pies and cake
Some busy sewing, others shop and bake.
Hanging around at Squares & Pubs at night
The youth plan their 'fun' for 24th Night.

I see shops decorated all along the road
With their décor, you they entice and goad.
I see Churches too join in the melee'
'Cos 'tis the time when Maximum devotees they see.

The Christmas Manger in a corner finds its place
As in Queue's to Confessionals the faithful race.
Open air services at places are even planned
As messages of Christ in Sermons are fanned.

I see Clubs & Restaurants' hanging out their Offers
The gullible they know, will fill their coffers.
I Skype Santa to see how he's doing
With Minus 23 degrees Record, says he's still shivering!

He's made a new coat and gown of red
All neatly hung & ready, near his bed.
A new coat of brown he's even painted the sledge
For his door, even made a new Wedge.

For no locks are needed he says up North
'Cos Robbing doesn't even form a thought.
In the Malls I see Parents shopping for toys
Both for Girls and even boys.

It's the time when the world wears a Festive look,
Describing it, an Author could write a book,
Hark! Christmas, I'm sure is not only about these various sights
BUT to Celebrate, the Coming of JESUS CHRIST!

(3.5)

What Christmas Heralds for you?
Composed by Leo DSouza Monday, December 3, 2012 at 1:25am

What does Christmas Herald for you?
Is it only' Feasting' & stitching something new?
Or is it 'Preparedness' for HIS Birth
That Heralds to Christians,' A New Life and Mirth'?

December Heralds the time for Christmas Joys
When kids write to Santa, for their 'desired' Toys.
House cleaning and sprucing, is now a common chore
As each one plan activities galore!

Old things doth make place for new
Everyone planning, what next to do.
The Shop's bedecked with Christmas Trees
To entice 'People', they never cease.

Stars and Buntings hang out bright
As the festive season, draws in sight.
Mother's recipes for sweets, suddenly reappear
Preparations are obviously, in full gear.

The Cake Trays are out, to clean
Ration lists contain, Chocolate tins and cream.
On Crossroads, as the signals turn to red
Gypsies peddle,' Santa Caps' for one's head.

At home, suddenly the Curtains begin to fade
Cushion covers to match, now have to be also made.
The House too screams, for a new coat
Cleaning the dust, gives you a sore throat.

Temperatures drop, but who does really care?
If' Sleeveless' is in fashion, that's what ladies wear.
The air is filled with a festive mood
Hotels & Restaurants', cajole you to try, their 'Xmas food'

On Christmas Eve, the Church bells peal
Carol singing begins, to make one X'Masy feel
Everyone's spruced up, their clothes to show
For Mid night Service, they decide to go.

On Christmas day, revelry is at its peak
Visiting friends & Elders, Greetings to give, Blessings to seek
Children anxiously receiving, their 'expectant' gifts
Their young hearts, with Joy, it Lifts.

Christmas Joy is truly 'Unpriced'
Stamped with the Blessings of JESUS CHRIST!

Chapter IV

Festivals Of India

India is a country with people culturally diverse,

Celebrating various and numerous Festivals, each having

their own special and unique characteristics.

My descriptions again may differ from other writers and

Poets who would be describing them in a completely different

perspective, but together I'm sure all would bring out

the essence of the Festival.

(4.1)

DIWALI . . . *Festival of Lights*
Composed by Leo DSouza Thursday, October 25, 2012 at 1:02am

Diwali the greatest Indian Feast of Lights
Takes Holiday excitement to all heights.
Preparations start a month in advance
Every Area, Every House, you just have to glance

Old things they make way for the new
While white-washing and painting goes on too.
Shops and Malls bedeck themselves galore
To attract gullible customers to their door.

All houses and colonies sparkle with lights
Shadow's dance with divas flickering bright
Indian houses resemble sparkling gems on earth
For once the surroundings have hidden all the dirt.

Wives shopping List's resemble a Roman Scroll
While husbands Purse strings . . . . take its toll.
Kids somehow get wind of latest electronic goods
While the more adventurous prefer trekking the woods.

It's that time of the year when
Writers and Poets like me, bring out our pen
Painting vivid pictures of happenings, to read
Of this bright and sparkling feast indeed.

Houses bedecked with divas and stars
Entreating God's Blessings on near & Dear ones of ours.
Aroma of Home sweets spread in the air
New Clothes Stitched or bought to wear.

Schools too for 10 days take a break.
So for Holidays, Peoples plans are made
It heralds a new year in the Hindu calendar
Bringing joy to households and lots of cheer.

Fire Crackers either crackle or light up the night sky
Bringing to children & all, a lot of Joy.
But Noise Pollution Rules, we all have to adhere
Instilling in children, with crackers, not to go near.

This feast keeps the Fire Deptt on its toes
Amidst the frolic, clanging bells, then off their Siren goes
Fire Tenders rush wherever fire erupts
Playing spoil-sport as the fun it disrupts

Parental guidance and control, is a must
As playing in fire . . . children unattended one should not trust.
A Little bit of caution . . . takes one many a Mile
Safety First . . . . Will always Bring a SMILE!

(4.2)

Holi—A riot of Colours.
Composed by Leo DSouza 12.02.2014 at 17:20 hrs.

Its a festival celebrated by all,
Man & woman, children both big and small.
With faces smeared in every imaginable shade
Starting with Red, Black, Blue or yellow, they parade.

To commemorate the joy of Pralahad
Saved from evil design, that Holka the Aunt had.
The Origin of this festival, it was
Smearing just Gulal* on forehaeads, for this cause

In some states this practice is still done,
While others, coloured water, adds to their fun.
It's a feast where many stay indoors
To avoid getting, with others, into fights and rows.

This is when you cannot recognize a friend from a foe
Or even your neighbour from next door.
All in gay coloured attire and abandon they roam
Drenching others with colour, outside their home.

Ladies form their own groups
Children throwing water balloons from, their hidden coup.
Bhang* consumed by tipplers, as they swoon,
Public Transports withdrawn, till well past noon.

The roads are stained with colours myriad
Somewhere more green or black or red.
If you're bold enough to venture out,
For help from others, it's futile to shout.

Modern youth indulge in even smearing silver paint
Those that don't are considered quaint.
This celeb starts early in the morn
Coming in hoards, they smear, then are gone.

By mid-day the crescendo is at its peak
By 2 pm it begins to dwindle and become meek
"Holi Hai" rents the air, all day, everywhere,
Looking like India procured a colourful Robe to wear.

---

1 Gulal = red/pink coloured powder. *2 Bhang = Local Brew *3 Holi Hai = Its holi.

(4.3)

DUSSHERA—Good over Evil
Composed by Leo DSouza 12th Feb,2014.

Dusshera is the festival of Good over Evil,
When Ravana's evil designs are in peril.
Mammoth effigies on vast grounds are erected
In papier mache, and elaborately decorated.

Being a National Holiday, huge crowds converge
To see again the Epic 'Ramayana's story emerge.
Rural & Urban people together shoulders rub this day,
Small time food thelas*, they make hay.

Prior to the end there's a fireworks display,
Lighting up the sky, in its own fabulous way.
Fire Fountains erupt, The sky sparkles in colours so vivid,
10 Headed Ravana's eyes, begin to glow red

The effigies packed with fireworks now all set,
To go up in flames—, crowds wait with bated breath.
Then suddenly with a Bang so big
The effigies blow up, The crowd in merriment, dance the jig.

The festive Curtains are now down brought
Another lesson depicting..'Good over Evil' is taught.

---

*1 Thelas = Handcarts selling foodstuff.

41

(4.4)

Ganesh Chaturthi
Composed by Leo DSouza 12ᵗʰ Feb,2014 18.30 hrs

This feast gives reverence to Lord Ganesh
Depicted with a man's Body & an Elephant face.
It's a 10 daylong Celebration
Mostly in Maharashtra, but also across the Nation.

Every home gives him a pride of place,
To purchase him, in the market there's a race.
Dancing with fun & frolic, he is home brought,
His blessings on all is sought.

Daily they perform 'arti'* and his "Puja"*
People assembling around from near and far.
On every square he is on display
Each statue dressed in fine array.

Celebrations have evolved into an entertainment
Songs & Dance, with evenings of merriment.
Loud speakers blare the latest Bollywood hits
Children even taking part in dance or skit.

Culmination of all this 10 day long devotion
Ends with the Idols solemn immersion.
It's the time of saying to him adieu
Invoking him, to come again, the following year.

---

*1 arti = Floral benediction *2 Puja = Worship

(4.5)

*1 Karva Chauth *2
(A one day Festival)
Composed by Leo DSouza 14th Feb.2014

The most solemn Custom followed by the wife,
Fasting from Sunrise to moonrise, for husbands long life.
Not a drop of water will she intake
Until the Moon she views, will she break.

To view the moon she can only through a flour strainer
The moon and husbands face together, so he better be near.
He pours the water slowly from a small pot
While she invokes God blessings, for the life he got
It serves as a bonding for the two
With full faith, no extraneous Rule could ever do.

The husband has to give her the first sip
Only then into her plate, her fingers she will dip.
Amazing to see, all wives young and old
On this custom, they from ages, maintain a stronghold.

Glossary: *1.Karva = means a 'pot'
*2 Chauth= means the 4th day of the full moon.

(4.6)

Pola—The festival of Bulls
Composed by Leo DSouza 14th Feb,2014.

Pola is the Feast of the Bulls, by the farmer
Worshipping the Bull, who works for him round the year
Mainly celebrated in Maharashtra State
Competitions too are held, with a village Fete.

They Thank the lord for the Harvest he does give,
And the bull, for toiling so that they can live.
Urban children, with wooden Bulls on wheels go around,
House to house, clickity Clack, the wheels do sound.

In villages, the Bulls are bathed and cleaned,
With Fresh Hay, as a feast, they are weaned.
A Tilak on their forehead, is put to show
How much they revere him so.

Gaiety marks the day for all
There's merriment by all both big and small.
It falls in August, on a new moon day,
The whole village enjoying being merry and gay.

Sumptuous meals of Five vegetables made into a curry
For the sweet dish, they make Puran Poli*.
A bull procession is held in the evening,
The oldest Bull honoured for leading.

He's made to break a rope, tied with mango leaves
Watched and cheered by men, children and Eves.
Following him are the village cattle like a band,
The order indicating the owners, social stand.

It's a feast held with great élan
Holding great meaning to the Farmers clan.

- *Tilak= Red mark made on Forehead * Puran Poli: Savory made with Gram flour and Jaggey*
  - *stuffing*

Chapter V

Kiddies Korner

Listening to little kids recite always enchanted me.

I always nurtured a desire to write Poetry that will

Interest the growing up kids, as well as the very young.

For ages, School going kids were always made to recite

Humpty Dumpty, Mary had a little Lamb etc. With this,

I hope to win over the kids, as well as the School teachers

with newer and interesting poems.

(5.1)

Alphabets and Me . . .

Composed by Leonard DSouza Friday, September 21, 2012 at 12:54am
(This is Composed and Dedicated against the Policy of
'Interviews for Toddlers' in Schools).

When I came for Admission for Nursery
At the Interview I was asked, if I knew A B C!
Seeing my nod, she asked me if I could recite my Alphabets
I boldly answered, Yes . . . bit by bit
Just when she thought she will throw me out
This is how I said it nice and Loud!!

Teacher taught me my A B C
But, didn't say what I should do with D
I then picked up E F G, do you know why?
Because I joined the next two and made it into HI!!

Next day I lay in bed, I was not well
So, I learnt in bed J K L
I laughed when M said NO to P
while in a Q stood R S T
While U and V did a (double u) W
The whole class was by now laughing when I said
Im ending this recitation with X Y Z

(5.2)

Cock-A-Doodle-Doo.
Composed by Leo DSouza Sunday, September 23, 2012 at 12:58am

Cock-a-doodle-doo
Asking his farmer every morning, what should he do?
He gets up daily at around five
And Thanks the Lord that he is Alive!

He jumps the fence and looks around
Everything is quiet, there's not another sound.
But he knows, to wake them, he has to crow
That's one of his self imposed and important chore.
So raising his neck he yells cock-a-doodle doo
Get up folks, I'm waiting for you!!
Ruffling their feathers, his harem of hens, cluck out first
Rushing straight to the water trough, as they thirst.

Glory the farmer's wife, getting up, switches on the light
Towards the bathroom, her, he does sight.
Cock-a-doodle doo he lets out one more yell
To wake the Cows and Pigs he has to tell
Another day's begun, then rushes to the well

Tim will now come with the water pail
He just appears every day, without fail.
In his pocket, he brings for him some grain
Throwing some in his direction again and again.
He rushes now back to the Pen
To check that left behind is no hen
Then in the Basket he gathers the eggs
Hanging each full basket on the kegs.

Bill the farmer walks through his fields,
Inspecting the crops and imagining the yields.
For the Cock-a-doodle, it's time to prune his feathers
He needs to look good for his 'chicks' mothers.
He eats his grain and scratches the ground
Sharpening his claws and picks anything he's found.
He heads behind the barns to rest
'Cos he knows in the day, there's shade towards the West.

Cock-a-doodle-doo is such an important guy
Sit back . . . . I'll tell you the reason why.
Then as he senses the sun go down,
He prepares to go on his daily round.

Hopping at the Pigs pen
He cocks his head & cockles at Mr. Ben
His friends greet him with a Grrrrunt
They know this is his own daily stunt
As he stately walks the grassy way
To tell the Cows, time to be on the way.

A cockle sound makes the hens turn their head
But, clucking femininely, follow him into the stead.
He cockles a sound for Billy to tell
Everyone's home, all is well.

That night Billy said, 'Cock-a doodle doo'
I'm so happy with you . . . .
Every morning we are awoken by you
With your signature call . . . Cock-a-doodle doo!!

(5.3)

Little Robin Red Breast..

. . . by Leo DSouza. July 2, 2013 at 3:31pm

Little Robin Red Breast
Why do you hop-without a rest?
I see you daily in my garden green
Picking little insects, your little eye has seen.

With a flip of your lovely tail
and a Tweet and Beep, everyone you regale.
You slyly and delicately pick those wheat grains
That my Mum-ma put in the sun, taking great pains.

Ever watchful of Pearly my cat
'Cos if she catches you, you wouldn't like that.
Little Robin why are you so bold?
And what in my garden, your interests hold?

It's definitely not my bed of Marigold
Could it be the Pansies, as their head high they hold?
I watch the Rose as she 'smiles' at you,
and flips her leaves, to drop the dew.

From up above the Custard Apple tree
You're being watched by Minnie the monkey.
As she comes to take a swipe
of the fruit, even though, they're not ripe.

Stripey the Squirrel, you she wants to test
Inching slowly towards your spilled grains, she eyes a fest.
Oh! Little Robin Red Breast, Hi I say
Seeing you daily, makes my day.

As I come back from school at noon,
I wonder, why, you flew away so soon.
Then I spied your nest, on the tree,
I was as happy as could be,

I love to see you bringing worms
To feed your three 'baby robins' turn by turn.
Their little 'peep-peep's', I love to hear
Now I don't let Pearly, even come near.
I just want to tell you Robin dear,
Please come to my garden, every year.

(5.4)

My Little Doggie Baby Boo..
Composed by Leo DSouza. Sunday, September 23, 2012 at 11:58am

I have a little doggie Baby Boo
His favorite toy is my Shoe.
He'll chew its laces every day
I just don't know . . . what to say.

He'll yelp and bark his baby bark
He thinks he's singing like a Lark.
He just loves to lap up his milk
Which makes his coat feel as soft as silk?

All day he searches for something to chew
His tastes are things most 'expensive' . . . too
My socks he picks and runs to hide
Impossible to find, even if you look far and wide.

At night he loves to sleep with me
Tucking himself, under my blanket, very cozily.
He nudges against me, his wet wet nose
He's my cutie pie, without saying it goes.

All my friends just love him too
So cuddly he is, my Baby Boo.
Without him, I don't know what I'll do
Cos I cannot bear to live without my Baby Boo.

When he's hungry, he brings his plate
And looking at my face, he'll whimper and wait.
Playtime he just loves to run and catch a ball
What the gully cricket boys lost . . . he has them all!!

If perchance, somebody should enter the house
He shows his dislike and gets very grouse.
When the postman brings the mail
He'll jump for joy and wag his tail.

When he wants to go for his stroll
He'll drag and bring the chain and roll and roll.
His walking time is fixed, every morning at Six
Exactly on time, in his head the alarm ticks.
In the evenings he wants to go at five
And expects that then, we should also get the vibe.

I dread to think of him grow up
Change to a Dog from a Pup
I know that as time and days pass too
Though grown, he'll always be, My lovely little Baby Boo!!

(5.5)

My School.

Composed by Leo DSouza Saturday, August 4, 2012 at 3:34pm

I still can recall my days in School
Where we were taught some Golden Rules.
My 1st Day at Nursery when I did cry
Seeing Mom leave me, I then, didn't know why?

I was taken into a room full of bawling kids
I had another idea of school, definitely not this!
I looked around at the Charts and all
I recognized 'Humpty Dumpty on the Wall"

While we were asked to sing and dance
I looked around and stole a glance
My eyes went across the road
At Urchins running after a hopping Toad.

Why couldn't Mom and Dad, like them, also let me be?
Instead of putting me here to learn A.B.C . . .
But soon this school I began to love
I felt at home like a hand to a glove.

Still couldn't understand the use of AB, C
When I could talk so fluently!!
I learnt to count from 1 to 10
What was their use. I didn't understand then.

I loved the 'Breaks' the Best
Running outside class, our speed to test.
From Nursery to KG, later we were sent
A New Uniform, my old one to a poor student lent.

Now we were a little bigger and smart
We jumbled the ABC's for a start
To spell out loud CAT, DOG and CART
I think with Numbers our teacher had a fad
Asking us to take two and then Add

Our little minds declared her mad, that's a fact
For suddenly now, she said take two and Subtract.
For Lunch break we thought we'd get a Plate
Instead, what Mum called "Tiffin", we sat and ate.

Years went by, to Middle School we went
Here these were the Best days we spent
In class at times, Mischief, without a care
Of the Teacher sitting in front, on the chair.

Breaks now were for Samosa's* to buy
Or look outside for a Girl or Boy.
We didn't like the School to end at one
Because unlike home, in School 'twas really Fun.

Our bags got heavier, it was now High School
'Concentrate on Studies' for all, was the Rule.
But, we still found time to play the fool.
To play a prank and still pose innocently Cool

Math's was now Formula's with COS and THETA
Teachers yelling, 'Concentrate Beta'
History dealt with Stalwarts and men now dead
Why did we have to memorize those dates in our Head?

Physics and Chemistry was all Levers and Acid
Some were keen, but like me, mostly Placid.
What good we wondered was Geography
Who cared if outside that was Coniferous or a Banana Tree!

All said and done, one day the Portals we left
Our last day in school we all wept.
School was where we all felt secure
With 'lifetime' friends, we were now mature!

We'll miss the peal of our School Bell
Or from the teachers, 'a shout or yell'
My school will for me forever be seen
My growing up from a Toddler to a Teen
And where my Life was molded and given a Sheen!!

- *Samosa = Savoury made of mixture of rice and wheat flour with Potato vegetable filling, triangular cone shaped*

(5.6)

My School Bell.

Composed by Leo DSouza Friday, September 21, 2012 at 10:39pm

There's no words with which I can tell
How much I loved my Old School Bell.
Hanging in a corner so alone
For years she has kept the same tone.

'Tung-Tung' in all corners she could be heard
Only Tunging, but without a word.
Living next door to School, so my Mum would yell
Hurry Monica!, 'I can hear the 1st Bell'!

She's in such a hurry, in the mornings, to Tung
Just when I step onto the staircase' 1st rung.
I think, why can't she at least let me reach
Then, let out her 'Tung-Tung' screech.

Yet when we have Hindi & Marathi, it seems she sleeps
Especially when our Homework's not done and our hearts do beep.
That's when we long to hear her 'Tung—Tung'
But, It seems, just then, she gets an infection in her lung!

Yet when it's our period to Sing
So quickly with her 'Tung-Tung' she'll ring
Even in the breaks, when we love to play
She'll break our game with her 'Tung-Tung' and to class drive us away

During Exams when our Brains go blank
Out of our Slumber, us she'll yank
For the paper we love & want to write the most
Stealthily she'll creep and ring, like a ghost.

But still we love our School Bell so dearly
'Cos she was always there yearly.
Friends & Teachers they came and went
But, she kept our time so dearly spent.

She would look down at us and stare
If, under her nose, with friends, notes compare.
But never once did we, her loyalty doubt
'Cos we knew she hung there, without a mouth.

One lesson I learnt from my School Bell
To hang around 'quietly' and never to tell
Secrets, kept in trust, and never to yell
If you want to be loved 'forever' like My School Bell.

(5.7)

My School Bus.

Composed by Leo DSouza Friday, September 21, 2012 at 6:19pm

We go to School in our school Bus
To ride in this we make no fuss.
Big lovely seats and windows too
Inside it's painted a lovely Blue.

Honk! Honk! He shouts along the road
Stopping along, for a Boy or Girl to load.
Clackety Clack his windows sound
As down the road he's daily bound.

His headlamps like two astonished eyes
As though looking for Girls and boys.
His yellow coat all shining bright
Looking brighter in the bright sunlight.

When it rains, two tiny arms wipe his face
As down the road at 10 km speed he'll race
Uncle harry who steers her around town
Is always dressed in Black and brown

When we get off, he looks so sad
He quietly goes and stands along his grey old Dad
We wonder what he does all day
While we kids in school learn, run or play.

After school he again takes us home
Then returns, whole night, to stand alone.
Like us, he has no one, of him to make a fuss
I just love my Yellow School Bus.

(5.8)

My 1st Train Journey—
Composed by Leonard DSouza on Saturday, August 18, 2012 at 2:53pm

Blowing its horn the Engine came
Bringing behind it the rest of the train.
Everybody quickly went inside
Pushing thru the door, that wasn't wide.

Our Seats on entering quickly found
Getting ready for the outward bound.
Grabbing the window seat as my place
Content & Happiness, all over my face.

Soon all the people their seats they took
For putting the luggage, under each seat they looked.
The driver then his whistle blew
The guard in return did it too.

We were now on our way
To our long awaited holiday.
Out of the window I could see
People and trees passing me.

The train began by now to go fast
Villages and scenes where just flying past.
Over bridges with Rivers below
On and On we did go,

Whooom!! Clak-tak-clak-tak-clak-tak
Another train whizzed past on the other track
Nothing inside it I could see
Because of the speed maybe.

At each station, sellers came
Selling Tea, Cold-drinks and for us kids a game
Mum & Dad had brought some food
So we sat to eat, getting into the mood.

There were other kids in the bogie too
We played with and made them our friends new.
Sleeping time so much fun we had
Climbing the berth, I slept with Dad
My brother slept with Mom he being small
Cos alone on a berth, he may fall,

Every station we stopped people left or came
All night and Day long it was the same.
The train sped on and on full speed
Like, to reach quickly, it understood our need

Beggars and poor kids came begging for alms
Feeling sorry for them, a few coins I put in their palm.
A Blind boy, with stones, played Music
And sang to earn for medicines for his mother who's sick.

Another boy cleaned the floor with his shirt
Keeping for us, the compartment clean from dirt.
In return he just pleaded for Rupees Two
As for his labor, he could eat too,
But, to give him, there were only few.

Finally we reached our journey end
Now looking to a nice holiday to spend
Outside the station, a taxi we got
And headed straight to our Holiday Spot.

I cannot blot out ever from my memory
Those thoughts of my First Train Journey.

(5.9)

My Grandfather Clock.

Composed by Leo DSouza July 3, 2013 at 1:28pm

Tick-Tock, Tick-Tock
Tick-Tock-Tick-Tick-Tock
Ticks away my Grandfather Clock.
Standing there, in the corner of the Hall,
Dark Brown in colour, and Oh! So tall.

He still has a lovely shine
As he continues keeping accurate time
At times, he lets out a 'Dong'
It's sweet chimes sound, like a sweet sweet song.
Telling me an half hour is gone.
And that I must, with my work hurry
Or at the close of an hour, I'll be in a flurry.

His Pendulum, silver coloured and bright
Swings continuously left to right
All even hear him, in the still of the night.

He's always perfect keeping time
Even though old, and not in his Prime.
He works all day and through the night
For him, there's no rest in sight.
Like a Clock, we too have to be
Always doing our work. . . . correctly.
Like him, others too we must guide
To live in Harmony . . . side by side.

My Grandfather Clock, teaches me Life
To be calm always and to ward off strife.
He's always his good old self
Never fighting, with the newer one, on the shelf.

He tells us dutifully, when to wake up each day,
Quietly hears Mother, 'Breakfast is Ready', say.
He hurry's Dad off to work
So his responsibilities, he doesn't shirk.
It's like he knows the Rule,
Telling us, when it's time for School.

We all love and follow him everyday
As he guides us when to Learn and when to Play,
When to eat, sleep and Pray.
He talks a lot, even though he's a Clock
Ticking away. Tick-Tock, Tick-Tock
Tick-Tick-Tock, Tick-Tock.

(5.10)

My Grandma's Cupboard.
Composed by Leo DSouza on Sunday, August 5, 2012 at 1:00am

Just like Old Mother Hubbard
My Grandma too had a Cupboard.
Whenever a sweet we'd want
She'd open it like a font.
I think the goodies in there grow
'Cos I've never seen her buy more.
One day I got a chance to see
When she opened it in front of me.
What I saw put me in a daze
She had been gathering things, I think, for many many days.
Inside the door were stuck pictures of us all
From the time we were Two feet tall.
Birthday cards we sent her, some years ago
Neatly piled and kept on the Cupboard floor.
Soft toys to her a present we had given
Neatly tied each with a Ribbon.
Her clothes were Oh! So very few
But, place for Jars of Biscuits, sweets and toffees too
Grandma's Cupboard was like a treasure store
Everything we wanted and even more.
If it was a cold case to me it seems
She would have had even Ice creams!!

My Grandma's Cupboard the best in the world
Had even 'Curling Pins' for hair to curl
Pretty Hankies kept in a box,
I even saw an odd of my baby socks.
Glass and Plastic Bangles of every shade
Bead Necklaces hung on a hanger she hand made
"My Grandma's Cupboard," for the World, I'll Never Trade.

(5.11)

PETA . . . my Gold Fish.

Composed by: Leo DSouza Thursday, October 25, 2012 at 11:26am

I have a little Gold Fish
'Peta' is her name
To continuously eat is her greatest wish
Her food, like mine, is not the same.

All day she swims in my tank
Up and Down she goes.
With her Golden glow, looking so swank
She just has no woes.
Her lips are so soft and cute
As my fingers, she does nibble and lick.
No noise at all like a mute
As gently her tail, at me she'll flick.

She watches from within, at little Kitty
Who too watches, in Hope and Patiently
Together staring, they make a pair, so very pretty
One full of Fear, the other with Anxiety.

Her marvelous fins, flow like a mane
With watchful beady eyes, she stares.
Swimming all day, yet her fins don't pain
I think, she searches me for comfort, everywhere.

I feed her, her pellets, every morn
She gobbles them up so very fast
Like she's not eaten, since she's born
At this rate, only a week, her food will last.
But still, her I love and will not trade
For any other Pet, no matter what
For her, 10 long years I did wait
To own her, My Goldfish and her Pot.

(5.12)

Wandering in the Woods
Composed by : Leo DSouza 01ˢᵗ Aug 2012.

This is the story of little Neharika Pandey
Who went wandering in the jungles one day?
She saw 'GOLU' the Bhalu in the woods
Against a tree. Eating honey he stood.

She spied MEENA the Tigress with her cubs
Close by unafraid grazed 2 little doves
"Smoothie' the Snake slithered under the bush
'Cuddly' the Rabbits in a Rush.

"Jumbo' the Elephant, Neharika saw, breaking branches
For herself and little Jumbo's lunches.
Meanwhile back home-Mum searched for Neharika
Who had wandered by now, a bit, too far?

Yellow and Black Butterflies she'd seen
From flower to flower, flitting for sweet pollen.
Exhausted now, Neharika beneath a tree, slept
While back home, Mum with anxiety wept
Search parties looking, her fallen hanky they spied
Then calling her name, they searched and tried
With a bunch of flowers clutched in her hand she lay
Waking her up, home at noon, they brought her that day.
Kids from this a lesson you must learn
Never to go out or wander away . . . alone.
Dangers, they lurk everywhere
You Might not be lucky like Neharika . . . that day.

(5.13)

Minnie & Rex
(Composed by Leonard DSouza)

Minnie and Rex were a Cat and Dog
They both loved eating like a hog.
Minnie a female was our Cat
And she responded to it, just like that.

Rex and Minnie one day found an old Hat
Tossing it around, they played on the Hall mat
Rex picked it up, hiding it under the chair
Making Minnie look for it everywhere.

Then Minnie would pick it up and run up the stair
In no time Rex bounded up there.
They would sleep cuddled together on a chair
Together, they made a lovely pair.

Minnie for Rex would from the neighbours bring a bone
Rex for her, a mouse would bring home.
They were a joy for us to see
Dog and Cat playing so merrily.

(Moral: Do good to others, as you would have them do to you)

(5.14)

The Clouds, Moon, Sky and Stars.
Composed by Leo DSouza on Monday, August 6, 2012 at 10:29am

Nature has endowed us Men, Women, Girl or Boy
With lovely gifts of Clouds, Moon, Stars and Sky
Unhindered we can watch them every day and night
Majestically along with others passing by.

The Sky is prettily dressed in her favourite Blue
With Clouds in Silver floating across it too.
'She changes her shades, depending on the light
In the evenings Grey and then black to bring on night.

The Clouds during day just seem to float
Creating fleeting images of a monkey, cow or goat.
They let the Sun behind them at times hide
Or move along just like on a joy ride.

At night the Moon lights up the sky
Casting shadows as across its face, clouds flit by
The moon lends its light to the stars
Making them glitter, in this Sky of ours.

To the Clouds she lends a Silver lining
Showing loving or depressed hearts a new meaning.
At times she too hides behind a dark cloud at night
But, as you look, she emerges again, looking more bright.

The Stars like speckles they seem to us
Each standing at their place without a fuss.
Some rebellious ones at times make a Dash
Leaving a trail behind, like a girls flying sash.

Young lovers seeing these Shooting stars, make a wish silently
Looking into each other's eyes so adoringly
All Stars have their own role to play without a doubt
Guiding Sailors to know their whereabouts.

God thru Nature gave us these lovely Gifts
to enjoy and admire and at times our Spirits to lift.
So let us like them also do our part
To make life better for others . . . let's make a Start.

(5.15)

The Sun.

Composed by Leo DSouza Friday, August 3, 2012 at 9:57am

The Sun he shines up in the sky
When he's up there, it's always dry.
He gives his warmth to each girl and boy
He takes no rest at all, but works with Joy.

He sends his Rays ahead, wherever he goes
Over Hills, Valleys and Meadows.
In winter, he's such a welcome Guest
In summer however, his heat we all detest.

During the rains, he wears the Clouds as a coat
We wonder what he does then, hiding about.
When the rains let up, he briefly shows his face
To get his warmth and things to dry, people race.

Seeds in Spring require him more
His heat to germinate and help their little saplings grow
His heat is used, Electricity to generate
But he being too hot, only few can tolerate.

Every evening he takes a downward dip
Behind the hills and trees and into the lake he'll slip
Colouring the sky in beautiful shades of Orange and Pink
And then he goes, for the night, to sleep I think.

(5.16)

A Cup of Tea . . .
Composed by Leo DSouza

A Cup of Tea!
How refreshing it can be
When I'm tired and feeling Oh! So weak
A Cup of Tea revives my spirits Peak.

A Cup of Tea when shared with friends
Drives misunderstandings down the bend
Executives with it, conquer many a deal
And a Bonding it makes one feel.
When someone with you Angry gets
A Cup of Tea . . . . Changes it.
Easy to make, even a child can
On a stove in a saucepan.

It's grown on Tea Estates in Darjeeling
Employment to women there, it brings.
Huge Estates on the slopes of a Hill
Growing in Climates really chill.

For those who find it hard to be awake
A Cup of Tea . . . sleepiness away it does take.
Ladies and Girls are always in confusion
Fearing Tea will spoil their Complexions.

But that's a myth everyone believes
I assure you, there's no such thing in its leaves.
Their Fields are very lush and green
Beautiful landscapes all around are seen.
Leaf-Picking time, women with baskets on their backs
Pick only the Best for the pack
A Lovely Picture, their heads popping up n down make
As they bend, the leaves to take.
The leaves are processed, dried and packed you see
Till it reaches you and me, to make,' A Cup of Tea'

71

(5.17)

Books . . .
Composed by Leo DSouza July 25,2013 11.52 am

Books have been mans best friends, they say,
But in to-days world, is an arduous way.
Our First were the ones, with Fairy Tales,
Then came our adventure trails.

Enid Blyton stories gave us the series on 'Famous Five',
While Boys on Leslie Chatteris', The Saint' series, did thrive.
P.G.Woodhouse books were there, with the famous Jeeves,
Voracious readers didn't believe then, in just turning the leaves.

'Biggles' soon were craved for, by the boys,
Girls turned to romance, graduating from dolls and toys.
Denise Robbins, Hermina Black, Ruby M Ayers, were there, just a few,
Till "Mills & Boon's' captured interest, everyone knew.

Hidden inside text books, they were found in schools,
Often breaking, the School's rules.
Earl Stanley Gardner, brought James Hadley Chase,
Della Street and Perry Mason, to crime spots would chase.

While Paul Drake would lend his inquisitive hand
Making it a threesome, in the Crime band.
Ian Fleming's James Bond Series, now hit the scene,
Demand for these, in all book stalls, a rise had seen.

To 'Famous Five' came, 'Hardy Boys' to compete,
The series of both, everyone vied to complete.
In between, the light readers, to Comic Books, had turned,
The Market got flooded, any number were churned.

'Phantom' Comics were now the craze
'Popeye', too some interest did raise.
A presence too made, 'Romantic' and 'War Stories'
Catching imaginations with adventurous glories.

Not to be left out, Magazines too hearts had won
From 'Illustrated weekly', 'Femina' & 'Filmfare', too made the run.
'Stardust' followed for the starry eyed,
'Sports week', sports lovers interest, tied.

Readers thus had a plethora of choice,
Labeling them, Good, Better and Nice.
Irving Wallace & Others were hits of yesteryear's,
Their collection was found mostly with our Peers.

Fueling the senses, were Harold Robbins and Mickey Spillane,
Though many looked upon them with disdain.
Ayn Ryand, Robert Ludlum, were not, for all of us,
Their readers, assumed a higher status.

By now the 'Idiot Box' was on the scene,
To sit with a book, now not many, were keen.
Fiction again surfaced, with everyone's sons and daughter,
Making a landslide sweep, was 'Harry Potter'!!

Readers now were found, Few and Far between,
Definitely none, who were bracketed, as 'Teen'.
However, Reading too has now changed its outlook,
Since stacking problems arose, IT Wizards developed . . . 'E-Book'.

Now thousands of stories, get stacked in just one Tab,
'Reading on the Go', emerged, now isn't that Fab?
So Books 'hard copies' or in 'E Form' will always be,
Readers can safely shed, their despondency!!

(5.18)

Twisted Nursery Rhymes in Verse!!
by Leo DSouza Saturday, August 25, 2012 at 2:44am

Humpty Dumpty Didn't sit on the Wall
Because he knew he would fall
He was watching Ole King Cole
Drunk, trying to climb the electric Pole.

The Spider had licked Miss Muffets Chair
While the Rats led Pied Piper away.
Jack and Jill refused to climb the Hill
Instead were searching for an energizing Pill.

The Bakers Man did not Pat-A-Cake
Being a Sardar, Patta Kake*, a walk he did take.
The Pumpkin was never by Peter eaten
He being already full on a plate of Biryani Mutton.

Did you know that Ba-ba the black sheep didn't have any wool?
Becos' he was Bald and outside, it was very very cool!!
Or that the Horn was not blown by a Boy in Blue
But, by the Woman who lived in a shoe?

The Gander's character was so very loose
That he ran after every little goose.
The 3 men got into the tub hoping to Rub her!!
Because she couldn't find a scrubber!

Mother Hubbard had grown old
Watching Willie Winkle nightly rob the citizens of their Gold.
Cock-a Doodle's wife swallowed Incy Wincey the Spider
Who was now spinning his web, inside her?

Jack Sprat who loved 'Fat' rang his Ding Dong Dinner Bell
While the little Maid brought her Milk to sell
Big Tommy Tucker quietly ate his supper
While Johnny put salt in his mouth instead of Sugar!!

Mary for her garden brought a bag of manure
Because the cockle shells, just wouldn't grow
Pussy Cat Pussy Cat, the Three blind mice had seen
Just where her plate of milk had been

The Queen like a tart, giving her heart for Free
Keeping her baby to Rock, on top of the Tree.
Now these Nursery Rhymes in twisted verses of mine
I hope will still jog sweet memories of Thine

My apologies to the Poets of the above Nursery Rhymes
For my liberty taken, to match Modern Times.!!

- Patta Kake= Affectionate term when addressing a Sardar.

(5.19)

Joey the earthworm..
Composed : by Leo DSouza January 16, 2014 at 1:59pm

Joey the earthworm lived in the ground,
Often Poking his head up, to look around.
The First time he came out of the mud
He fell madly in love, with the rose Bud.

He'd crawl to his aunt Moo's house
Lying still, sensing danger from the garden mouse.
Her house was there under the flower pot
Living with her children, who were a lot.

He'd slither and slide daily in the wet mud
Just to see his love the bud.
He got jealous, her face to see
Kissed so lovingly by Mr. Bee

One day his Mom crawled after him
leading him near the pond & its brim.
He peeped in, enchanted with the silvery water
But Alas! the Angler seeing his Mom, caught her.

He cried, but hid, seeing the anglers grin
He had to stay Free, or himself land in the tin.
He hurried to tell his Uncle Joe
Of Mom's plight, and to help her so.

But Joe went visiting under the sink
To see daughter Tootsi's baby, long and thin.
Joey now sat under a brick to think
His Hopes on A game plan, he had to pin.

He desperately crawled among the leaves
following the Anglers footsteps with ease.
He saw him sit beside the stream
When Joey to Mom, 'Be careful' did scream.

Then he spied, behind a rock, Toby the Toad,
Doubling his pace, to him, his problem, did unfold.
Toby said, 'Yes' he'd be glad to immediately help
Instead of waiting, to hear her yelp!.

He hopped, rushing through twigs, and bush
Reaching the stream, near the Angler, in a hush.
Toppling the tin, with a kick, upside down
As the angler cursed & looked at him with a frown.

Mom took her chance and scooted fast
Hiding under leaves, till united with her son at last!
Together they crawled away, heading home
Thanking Toby for his help, their friendly gnome.

(5.20)

My Garden Friends..

Composed by: Leo DSouza January 21, 2014 at 1:26am

Humpy is my pet garden snail
With her house on her back, and a tiny tail.
Crawling along feeling her way
Clocking just 1/100th of a mile a day.

Never in a hurry, has all the time,
Crawling always mostly in a straight line.
One thing I could not at all fathom
Seeing her pace, where did all the babies come from?

No special solutions to give a sheen
Yet, she always keeps the garden clean.
She rids the garden of the infamous Garden bug
Assisted in her work by Slimy the Slug.

Every Bird hovers over her watching with keen intent
Hoping she'll falter, eyeing a 'meal' they contend.
The small red ants is what she hates the most,
Knawing and attacking her live, inside her own post.

Zebu her friend, the squirrel, would never cease
To playfully take a jibe at her, just to her, tease.
Smiley I called Lizzy, as she'd squint and peer
Flickering her tongue, searching morsels, to swipe clear.

Kitty would gaze intently and even extend a paw
Towards Humpy, but find her too small to gnaw.
Croaky my froggy friend, would of her take care
Challenging all and sundry, whoever did dare.

Cocky the Cockerel with his sharp and deadly claws
Colourful plummeting feathers and without any flaws
Would scratch the mud throwing towards Humpy the earth
Then cock-a-doodling-doo, laugh in mirth!

My friends in the garden I love them all
In their own small way, they have a ball.
Never with each other acting mean
Their only mission . . . 'Keep the Masters Garden Clean'!!

(5.21)

A Bus Ride to an Indian Zoo
(Composed by Leo DSouza)

Two friends named Hari and Arzoo
Went for a bus ride to an Indian zoo.
On the bus were other kids too
Into their games they included also these two.
They saw passing on the roads, cars whizzing by
Stalls of all eatables and chai*.

We passed the Pani—Puri* man
Our little mouths to water began.
Thelas* we saw all laden with fruits
Gardner's from lawns, removing weeds with roots.
Tourists walking into the Malls
Roads lined with all kinds of stalls.

Reaching the zoo, tickets we bought
Into the toy-train, some seats we sought.
The Zoo lawns were oh! So very green
Bedecked with flower beds, could be seen.
Equally excited were the Monkeys, like we
Seeing them darting about, jumping in glee.
The Birds in cages our eyes did meet
Flying and chirping, each in their own tweet.
Spotted Deer and Gazelles were also there
Tigers & Lions in Cages, for those that could dare.
The Peacock his Majesty spread his tail
Dancing away following the Pea-hens trail.
Our return ride in the bus we thoroughly enjoyed
Seeing the city's lovely sights, we sighed.

There were Statues of old leaders at every square
Standing so upright, we could only stare.
The occupants were in a mood to sing
Having enjoyed the day and everything.
An aunty opened a box of sweets for us
Passing it around for all in the Bus.
It had rained near our home so it was cool
Today we enjoyed our Zoo ride, tomorrow its back to school.

Chai= tea, *Pani-puri = Small Round balloon shaped puffed savory made with rice/
wheat flour deep fried stuffed with diced spicy potato and served with Tamarind water.
*Thelas= Hand carts.

(5.22)

Pets
(Composed by Leo DSouza)

Kids love to own a Pet of their own
Unimaginable ones too with them have been known.
Mrinal in a box kept a Spider
That would walk around and sit beside her.
Nina she had a yellow frog
While Sunil in his pond a croc
Pramodh had a pair of white Mice
Seeing mice so tame.. was very nice.
Deepak had a huge Bulldog
In Tambi's backyard, there was a Hog.
A Squirrel poked out his head from Jim's pocket
The huge Alsatian of Rajesh, he had to lock it.
Manoj had a tank of Aquarium Fish
Nigel the naughty one said, "they'll make a tasty dish"
Abdul he had a pair of white Pigeons
While Suzie kept in a basket, her two small kittens.
Raju's pets were some Rabbits
Cleaning their cage, for him, just had to be a habit
Nothing to beat little Mukesh with his Beetle
That crawled one day into the kettle
The kettle was cold, that was good
Otherwise, he would have burnt his little black hood.
Dorothy would always sit and cry
Because she couldn't catch and keep her pet Butterfly.
Monica had a Parrot that talked and sang
Wanting water, his tin he would bang.
Neil had a cageful of love-birds too
Akshay's favourite was a colourful Cockatoo.
Robert had a tortoise, he named 'Slow'
'Cos it took him hours, anywhere to go.
Jaya's guinea-fowls looked lovely all spotted
While Sarah's Lady-Bug was black dotted.

Keeping Pets taught Children to be kind
To Animals and even Mankind.
Encouraged, they'll grow to love animals and save Ecology
Making for us, our World, a better place to be.

(5.23)

Cleanliness
(Composed by Leo DSouza)

About Cleanliness is very important for kids to know
To live and be healthy as they grow.
Before and after Eating, their hands to wash
Instead of saying . . . . "Oh Bosh"!!
They need to clean behind their ears and under toes
'Cos that's where the 'grime' collects and stores..

Daily Baths and change of Clothes
Saves them from unwanted sores.
'A Healthy Mind in a Healthy Body',
Is true and applies to everybody.
Washed and ironed clothes they must wear
And Socks, without a tear.
Shoes well polished every single day
Toward Cleanliness, that's a sure shot way.
Room's maintained all in order kept
Dirt from the floor daily swept.
Clothes not all strewn about
'Cos they'll be crushed, cannot be worn to go out.
Hair all neatly combed or use set-wet gel
To look tidy, so peers don't have to yell.
Cleanliness is 'the mark of a man'
So kids, just follow, all of you MUST and Can.

(5.24)

Old Grandpa's Walking Sticks

I still can picture my Grandpa at 76
Walking everywhere with his walking stick.
His walking stick was to him, like a friend
Every morning he'd take out one to tend.
He had sticks of so many kinds
Antiques some, today the likes you will never find.
A Pair of entwined Snakes with hoods that met
Beautiful to look at, supported his wobbly feet.
One with a Dogs head carved as the knob
Any Roadie troubling him would get a clob.
He had one with the Knob and tip of steel
Which he polished daily, I liked its feel
Of his walking sticks he was so very proud
New ones gifted, put him on No: 9 cloud.
Everywhere he went his stick had to go
When young, we couldn't understand the reason, you know.
Wearing a suit and well polished shoes he wore
With a Solar hat on his head and his stick he'd go
Somehow outside he had a daily chore.
What it was, no one ever did know.

One day he lay in bed very sick
But still, he asked for his favourite stick
He fondled it and held it like it was a magic wand
As he slowly slipped away, to a land beyond.

(5.25)

My Uncles Bicycle
(Composed by Leo DSouza)

My Uncle Bob had a very funny bike
I've never seen another . . . look alike.
Green was its frame and mudguards Red
His seat was handmade. So he said.
The Bell a cracked sound it did make
Yet proudly, to ride it, out he'd take
Each time he rode by, people had a frown
They wondered if, "A Circus' had come to town.
He cycled everywhere he could
Up the Hill and path into the wood.
With his bicycle he was famous you know
'Cos I saw people waving and smiling as he did go.
In the Stand his cycle would stand out
Who else would a Technicolor bicycle flout?
The only cycle with all colours galore
Even a Paint box, couldn't accommodate more.
If only 'Looks could ever kill'
It would be My Uncles Bicycle!!

(5.26)

My Great Grand dad's old Tick-Tock.
(Composed by Leo DSouza)

Adorning our Hall there was this Clock
All day-night long going Tick-Tock
In a corner it proudly stood
Still gleaming in its polished wood.
He chimed every Hour and even half
Its loud chimes would at times cut short our laugh.
This Clock belonged to my Granddad
Chiming right through each one's life it had
With a pair of beautiful hands in front of its face
Slowly moving round and round with grace.
Its pendulum continually swinging left to right
Shining and gleaming, even in dim light.
Granddad, So very proud of it was he
Those days he bought it he said for just 25 Rupees.
Our neighbours all looked at it with envy
While Granddad's face would light up with Glee.
He wouldn't part with it for any Fee
As the years passed we all found
We too couldn't do without its sound
Now he stands a Chiming Reminder
Of my Granddad, who was to us, very Dear!

(5.27)

The Big Top.
Composed by Leonard DSouza

The Big Top or Circus we call
Is enjoyed by us all
The Knife-Thrower, throws his knife'
So many things we children get to see
For just a small Entrance Fee.
Men & Women swing the Trapeze
Catching our breath, our hearts freeze.
In the beginning as we eat Pop-corn
The Animals & Artiste on Parade come along.
Beautiful white Horses
With their Bosses.
Elephants holding each others tails
All the children to regale.
Girls standing on a Galloping horse back
Steady . . . like on a Rack
Around the arena they take a round
To the Bands Music and sound.
The Clowns come to make us laugh
They make up the comical staff.
The Juggler Juggles Balls in the air.
Makes us wonder and stare.
On a tight Rope walking is a man
He doesn't fall but . . . He can

A Parrot riding a cycle is there
Dad told me, earlier this was done by a bear.
The Tigers and Lions acts were something of the past
Protection of Animals Act, removed them fast.
Camels, the kings of the desert are only for show
Here, they just walk past and go.
The Knife thrower throws his knife
The woman tied to the wheel, is his wife,
The Hippo opens his 4 Ft mouth wide.
One can see down his throat, inside,
Seeing him we get such a fright
Poms & German shepherd dogs are few
Walking on their Hind legs two
For us Children, we love the clowns
Whenever the Circus comes to Town.

(5.28)

A Pretty Flower
(Composed by: Leonard DSouza)

There was a Pretty Flower
Just a flower
I've seen
Growing in my Garden green.
Two days ago in the garden I fell, with a thud
Looked up, in front of me on the tree, was a bud.
Everyday as her I would see
She grew bigger & bigger steadily.
Visited by bees and butterflies
She grew into a pretty flower so coy.
In her yellow dress she outshone
Around her, her sisters, different colours adorned.
One day a Party she had
All the flowers were so glad.
The Roses came out in Red, Pink and White
Making with others, such a lovely sight.
Marigolds in Orange and Yellow too
Swaying together were the Hollies few.
It was the season for Pom-Poms to show their head
With their little hair like bristles, they shyly said,
"Wow, so lovely to see all my friends'
A Day together, it's lovely to spend.
The Bougainvilleas' with their arms so long
Watched to see who's coming along!
My Pretty Flower so happy, she wanted more
To come to this her Garden Show.
They all said that they were sad
When Humans acted so bad.
Breaking them for Pooja and Altars everyday
Which God to do this, to them did ever say
They did express
In utter distress

Man from other's gardens rob us with ease
With 'Robbed Flowers' their God to appease
Which God taught to 'ROB", they demanded to know?
For GOD himself created us, our beauty to show.
They felt that when they dutifully grow
Why cannot 'man' on them some mercy show?
The Flowers appeal to the kids in school
Their thoughts to pool
Educate the elders and make a Rule
Not to do the same and only themselves fool.
For God created Nature to live alongside man
If all try, they definitely can!

(5.29)

A cheeky little Rat.
Composed by Leo DSouza on 3rd Feb 2014 7.30 pm.

I've been called a Cheeky little rat,
Mortally scared of Tommy the Cat.
I used to nibble at everything that,
I saw even the House Master Robby's hat!

I would love to roam especially at night
With no worry of having to scamper with fright.
Under the table and places where there's no light.
Just so I could get something for a bite.

I didn't like the injustice to me shown
When here itself I was bred and grown.
Yet seeing me they let out a shriek
At these times I felt, Life was so bleak.

I would quietly from my hideout . . . eye,
Toby, the house dog's plate . . . you know why?
'Cos that's where I could quietly sneak
And Grab a quick morsel, so to speak.

My favourite was to dart near Jeremy the kid
Grabbing his cube of cheese and which in my Hole I hid.
Among the old cushions, my home, in the Attic
I felt very comfy and ecstatic.

I enjoyed when the Master Robby me, tried to chase
Seeing me darting, he got all red in the face.
Then there was the buxom Bella a grumpy maid
Looking brazen but, inside was very afraid.

But alas I too have now grown old
The house now deserted, long back being sold.
I too now await morsels my Grandkids bring
As memories of the past, a bell will ring.

(5.30)

Pitter-Patter Rain
Composed by Leo Dsouza July 16, 2013 at 5.26 pm

Rain Oh! Rain, my Pitter-Patter Rain
Falling from high, yet you feel no pain.
So pure are your drops and so so clean
Like transparent silver balls, how innocent they seem

Each singing their own tune . . . Pit-pit-pat
Music to everyone's ears, I'm sure of that.
So soothing it's to hear your drizzle
Falling from roof tops, to form a trickle.

Pitter—Patter, Pitter-Patter, unmindful are you,
Falling and dampening everything, old and new.
Rain-Oh! Rain, my pitter—patter rain
Some enjoy, others think you are a pain.

From the preceding heat, you bring such relief
In joy, sprouting from the trees, come a new new leaf.
Your presence, entices some to stay on in bed
Cuddled up, specially the newly wed.

Kids they love to go out and get wet
Specially, when parents, are not home yet.
Pitter patter, Pitter Patter, as you continue to fall
Drenching people, from top to toe . . . . all.

The animals quiver their coats, now and then,
to shake their wetness off, caused by you the Rain.
Birds too with a watchful eye look out
For that courageous worm, be it thin or stout.

Frogs and Toads, you, a guttural welcome give
'Cos, this is the season, for which they live.
This is the time of year, when clothes don't quick dry
And kids on purpose don't try to be dry.

93

The potholes, they seem to disappear,
I'm sure, it's you they fear.
So tempting on the road, the little puddles seem
Splassssh! Splasssh! a passing car, makes you scream!

Your intensity sometimes a hurdle does create
When to appointments, people get late.
The roads a silvery clean look do sport
As though they've been given, a fresh new coat.

Rivers this time, speed up their flow
Banks, giving more space, for the water to go.
But, when you come down, steady and strong,
On the banks, people hesitate to throng.

To give you company, Thunderous clouds, they Roar,
While Lightening Bolts, spark the skyline, more and more.
Your Pitter-Patter, Pitter Patter still, to hear is a pleasure
For farmers, your coming, is a treasure.

While weathermen go out, to measure your fall,
For sports lovers, it's the time for Football.
Rain Oh! Rain, my Pitter-Patter Rain,
we look and long for you, year after year, again and again.

Like other Seasons, you too, teach us,
EQUALITY, falling on everyone, without a fuss.
No Caste or Creed, matter to you ever,
I hope, to emulate you, man too will Endeavour.

(5.31)

Clap . . . Clap . . . Clap . . .
Composed by Leo Dsouza July 21, 2013 at 6.38 pm

Clap . . . . Clap . . . . Clap,
Every Girl and Boy.
Clap . . . . Clap . . . . Clap
To show your JOY.

Clap your hands for all that's good
Clap yourself into a mood.
Life is full of so much Fun,
If only you Clap,.. yes Clap, everyone!

Clap . . . Clap . . . . Clap
Every Girl and Boy.
Clap . . . . Clap . . . . Clap,
To show your Joy.

Now Smile . . . . Smile . . . . Smile,
Every Boy and Girl.
Smile . . . . smile . . . . Smile,
'Cos a smile, drives away a Surl.

Put on a smile, whatever you do,
You'll find the work enjoyable too.
Wear your Smile, everyday in Life,
It cuts through barriers, like a knife.

So Smile . . . . Smile . . . . Smile,
Every Boy and Girl.
Smile . . . . Smile . . . . Smile,
'Cos a Smile drives away a Surl.

Now Clap your hands and stamp your Feet,
Offer your Smile, as new people you meet.
These in addition, to good things you do and talk,
Making Friends then, will be just a Cake-Walk.

So Clap your Hands, Stamp your Feet,
Add your Smile, and you'll always meet,
Success. As you walk life's mile,
Driving away Hatred, . . . if even for a while.

So wear your Smile and Clap . . . . Clap . . . . Clap,
You'll be a light hearted chap!
Stamp your Feet and Talk . . . . Talk . . . . Talk,
You'll never be alone, in this world, ever to walk!!!

So, Clap . . . . Clap . . . . Clap
and Smile . . . . smile . . . . smile
Remember good things, as you Talk . . . . Talk . . . . Talk,
You'll always have company, as you, Walk . . . . Walk . . . . Walk!!

(5.32)

Plight of a School Girl!
(Composed by Leo DSouza)

My life has been in such a mess
When you hear all, you'll agree with a 'Yes'.
First I got no choice to choose my Mom and Dad
And if you think,' that's not bad'
Just hear about the childhood I had.
Because I was a girl, I could not wear a Pant
Without my mother, 'rave and rant'!
I loved to play with Guns and Cars but, was given a doll
Was not even allowed to play 'Football'
By Mom I was told when growing,' stay far from Boys
'Cos they are rough and will make you cry.
A little older and she said,' Beware of Boys'!!
You are growing and should know the 'what's and 'why's!
Now, this I didn't understand why
'Cos I'm sure years ago, Mum was a girl and Dad a Boy!!
And if Mum didn't follow it . . . then why should I?

Which school I wanted to go to, they never did ask
Was it for them such a difficult task?
Like a lamb quietly followed their choice
Never getting a chance, my Opinion to voice.

Now in school, Oh! My God! What Pressure!
For every mischief I did, my mother, I had to fetch her.
I never understood in Nursery why the teacher insist I sing and dance
When in actuality, outside I wanted to prance.
In KG I was asked to 'say' my tables, if I could
I look around, all the tables in class, had no mouth but made of wood!
Each time the Bell did ring
Out another textbook the teacher would bring.

We'd just get used to the new one
When the Bell rings again, she'd say, its break time outside run.
Now break time I understood differently
Not finding anything else I'd break from the garden a tree.
Entering the class my classmates the teacher told
I was always the only one, in the corner, my ears I'd hold.
The higher classes I had a little more fun
With a magnifying glass and ray's of the sun.

Now in Middle and High school, no spare moments we had it seems
Forever for some function forming some or other Teams.
From the 1st day there's always some function or other
For Studies the Teachers didn't, so why should we bother.
At the Investiture a Cabinet team we'd install, with great Fuss
Later those ungrateful girls would, only us boss!!

We had So many extracurricular activities in our school
No time for studies, but plenty to play the fool.
We have Mothers Day, where moms of all ages come that day
What we don't do at home, we have to for them dance and sway.
Then on Father's day we see so many doting Dads
Each coming with their own Fads!
Grandparents Day we see the old come wobbling into the Hall
Thank God! We didn't have to provide Rocking Chairs for all.
Rickshaw wallahs day we see these days just a few
Imagine us dancing for them, like we are 'performing animals' in a zoo.
Being in a Convent, we have Nun's Birthdays and Feast to celebrate
As though we don't have enough on our Entertainment plate!
Who wants to be stuck in Stalls at the fancy Fete?
When more interesting happenings are at the Gate!

Oh! I forgot we also have the Republic Day Parade on K P Ground
So many leave from class but only half reach the Ground.
Independence Day we in school hoist the Flag
Thank God that day . . . . No Bag!
Our Sports day takes so much of our time from our Hand
What Charm the school gets from it we don't understand
We are made to March Past the crowd all ogling at us
Then expected to run races like slaves in Roman times, without a fuss
The PT is so colorful, that's a fact
Just to highlight our acumen, the PT Instructor maybe, lacked.
At Times the ZP authorities decide we must attend a rally
Walking down in the sun and narrow alley
Often the teachers are sent on Training or Election Work
The School stands still 'cos on duty is only some Peons and Office Clerk
By the time all this is over its nearing March end
Tuitions is the only way out now for this mess to end
When will our Government let our Teachers, teach?
Or will our Education Deptt only fresh ideas Preach?
God save us students and our plight
Now tell me . . . wasn't I right?

(5.33)

Circuses, have their charm . . .
Composed. by Leo DSouza. July 23,2013 at 2.43 am

A Circus had come to town,
With a huge big tent of brown.
Animals like Horses, Elephants and Doggies too,
Camels, Ducks, monkeys and a Cockatoo.

Bhalu the Bear would stare with his round beady eyes,
The Great Hippo so huge, thick folds on his thighs.
Moti the Pomeranian dog, on a bicycle,
While the Cockatoo, feigning to be ill.

Monkeys were there, a Rickshaw to ride,
Elephants, a game of Football, they tried.
The Children with joy all clapped,
As each Clown, another's back he slapped.

When a Circus comes to town, all enthusiastic they will be,
Children worry Parents, to take them to see.
On their minds is also Pop-Corn and Monkey Nuts to chew,
Ice-Cream and & Ice-Gola's* sometimes too.

The Trapeze act is frightening, kids say for us,
'Cos they swing across without a fuss.
As they put the lights off we see,
Men and women, swinging end to end so fearlessly

Dressed in Luminous suits, a sight to Behold,
It's the Pinnacle of Acrobatics . . . . worth in Gold.
The Human Cannon and Well of Death,
Makes one and all . . . hold their breath.

At the Beginning, in full attire, is the Regal Ramp show,
Men and Animals come with Fanfare, take a round and go.
The Tigers and Lions are missed these days,
Funny are the Animal Activists and their ways.

Here was a Source, when Animals who were aged,
Got at least 2 square meals, even though they were caged.
Instead they today, they are kept in the zoos,
Where youth Harass, Half starved, and in full Public View.

A lot of Circuses have lost their charm of old,
Struggling to Pay artists or even them to hold.
A day, will not be far I think,
When the Big Top will permanent into the quagmire of this world
sink.

(5.34)

My Magical Tree.
Composed by Leo DSouza June 23, 2013 at 14.20 hrs
(A little Childs Dream)

Last night I slept and a dream, I dreamed
Making me smile, everything, so real.. it seemed.
Just outside my window sill I saw,
Tweeting and Chirping, Sparrows and Robins, singing galore!

Shifting my eyes—Oh! what lovely trees
Hanging on branches were 'sweets and Toffee's'
Fruits like apples and Mango's, all on a single tree
Bringing smiles in my sleep, I even saw a bumble bee.

Excited I was, for other branches even had toys
Different things for Girls and little Boys.
I saw 'Spiderman' and 'Harry Potter' having a chat
'Robin hood' too, with his beautiful Top-hat.

'Tweety Birds' singing a melodious song
with 'Angry Birds' just flying along.
What a wonderful tree I thought I had
Everything 'good' and nothing 'bad'

No markets to go, where Prices are hiked
Just have to stretch my hand, pluck what I liked.
I saw Dolls for sister Betsy, which she loves
Even what I wanted, a pair of 'doves'

'Coke Bottles' hung there with packets of 'Lays'
'Biscuits & Chocolates' with 'Corns of Maize'
This tree was like a little 'Super Bazaar'
Everything so close . . . nothing seemed very far.

Suddenly I heard a 'bang' so loud
I felt some droplets, like rain from a cloud.
I slowly opened my eyes and looked around
I had fallen from the bed . . . on the ground.

My glass of water had spilled on my face
My dream shattered . . . I was in a daze.
Gone too was . . . . my 'Magical Tree'
How I hoped and longed . . . . it, like that, could be.

Chapter VI

Giggles

I always believe that a reader must be given a variety of poetry,

instead of following only a stereotype pattern of writing.

I therefore decided to tickle the taste buds of all kinds of Readers.

I have taken the most ordinary things in one's day to day life and

given them a very humorous twist, so that they can be enjoyed by all.

I Sincerely hope that my efforts will bring a smile of appreciation

on the faces of my readers.

(6.1)

Animals 'Thoughts' on Man!!
Composed by Leo DSouza Thursday, October 4, 2012 at 3:44pm

Man first stepped in the forests when,
Each animal quizzically looked as, to them, this was an alien.
Each wondered what this stranger was like
'Cos besides his limbs, he was carrying a spike.

The Elephant, flapping his ears, looked him up close
Like himself, he didn't have a long long nose.
His ears too, not fully formed he found
'Cos he couldn't flap them at all around.

The Monkey said, 'he looks so much like me'
From his head down till down below his knee.
But, what's that he's wearing over his skin
Has he got something to hide, within?

The Grizzly Bear said, 'He's definitely not a monkey
'Cos he has no tail to swing from the tree.
He walks on two's, his body has no hair
Oh God!, he thought, this creature's come from. Where?

The Tiger seeing him was quite amused
he was devoid of stripes so, how his enemies, will he confuse?
What will he do in this Jungle of ours?
He cannot camouflage himself too, in the grass.
His Mate too looks so mild and meek
Always pushing him in front, egging him to speak.

The Lion too saw them both and gave a roar
Who's this fool he wondered, and looked to see, if there were more.
The 'mate', the Lion felt, must be daft
'Cos on her head he spied a scarf,

The Spotted Deer and antelope with quivering tails
Shifted their heads to look at both, male and female.
They mused, one looked so brown, the other so pale
Like one was overcooked, the other 'Stale'!!

The Giraffe looked down his long neck
Such crazy creatures he thought what the heck!
The female's soft cheek, he wanted to peck
But, to bend so low, it would strain his neck!

The Jackal, Hyena and Wild Dogs too
Curiously watched from afar, the movements of these two
Something's definitely wrong with them, they thought
Otherwise around them, why they've wrapped so much cloth?

The Hippo with his little brown eyes
Watched them try, to drive away the flies.
Then looking up, as though asking GOD, in the sky
The reason for making such creatures . . . Why, Why, Why??

The Snake half stood and opened his Hood
Who are these, he wondered, roaming in the wood?
His hair so short, her flowing mane
In making them, was GOD going insane?

The Dog and Cat from the village, were the only two
One wagged his tail, the other began to mew
They both smiled at each other and instantly knew
Friends among animals, they'll have just a few

They then decided, then and there
That next, for friends, they will search, the Sky and Air.
But, for now, they must move elsewhere
If in this World, according to GOD's plans, they have to stay.

(6.2)

A Weekly Market Place.
Composed by Leo DSouza On Saturday, August 4, 2012 at 6:44am

Have you ever been to a weekly Market Place?
To see each veggie neatly heaped in place?
When I was young in our small hometown
I would often love to go just to roam around.

To see the vegetables laid out was a delight
Palak* & Methi among the greens made a pretty sight.
Brinjals* in Purple and Tomatoes in Red
Cauliflower and Radish to the Turnips said
Come on lie beside me on the Matt
I'll see you're protected be sure of that!

Green chilies were hot, Cucumbers cool
While Flat beans, eyed us, lying near the stool.
French Beans all curled up also lay
Envying Cabbages, snuggly wrapped in leaves that way.
Onions beckoned us with their Red open coats
While Potatoes with eyes, watched us count our Notes.
Fatso the Pumpkin sat like a king
Watching Ladies Fingers without any rings

Green peas in a heap, were constantly tossed around
But dared not jump, for fear of rolling on the ground.
The Grain Merchants had heaps of Rice and Wheat
Different qualities, in heaps so neat.
Sacks of grain stacked one upon another
I pitied the ones below, beginning to smother.
The Fish section was a separate enclosure
Cat Fish, & Pomfrets and Fish from the River

Lobsters and Sharks lay side by side
Each Fish with their Eyes open wide.
A buyer would bend and open their Gills
to check their color, whether Fresh Red still.

The Mutton shops were a gory sight
Legs and Torso hanging, Heads on another side.
While I used to Shake and Shudder,
Someone would come asking for Liver.

I would watch but writhe in dreadful Pain
As the butcher opened skulls to remove the Brain.
I loved the knick-knack stalls the Best
What a variety they had, for our eyes, it was a fest.
Small dolls for girls and cars for boys
Glass Marbles, Hair-Bands and Oh! So many toys
They were called the Poor Man's Mall
From Tumblers, Cups, Mugs & Strainers, they had it all
The Cost was,' anything for a Rupee
So, Market Places were really fun you see.

You could even buy your Oil and Ghee
For Pickles & Masalas this was the place
All authentic Village Stuff . . . . in this Market Place.

---

*Palak = Spinach, * Brinjals = Egg fruit.

Chanella Cubbins : this is so beautifully written Leo. u have painted a picture . . . a masterpiece in words. So simple and yet so beautiful and stirring. To anyone who has been to a market place and experienced this . . . . it is a walk down memory lane. To those who have not . . . . it's a picture on their wall to marvel at.

(6.3)

Clothes . . . Owners Wear!!
Composed by Leo DSouza. Saturday, August 18, 2012 at 4:12pm

My Owner he is short and square
His dress sense makes everyone to stare.
At times, I'm embarrassed, as a garment of his,
Though wearing me he is in utter Bliss.
He wears me daily because I'm his favorite Jean
But, I too like to be washed and kept clean.
He likes night & Day only me to wear
I tried my best and succeeded in developing a tear.
Unfortunately for me, Torn Jeans became a fashion
I now became his true Passion.
The T-Shirt he wears as a top
Make me feel to go flip-flop.

My Cousin the 'Trouser' looks proper and trim
But never suited the likes of him.
Slogan T-shirts soon became a craze
But I was embarrassed invariably by their phrase.

My foreign cousins' Low Waist Jeans'
Make me laugh, whenever, in them he's seen
I'd walk alongside them in constant fear
Of it slipping & everyone laughing ear to ear.

They had their forks below the knee
I often wondered what he'd do to P
Each time they participated in a run
I silently lagged behind to see the fun.

My female cousins were a varied lot
Some 'OK', others made their owners 'Hot'!
The older gen, the 'Gowns' now gone old with age
But their Grandchildren's 'Micro-Mini' brought a Blush on even a sage.
The Maxi's and Skin fitting' were of a different era
To see the owner better, one had to go nearer.
The 'evergreen 'Sari' lengths the same but, changed the wearing style.
They now subtly slipped below the 'Navel' sublime.
Their sisters, the 'Choli's'*now more alluring
Small they shrank, the midriff baring

Cousins from Indian Origin too underwent a change
More in Outlook and in Range.
Kurti's* came exposing a lot of Thighs
Evoking from interested quarters. Some silent sighs!!
Salwar's* they gathered a lot at the waist
How well they understood, the Male taste!!

The bathing suits that the girls did wear
It almost looked like there was nothing there!!
The boys and men continuing themselves to indulge
But not succeeding to hide their bulge.
Clothes the owners wore, I swear
Have been turning heads and getting a stare
We as garments just have no voice
Of choosing a body of our choice.
We just have to go along like a tool
And let the owners, make of themselves a fool.

---

*Choli = Small Blouse used with a sari. * kurti= Shorter version of the Punjabi dress
known as Kamees worn by ladies. * Salwaar= lower part of a Punjabi dress.

(6.4)

Experiences at a Railway Station.
(composed by Leonard DSouza on 13th Aug 2012 10.30pm)

Railways are our Nations Pride
Trains running every direction far and wide
India's cheapest mode to travel by
As Bus rates are exceedingly high
And Air Travel rates . . . touch the sky.

However most Railway stations are a sight for sore eyes
Filth, Garbage and infested with flies.
Crowds on platforms is nothing new
Though with Valid Tickets, there are very few.

Outside the Station there's always one or other racket
One has to watch for a pick-pocket.
The 2-Wheeler and Car Parking is such a disgrace
Finding your vehicle later, you become Red faced.

You can park but, asked not to lock the handle
They then shift your bike at their will
You're lucky if it's in one piece still.

For your Luggage you try and engage a 'Coolie'*
They are there big, fat and burley
Their rates are always higher than prescribed
Quoting high it seems, from birth they've imbibed.
They'll quote and then stand aside
Knowing they are taking you for a ride!

You either agree or your luggage yourself drag.
God help you if you have more than one bag.
The Platforms are like a concentration camp
Limbs spread out are people, sitting on bags avoiding the damp

In between you'll find Thelas* of books and toys.
A guy in Khaki with a kettle shouting 'Chai*
You'll also see a dog so comfy having a sleep
An invalid's car, behind you makes a Beep.

An attempt is made to swab the floor
Then within seconds again, trash, someone will throw.
And then when a train slowly pulls in
Commotion erupts and there's an extra din,
People running helter skelter for their coach
While the waitlisted for the TTE does search.

The Tracks are filthy, water bottles, paper packets lie strewn
This is India, to this we have to get attuned.
Whether the Station has Platforms 1, 20 or 7,
It's for the beggars a 'Haven" and drug peddlers 'Heaven"
Commuters are just jostled and pushed around
Rarely a place to sit will be found.

Their Booking Office is infested with touts
Hand-in-glove with Counter Staff showing their clout.
'Agents Counter' is banned for the common man
But at general Counters, Agents men places capture, all they can.
The announcements made are so muffled and unclear
Listening to them, your train you'll miss is the fear.
Enquiry Counter's are the best, they test your Fate.
When the train's on the platform, they insist it's 2 hours late
Some Stations are painted and maintained so clean
Smaller ones in villages, just a tin shed are seen.
Unless the Public don't get on their back
They'll not bring the railways, on the right track.

---

*Coolie = Railway Porter. * Thela = Hand cart. * Chai = Tea

(6.5)

GOD Please Redesign Man!!.
Composed by Leo DSouza Friday, September 28, 2012 at 5:40pm

God, please make man with New Organs to grow
Replacing faulty ones and those that go slow.
Often I think, Ponder and for these things yearn
'Cos it'll take years, to do this, if left to man, to learn.
God, this will help Mankind from the Doctors 'Fleece'
Rich or Poor, we all join in, to Request you please.
The Doc's they think they are above YOU now
And make man literally, to them, bend and bow.

If today one goes to them for just a headache
Unblinking, they'll recommend, you a Blood Test take.
For even a normal Cough and cold
The Markets flooded, with medicines untold.
If a man, to a doctor, he does venture
That alone raises his Blood Pressure!.
If forbid, your Leg pains, you say
Without an examination, they prescribe an X-Ray.

If some irritation exists on your skin
Smile bursts on their lips, and their eyes begin to glisten.
For they know now they've got you in their trap
With Numerous Tests, whose Results are mostly Crap!!
If in auto mode, when damaged, grows another artery
2 1/2 lacs man would save on Angiography!!
There wouldn't be need for Angioplasty, or to put a stent
As an old artery would follow, when the old one went.

If one's Hips crack on falling, or do fail
No Plates or screws would be needed, to impale
Self replacing bone plates, could take their place
Man wouldn't have to, with operational pain grimace.

If his or her Knee cap gets old with grace
Lovely it would be, to see a new one, slipping in place.
When one kidney begins to fail and flop
Give the other the ability, to pick him up!

If the Liver's unwell or the Spleen
Both, each other, you could, make them wean.
Man would not have to depend on, these Quacker Nuts
'Cos he could recuperate, with his own guts!!
GOD, you've already done it for a broken bone
Healing itself, internally, on its own.
All the Doctor does, is put a plaster
While squeezing your purse a little Faster!

Now the Retina with age does go weak
Our normal eyesight, gradually, it becomes bleak
So install at Birth, 'A Setina', like a Set Top Box
So our eyesight will always be, as sharp as that of a Fox.
Now for those Pearly whites, you gave as Teeth
Just as the 'Permanent' push the 'Milky ones' off their feet
In case of malfunction, if new ones, old eject
There'd be less toothless grins to Project!!

For all the sicknesses on man, you did bestow
This, 'Forever Good Health' you could Restore.
Man won't have to even go 'off his head',
The World having, 'more sane people' instead.
With Medical Insurance, so many Companies, innocent people bag
The Less fortunate's Medical Bills, their faces, sag.
Making illegal money thus, is many Hospitals Obsession
The Doctor's line is no longer, that of a Noble Profession.

It's been ages, since you created Adam and Eve from Dust
Man progressed, using his brains, not letting them rust
But, if for all I thought, Imagined or ever did yearn
If you let them Happen God, I'll be a Second Jules Verne!!

(6.6)

COOKING!! . . . And What the Ingredients Feel & Say
—Composed by Leo DSouza

Cooking to watch is such a delight
Be it morning, Noon or Night.
Some Big Chef's once held a Demo in our City
If I hadn't gone, it would have been a Pity.

The Crowds came in hoards, to watch in Awe
Dishes that hadn't been prepared here before.
While everyone saw the Marvels of dishes unfold
What I heard and saw, no one about it, ever told.
These ingredients, I felt, came to me, their feelings to unfold.

To the Common man it was just the Onions cut
I heard their dried coverings Cringe, but
Being dismembered, their insides did vie
Flicking their saliva at the Chef, making tears come into his eye!
The green chilies, as he, their Bellies split in half
Imagining Smoke from his ears . . . they began to laugh!

The Potato peels he put aside to throw;
In protest, few jumped down, causing him to slip on the floor.
The Tomatoes felt naked as he peeled their coats
They said to me, in protest, they would in the gravy, just float.

The Green peas whispered to me that He behaved like a sod
Separating them from their cozy Home . . . the Pod.
The Italian Section Chef had planned a Pasta Delight;
But the Pastas, flexing their muscles, decided to fight.

Broccoli they, to each other closer did nudge
To demonstrate that they too had a grudge.
The white sauce decided to become a Paste,
The Chef's now scurried and huddled in haste!
The German Chef's Sausages, like their mother did grunt,
Jumping into the salad they did a stunt!
Hopping around the dish making the fried eggs flip,
Sometimes their ends, into the sauce they would dip.

In today's world where everything is 'Made in China'
The ingredients stood united, even the Pudina and Hara Dhania.
I returned my gaze to Reality's front stage,
Thunderous Applause from the audience I gauged.

The Ingredients siblings watched with faces aglow
As from the stage came voices, "More, More give us More "!
The applause by now was making them deaf
Then, they realized, it was not for them but, the Master Chef!!

(6.7)

How Birds & Creatures Reacted to Man . . .
Composed by Leonard DSouza Thursday, October 4, 2012 at 11:58pm

When Man's Tryst with Animals didn't break any ice
Turning to winged creatures and crawlies, he thought it would be nice.
So with his Mate they went on a Bird watching Spree
Because amidst Nature, he felt so free.

When Man sought friends from the Sky and the Trees
Hanging there in the branches, spied a hive of Bees.
Whizzing and Buzzing around they watched in awe
To them, Man was a funny creature they ever saw.
No wings to fly, he had on his back
Instead he and his mate carried a bag pack!

To the Butterflies flitting from flower to flower
Their tranquility, these two, had begun to mar.
No colours for beauty, just one, from head to toe
Truly, they mused, Man's a real specimen so.

The Cuckoo with his long tail so brown
To him, without feathers, man looked a clown.
Instead he wore something, he called a gown
Which made him and the Crows together frown.

From high above in the Sky
The Eagle spied, these two creatures, walking by
From that height, he just saw, mops of hair
With something on their feet, they did wear.

The Parrots screeched and flew up in fear
Were these two come, to take their babies dear?
Wild Ducks took off with a flap
Wondering why these creatures, are wearing a cap!

The Pea-cock got disturbed from their courting dance
Seeing Man & Woman, the Peahen got into a trance.
The Partridges scurried into the thick dense bushes
While their young, took shelter, in the Rushes.

The Mynah's and their cousins the Starlings
Wondered, what kind of birds are these with no wings!!
The Kingfisher darted and hovered over the pond
Knowing with these two, he'd have no bond.

The tailorbird missed a stitch, in the leaves he was sewing
Wondering, in these two minds, what was brewing!
The Crickets and Bugs, picked up a leaf, to quietly observe
How these two, to come here, had the nerve.

The Ladybird, in a Royal coat of Red
Was hoping, these two, wouldn't step onto her bed.
The Crawly Caterpillar, on the branches as he tread
With his feelers, tried to sense, if they were wed!

The Tortoise with his Shell, as he plodded on,
Wondered who were these visitors, early in the morn?
The Fish in the Rivulet and pond, wagged their tails and did stare
With Black beaded eyes, as they came up for air.

The earthworms arched their backs, with each sound
From the feet of these two, as they thumped the ground.
By now Man & Woman realized, Birds and Insects were far too many
But, Together, if they were kind, could live in Harmony.

So getting down on their knees, took a decision so very Bold
To Tell GOD, they're happy to live, with the Gifts of this world.
Then turning, they walked back to the village and town
Where they decided, they'll make home and settle down.

(6.8)

Life in Mundane Inanimate Things!!

Composed by Leo DSouza on Monday, August 6, 2012 at 3:53pm

Even Mundane inanimate things have life; did you ever stop to think?
No, my friends, I'm not going over the Brink!
See I'll explain that this is true
With examples of a few mundane inanimate things too.

The very slippers you use as you get up from sleep
Didn't you hear them wince at your weight, wanting to weep?
See the bristles of your tooth-brush, their face in disgust
Having to clean your teeth of the morsel's crust.

Your poor water tap, as you twist his top
To get water, inside him something goes 'pop'!
That Cup when uncaringly you pour your hot tea
Singeing his insides . . . . did you care to see?

The loyal doors as you pull behind you to close
Ouch! He grumbles, 'cos you hurt his nose.
Your Guard, the security Lock, as you twists his insides with a key
He creaks in pain; maybe you pricked his only kidney.

The Road you walk/drive on, crunching his face
Did you ever look back to see his grimace?
On the Table at work, as you put your bag
He cringes in pain, you hurt his back.

That pen you use to write and sign
Grumbling, cos her tips, like your nails, can't be painted to shine.
Those Buttons on your dress how they choke
Strangled with buttonholes round their necks you yolk.

The walls of the buildings you pass by everyday
Admiring you but, about their painted faces, no praises at all you say.
Life can be so enjoyable for everyone
If, for mundane inanimate things too, small things can be done

Treat them nice, they are yours, treat them well
Don't give them reason, to give up on you and yell.
So next time any mundane inanimate thing you see or use
Don't let them think, that them, you are going to abuse.

(6.9)

MAN—A default by GOD?
Composed by Leo DSouza, on Friday, November 26, 2010 at 11:32am

This Man's made up so funnily . . . . have we ever thought?
Was it deliberate- . . . . or a 'lapse' on the part of GOD?
He created him 'First' but, let the woman dictate
To eat the 'apple' . . . . now see our Fate!!

Physically too he is full of flaws
That don't define any scientific laws.

He has 2 'Drums' . . . . that none can 'beat'
Given 'two heels' . . . . yet, flat are his 'feet'
If you try . . . . it's quite a tale
Trying to hang a picture with his 'Nail'

Without being scourged . . . . he has two lashes
But, no signs . . . . of any gashes.
No 'strings' attached but . . . . there's an 'elbow'
'Hair' cells are 'dead' . . . . yet they continue to grow.

A 'Cap' for the knee but . . . . mostly a head that's 'bald'
If that's not silly then . . . . what's it called?
'Tis said . . . he talks from 'back of his head' . . . . in spite of a mouth
Yet he's capable of holding . . . . his clout!

His 'feet' are not 'measures' but a walking aid
That hold him up and . . . . Helps his gait.
Not a 'cow' but . . . . does have '2 calves'
Acts like a 'goat' so say . . . . the better halves.

He Possesses no 'numbers' but . . . . has 10 'digits'
From childhood his mom says . . . . was a fidget!
He can 'screw' even . . . . a 'nut' he's though
Endowed with 'things' that . . . . don't 'bounce' or 'crow'

Rear of his head is termed . . . . a 'nut'
Has no 'horns' but . . . . a deadly 'butt'.
With 'no horns' . . . . in-spite, his trumpet he can blow
Some 'gum' that don't help to stick . . . . anymore.

Enamel are his Teeth, ... called 'pearly whites'
They're deadly if and when he decides to . . . bite.
'Two palms' that he can shake and sway
No leaves at all . . . . leaving all in dismay.

A nose that's 'fixed' yet . . . . it's said to 'run'
An explanation for which . . . . there is none.
Two holes they do possess that . . . only sometimes 'leak'
A scientific reason to this . . . . seems very bleak.

(6.10)

Marie's Favourite Shoe..
Composed by Leo DSouza Sunday, September 23, 2012 at 12:49pm

Oh! How everytime Marie love's to
Wear her very favourite shoe.
She loves that little white Bow
Just below her little toe!

Whenever, it's she's worn
She stands out and amongst others outshone.
She wears it everyday for a walk
Even though she can't, to it she'll talk.

It keeps her company when she's out to play
I'm sure, if it could, it would have lots to say.
So snug Marie says, it keeps her toes
And willingly follows, wherever she goes.

Her other shoe friends of white and blue
Get jealous of her too
Even the Red, Yellow and Green
Who had in that coveted place once been!.
Shake off their collected dust
Deciding to 'stand united they Must'

Marie then gently sits with them all
Explaining, her interest in them, had not waned at all
It's just that this her favourite shoe
Is now in fashion, but she Loves them too.

So a truce with them she has reached
Assuring that, in them her trust, she has not breached.
Now a Plan she's put in place for each shoe
What day to wear the Red, Pink or Blue
And in rotation the others too.
But secretly, she still has this her favourite Shoe
With her tiny little Bow
Just above her little Toe!!.

(6.11)

The Irritating Little FLY.
Composed by Leo DSouza Saturday, September 22, 2012 at 2:25pm

Buzz . . . . Buzzzz . . . . Buzzzzzzzzz,
He flew all day
Sometimes here and sometimes there.
Eventually heading straight for my hair.

It was the Hair Oil I think, he liked its scent
'Cos he followed wherever I went.
If I escaped and sat in the Hall
He'd follow my scent and pretend to climb the wall.

Buzzz . . . . Buzzz . . . . Buzz . . . . on and on he'd go
Heading for my Head, face and toe.
No matter how much I try
I couldn't get him away to fly.

He'd hover even over my food
And get me off my appetite and mood.
I couldn't understand or see
In this big world, why he only found me?

Why? . . . . Why? . . . . Why?
You silly little Fly
Don't you elsewhere, even want to try?
To Fly . . . fly . . . . Fly?

I'll wave my arms across my face
As in front of my eyes, he continues to race
Or settle on my outstretched knee
Even if it was only momentarily!

If when flying around, at him I swipe
He'll land on my forearm & his face he'll wipe!
With Big Black eyes at me he'll glare
'Try Swapping at me", to me he'll Dare.

At awkward moments he'll sit on my nose
Just when both my hands are full, as though he knows.
I shake my head from left to right
It makes me look a funny sight.

I swear if in the next world I have a say
I'll ask God to let me have my way
"Make me a Fly' to him I'll Pray

So I too can worry my friends' every day.
I'd love to Buzzzz around while they cry
Seeing me . . . The Irritating Little Fly!

(6.12)

The Waiting Room in A Doctors Clinic!!
Composed by Leo DSouza Tuesday, September 4, 2012 at 12:01pm

The Doctors Clinic is a place no one wants to be
Because you walk in with a cold but walk out with Acne!
A Visit to a doctor's clinic can also be fun
Entering you spy a boy in a corner, with a Nose run
As he vehemently intakes the 'run' with a sniff
Thank God it's unscented or, you'd get the whiff!!

Look around you hear Groans from the lady in blue
With patients acting Doctors, advising what to do.
You smile as you see that guy with a shoe bite
Makes you wonder why he bought a pair so tight!

Old Uncle Harry's there with a cough that's bad
Maria troops in because of a Fever 3 days she's had.
Little Bobby's mischievous pranks, in school he scraped his knee
For his mischief, the Father now burdened with the Doctor's Fee.

Rajni the servant's daughter bitten by a dog named Zee
'Cos she wanted to examine his Bone more closely!
These all sit and wait so patiently
'Cos the Doctor's time to come is 6.30.

Meanwhile Rakesh is worried about his uncontrollable Bowels
While 2 little Babies deafen you with their howls.
Lucy is also waiting for a certificate to say she's Fit
Recovered now from her tongue she had badly bit.

There's Mr. Sharma's son with a Stomach Ache
I believe yesterday, he ate too much cake!!
Old Mr. Thorat he's walked in with a bad throat
His voice is now more of a croak.

Mansi dreads the Injection she has to take
The Last time her shriek, even the dead did wake.
Then there's Rev Sr Jane, who's being treated Free
Because the Doctors daughter is in her school in Class III.
There's Anjali too, with her head on her dad's shoulder
'Cos learning to ride a scooty, successfully hit a boulder!!
It's funny the Stethoscope he hangs around his neck
Even for a toe ache he uses it . . . what the Heck!!

Wonder if from it what he gets
It's just a show gadget . . . anything on it I'll Bet.!!
Otherwise explain which Heartbeats you get from a' back'?
Or does he think. . . for his patients this is the best way to make a whack?

The changing Seasons also add to all the Fun
In Summer people come, 'with a touch of the sun'
Now why on earth would they do that you think
But, then man is known to often go off the brink!!
The onset of monsoons is the Doctors days of Bliss
Half the town are down with 'Conjunctivitis'!!
The Doctor has to count and doubly check his fee
'Cos the patients plea.. 'Doctor Sorry, I can't see'!!

The Rains bring colds, skids and falls
Created by 'God' for the worldwide citizens all
The other Seasons too contribute their bit
Bringing "Viral's" when no other' Tag' can fit.

Oh! to be a Doctor is everyone's Sigh
Why my Profession didn't correctly choose I?

On: A Waiting Room in a Doctors Clinic:.
Such a vivid description.. I could picture every patient sitting there..
Amelia Nazareth

(6.13.)

Trees.. What they Teach.
Composed by Leo DSouza Monday, October 22, 2012 at 1:17am

Have you heard of a Tree that can Speak?
It's True, so here, see How, I'll give you a peek.
Didn't you ever hear our leaves whistle?
Whether we are Bamboo, Pipal or Thistle.

Our Best friend is' wind' who hovers round
Dancing between us, without a sound.
You know, when man doesn't think of us first
We droop our leaves, telling him, we thirst.

We move our branches, as though by magic
But, not too vigorous, lest it turns for us, tragic.
When it's warm we rustle our leaves
To give man & others around, some breeze.

We spread our leaves creating a shade
To protect our roots and to cool man's head
In our branches, birds seek to build their nests
So in the evenings, they can return and rest.

In return we ask them, our seeds to carry
And to scatter around, 'cos we can't move to marry!
When Seasons change we are the first to tell
We act and are looked upon, like a weather Bell.

In Autumn, we shed our leaves, little by little
Not wanting our tender branches to get brittle.
With our fallen leaves, we carpet the floor
Our leaves of brown and yellow, add lustre and glow.

In monsoons, our roots take up water to store
'Cos in winter, our saplings need moisture to grow.
Summer it's too hot for most of us too
The earth around our roots is crusted anew.

Just looking at us one can tell
It's changing Season, as sure as Heaven and Hell.
From Trees we get a lot to learn
The most Important . . . be satisfied, never Yearn.

Stand tall and always give
If, happy in this world, you have to live.
Like our branches, spread love far and wide
Be very Open, have nothing to hide.

Lastly live your life like a Tree
Give everything Off you . . . Willingly.

(6.14)

Useful and abused..Vessels of Love!

Composed by Leo DSouza on Thursday, August 16, 2012 at 9:37am

We are a very very big and very helpful family
Dekchi's,* Thali's*, Pans, Spoons, Forks, Knives and Plates like me.
We are all made or manufactured but, never born.
Our ancestors were Leaves who, are to villages gone.

When freshly made, we are packed from mothers house and sent
To beautiful places where earlier my cousins too went.
Here we are dusted daily and put on display
Till our Foster owners come to take us away.

We've given ourselves to humans for ages
In spite of our valuable work, get no wages.
Our work and miseries to you I'll relate
Starting with me.. The Plate.

We are made tough to hold hot food
Or greasy things, depending on humans mood.
We stand smiling and sparkling on a rack for use
Never once on them playing the Ruse

But they bang me with the spoon
If the servings don't come off soon
What fault is it of mine?
"Getting banged like this', I whine.

My face has so many scars for life
Left behind as they cut me with the knife.
The Forks the only ones to us are so kind
Poking only the Meat or Potato, which they find.

After their fill, we are unceremoniously dumped in the sink
Whether we are hurting they don't stop to think.
The Spoon, arms or helpers, to the plate we hang on the hooks till used
without us they cannot cook or serve, yet, are abused.

Our ears they bang on the face of the Plate
Serving themselves hurriedly, cos they're getting late
Titles like 'Cooking', 'Serving', 'Table' and 'Tea' on us they bestow
Only for themselves to recognize us so!

I hope one day they realize soon
Any name they give, we all are still a Spoon.
We get singed when they cook but, who cares?
When into their mouth we go, at their monster teeth we stare.

Our babies are kept only to stir their Tea
Hearing our kiddies wince in the heat, we sob silently.
Though we glisten with pride we too have strife
'Cos we have a wife, 'The Knife', to cut others down to size!

With her help, we help them to cut
Veggies, Meat even tough things on their plate but,
To them that's our only job they feel
When they finish, they let us keel

It saddens us when we are dumped in a basket or tub
Or in the mornings when their' help' us vigorously scrub.
We almost drown when the tub is filled with water
Some of us even gulp down the soapy lather.

We do stomp and tumble amongst ourselves for fun
While the 'Help' pulls us to scrub, one by one.
When will Humans ever realize our plight?
And treat us with dignity, so we don't amongst ourselves fight.

With time, this scrubbing makes us lose our luster and sheen
Others to replace us now, are very keen
But life for us too ends after our use
And we all retire to live in recluse.

---

*Dekchi's = Deep cooking vessel * Thali's = Lids for vessels

(6.15)

A Mosquito's Escapades . . .
Composed by Leo DSouza Monday, August 13, 2012 at 1:17am

I love to buzz around and take a quick bite
My hunting time is mostly at night.
Dark, Gloomy rooms even in the day
Entice me as long as hot blood flows that way.
I've stolen a bite and taken a deep suck
I take all risks and try my luck.
I love buzzing near a human ear for sap
And enjoy seeing them, their hands flap!
My brother and I daily have a favorite match
We prick a human, then, from a window sill, watch him scratch.
We keep our score and laugh with glee
As he or she, swings out at him and me.
Our favorite spot is the ankle and the neck
Even if we get an attempted swap, what the Heck!!

Buzzing in a dog's ear is so much fun
Seeing ole Rover flap his ears and run.
We dodge and hide inside his coat
Or jump into his water bowl and float.
Ladies skins are so nice smooth and soft
On their awkward places resting, I feel like on a loft.

My brethren used to have a field day before 'Good Knight' came
Then slowly we learnt to overcome the same.
'Mosquito Coils' came in Green and Red
'Mortein' was brought to make sure we were dead.
'Odomos' the Cream came next to protect them against us
That smell for us was disgust.
Men never stop; it's now 'Odomos Spray'
On them we now either slide or fly away.
For some Intellect, a Professor we bite
Then Nip a Lawyer to set things right.
That Doctor is quite a guy
When he blames us, slapping the Nurse on the Thigh.
At the club, that Sexy dancer was the best
Watching her juggle as we bit her chest!
We would have given everything for the rest
But, for our slim legs, it was quite a Test!!

Because the Priest was trained to absolve and forgive
Biting him, we got another chance to live.
With the Nuns, we got into a Habit
Our little bites, they seemed to like it.
With the Chemist we were scared of being drugged,
Biting a Spy we could have got even bugged!!
A Nip at an Army man was also fun
Especially when unloaded was his gun!

In our life we learnt to buzz around
And feast whenever a victim's found.
Not a Night goes by without a 'HIT',
But, still we take our bites, bit by bit.

(6.16)

What If . . . ?

Composed by Leo DSouza Friday, October 5, 2012 at 11:32pm

What If . . . . I often wondered, would be the likes
Of Man if, like a Tiger . . . he too had Stripes?
Or like a Zebra . . . his stripes were Black and white?
With ears on his head . . . upright!!

What If . . . . within 10 minutes of Birth, he could stand and Run?
Wouldn't we have had 18 more months of fun?
What If . . . we too were blessed with "Instinctiveness'?
For many, wouldn't land themselves, in a mess.

What If . . . . our body too was covered with hair?
No worries we'd have of fashion or what to wear.
What If . . . man was given a Tail?
There would be no need of Transport: Air, Road or rail!
'Cos man would swing himself everywhere by his tail.

What If . . . we had eyesight or claws, as sharp as a Hawk?
We could swoop down on our food, and no need to eat with a fork
What If . . . we were given like a Camel, a Hump?
To store food, which excess if any, now we dump.

What If . . . like an elephant we had a Trunk
Ten times to drink water, Class, we wouldn't bunk!
But Then I often think . . . . What If
Like a Hippo, we were given a huge midriff?

We wouldn't even have the Gift of Laughter
So What God gave us, Let us look after.
It's more fun to live with Competition that's stiff
Because as long as we live, we'll always have a . . . . What If!!

(6.17)

Animal Meet!!..

Composed by Leo DSouza. August 4, 2013 at 3.24 am

One day Cows, Sheep, Goats and Pigs, planned a meet,
To Register their protest, together stamped their feet!
Objections they had, 'of having to die',
For Mans appetite, which till now, they had to satisfy.

On one side said the Cow, they call me a GOD,
In the blink of an eye, to kill me, they give a nod!
My milk they use for tea and Coffee
Or even to bring up, their own Baby.

Why!, they even take my wool for sweaters, said the Sheep
And now plan to put me, permanently to sleep!!
To deserve Death, have I done them any harm?
Why can't I be allowed 'freedom' on a farm?

Don't you know, down the years, man's become a glutton?
Killing me, even a goat, just to eat me, as Mutton!!
My milk too they take, depriving my poor kid,
My Tears well up, I can't understand, what harm to them I did?

Hi everyone!, Don't forget, Here I am,
A Pig . . . . Me they kill, for Breakfast to make Ham
Why can't they leave us to live like pigs?,
And turn their appetite now to eating figs?

Will he explain, which Religion advocates killing of an animal?
So that his own hungry desire, to fulfil?
It's not Hinduism, Islam or even Christianity
And that's the truth and a certainty.

So why and when did this Slaughter begin?
When GOD made, for all of us, this Earth, to live in!
HE gave us to enjoy, the 'Fruits' of his toil,
Who then gave man, the right, this 'Offer' to spoil?

A Unanimous decision, these animals did take,
When 'Slaughtered', a loud voice, they'll make.
And die with their eyes open wide
So one day, man can hang his head in shame, and face hide!!

(6.18)

Mini Skirts . . .

Composed by Leo DSouza (written by me 40 yrs ago for My College Magazine)
Re-witten July 26,2013 at 4.06 pm

Skirts are as we all know what
Divided from the blouse by I'll tell you knot
Some are long and some are short
But these are some of the shortest sort

As mini skirts they are known
And by modern girls they are worn,
Their length is quit above the knees
Its scandalizing what one really sees

With them stockings they too wear
But made of net so there's plenty of air
They Made many an old man Stop and Stare
Even though by now, he lost a lot of hair.

And with the coming of these skirts,
Many a cloth merchant has lost his shirt
While the Skirts went up, his Profits fell
He hoped this was, just a short spell.

(This was in the Aloysian(College) sometime late 60's
but the remainder of it is untraceable . . . . so I have composed these
in continuity today 26.07.2013)

When Previously he sold, for a Skirt, three metres
Now it was 3 skirts to a metre.
The Tailor too, to make them more swanky,
Somehow, found extra cloth enough, to even make a hanky!

Now, though for them it was a Fad,
They just couldn't convince their Dad.
'Cos he was always hoping for 'No Breeze'
Then to divert young guys attention, he would Sneeze!!

Mum of-course, just held no grouse,
Knowing the balance, would make her, her sari blouse.
Brother's would far away from sisters, run,
As their friends would jeer, and often make fun.

The Boys alternatively were drawn like flies
And 'stared or glared' with google eyes.
It just gave them thrills to see titillating skin,
And more, if the material happened to be thin.

The Religious men in Shrines and Holy places,
In embarrassment and shame, covered their faces.
Silent prayers they raised, to their deities,
'God Forgive these girls', before they become Ladies!!

(6.19)

Adoption Terms from a Cat
Composed by Leo DSouza Feb 23, 2014 at 11.00am

I am the kitten that grew up next door,
From young I eyed your sprawling Bungalow.
Your garden patch I've seen, so nice and green
Lush lawns and windows, so clean.

I waited eagerly for 'owners' to come to live
So to you, my Conditions, I could give.
I have decided to be your cat
You have no options, this way or that.

I've watched cattishly, your goods unload, from next door
Predeciding to Covet those beautiful rugs and Roll, galore.
When you came I saw you had no pet
But life will be lonely, as older you get.

So you're lucky, I've decided 'you' to Adopt
But be sure on my Terms, I'll never be soft.
Just a morning cup of Milk I ask
For you I'm sure, that's no big task.

No leaving me to fend for myself
Just reserve my meat in your Fridge shelf.
I like Cuddling, but kids are not to pull my tail
If they do, I'll scratch them till they wail.

Allowed I must be, to inside bring, my kill
And peacefully eat it till I have my fill.
It may be a rat or a Chicken breast
Near me a 'No Disturbance sign', when I Rest.

Tell your wife, at me she'll not scream
I'll not touch her facials, "Fresh Cream".
I promise to all, I'll be very nice,
I'll even rid your house of Mice.

I'll let little Johnny his fingers run
Through my fur and have his fun.
I'll not spoil Granny's knitting woolen ball,
I'll even come, whenever' you call.

When my little kitties come, them, you won't sell,
But like little 'kittizens' you'll treat them well.
They'll like me, find a home, when time is right
So, don't ever shout or start with me a fight.

Outside in a corner, keep Sand in a tray,
So I'll ensure, my business, won't cross your way.
Since you have 'No Option', this way or that,
You'll be my 'Adopted' and I your CAT.

Chapter VII

Poet's Mindview

Here friends, I present you my thoughts on a variety of topics.

It may not be your 'Cup of tea' some of you may 'Scorn this poet friend'

and we may be on 'Crossroads' on our views. But, in 'Our fast Changing

World' our 'Bonds of friendship' will strengthen when you read and

Appreciate my works, till one day maybe this 'Poet goes Blank'

(7.1)

A Poet Friend's Scorn . . .
Composed by Leo DSouza. Saturday, August 11, 2012 at 3:12pm

My Friend also some Poetry does write
But both our focuses'..On a different sight.
Greener Pastures a Life to make
Went this friend for family's sake.
The New land offered No comfort like here
Life was a struggle and so very dear.
The Only consolation . . . it was a foreign land
But every chore, one had to do by hand.
No servants like in India galore
Each to his own for sure.
This poet friend had to struggle
Hoping in time, will end the trouble.
In between jobs this Friend Poems wrote
Anything to keep from rocking the boat.
A bitter lesson learned
'Cos here all the boats were burned.
Varied jobs were undertaken
Just to keep from being forsaken
A Chance meeting we did make
Catching up for old time's sake.
But when this Poet-friend came to know
About my works, a little interest, in them did show.
An undercurrent sweeping I could feel
Was it Jealousy? Definitely not Sincerity for real
Sharing my works I continued to do
at 1st Appreciation came, then it dwindled to a few.
This friend compiled Poems into a book
Though quite a while it took
A copy to me was promised of the same
But it never really ever came.

Instead I got a note, at which I did stare
'Cos I was told, my poems with this friend no more to share.
I knew then that I was right
Jealousy had resurfaced alright.
But I still ask God to bless this Poet Friend of mine
and let the sun in that hemisphere shine.
Not quite one to pick a bone
Decided, this friend, I'd leave alone.
Though not considering myself, 'A Poet Born'
I had encountered, 'A Poet Friend's Scorn'.

(7.2)

A Tsunami Hit and After

by Leo DSouza on Sunday, May 6, 2012 at 11:16am
(Composed and dedicated to all the souls lost in Tsunami's the world over)

The people holidaying on the Beach when it hit
Suddenly disappeared . . . . what happened was, beyond my wit
Beach-side stalls . . . now turned a mass floating around
No owners, no wares, all swept away or downed

It was just a mass of water on every side
taking people—houses and vehicles in it's stride.
Tumbling cars—like empty matchboxes could be seen
Dead animals too floated in the stream
Perched on high-rise buildings—stranded there
Rescue only possible for them, if someone will dare.

The street lights were gone . . . signal lights uprooted out
No need for Police now . . . to show their clout
Traffic on the now waterway was . . . a free for all
Vehicles minus drivers, somersaulting and over each other fall
No mercy to Ladies or Children was, by it shown
All swept away equally, fast racing away and down
Mothers clutching babies to their chest
Crying and yelling, hoping for the best.

From sturdy buildings that stood the test
Howls of dogs, mews of cats rose above the rest.
Waving hands seen from an upper floor
Sadly watching their belongings . . . speedily go.
No landmarks in the city spared or left
Bill-boards bent, weaker structures, in half were cleft.
Hospital boards dangling from the onslaught
Told their own stories of patients drowning, unaware caught

Some survivors, to wooden planks, clinging went
But, to whom 'S.O.S' messages could be sent?.
Enterprising 'looters', trying against fate their luck
on makeshift boats..from debris they grab and sometimes having to duck
Plaintive cries of animals, from owners lost
Hoping to be rescued and relieved, from this holocaust
Those that could went to higher land
Wading thru chest deep water, Slush and sand

To add to the woes . . . the rain came battering down
Drowning now, except the gushing water . . . every other sound.
Dogs, Pigs, cats, horses, all were there
Joined by bullocks and mice all floating everywhere.

God's wrath, it seemed, was sent down to all
Sighted also was a baby girl, clutching her doll.
all night long it lasted, this havoc
Man's ability and ego, as though to mock.

The morning after, calm it brought
Survivors around . . . some or other Help they sought.
Rescue Teams had by now boated by
Calling for survivors and responding to any cry.

Animal-aid workers too chipped in then
side by side, assisting some Army men.
Scaling pipes, the trapped, to reach
Creating dams with things, the water to breach.

Finding survivors was no small feat
Combing the buildings. Inch by inch, feet by feet.
Wounded given First-aid on the spot
While shifting others, on stretchers they got.

Sirens Sounding, beacon lights showing, it's coming. Help
Now there was Hope for every Cry and Yelp.
the morning brought receding water and it's signs
Massive destruction lay in front as though, hit by mines.

Slush covered roads and filth littered the place
of a town, known for it's neatness and Grace.
Carcasses and bodies, strewn, all over they lay
in lanes, drains and all along the Highway

Disposal squads took up the burdensome task
From the stench, their faces, behind a mask.
'Twld take days and months, who's who, to know
Photographs taken their next of kin to show.

Enmass the mutilated bodies, the Govt decided and burnt
to avoid an epidemic . . . it is learnt.
So, with tearful eyes, the living the Dead . . . did dispose
And to re-build the town together..a cause . . . arose.
Slowly clearing the rubble brick by brick
the Town, in Six months . . . rebuilt..with a magic stick
Memories of those . . . forever gone
will always be dear and . . . linger on

There's Tsunami Alerts now put in place
To avoid such disasters, and in future to Face,

(7.3)

A Wedding..

Composed by Leo DSouza on Tuesday, November 27, 2012 at 9:57am

A Wedding, is between loving persons two
But involves, Relatives and friends quite a few.
It's about 2 individuals that met one fine day
Attracted to each other, along the way.
Meetings at times, Clandestine or just Open
Slowly bonding them, to situations of Win-Win.
Sharing ideas, likes and dislikes
Till their minds, for each other, begin to psych
Dreams and aspirations, they begin to share
As they plan, preparing for their Big Day.
Relatives, too excited, also start their plans
As both sides Parents, put together, heads and hands.
Deciding Venues, Menu's and list of Guests
For both sides, this becoming, a Prestige test.
If financially balanced, they both are
No Problems arise . . . by far.

But, where burden's, on the Parents of the Bride
They begin to 'beg + borrow' to save their pride.
Often the Brides family gets heavily in debt
If, on them alone, expenses have to be met.
At times the 'couple' in love, are unaware
Of this turmoil, each of the families share.
'Shopping' is paramount on everyone's mind
Each vying for attire, of a unique kind.

The 'Bride and Groom to be', search the Stores
for 'things' in her head, which no one knows.
Her visualization of a Dress, to resemble a Queen
And to fulfill her wish, he's always keen.
Some 'Grooms' have fanciful taste, even though males
For 'frills on shirts' or Coat with tails.
Travel plans are chalked and made in advance
Not leaving anything to chance.
Both sides 'houses' get into a flurry
Invariably 'Times short', so they have to 'hurry'
On the day there's full commotion
Some looking for Oil. Brushes or a Lotion.
Nothing seems to be quite in place
The state of the house, in total disgrace.
At the Church/Temple, everyone's at their best
Except for that baby, yelling, and being a pest.
All eyes are fixed on the couple now
Going thru the Rituals, as they take their Vow.
Gay abandonment follows, at the Reception Hall
Everyone's come to enjoy, and have a ball.
Their cups of Joy, now filled to the Brim
It's now the Brides last days, of remaining 'Slim'
The hours tick by, the night is almost through
All get ready, to wish the Couple, an 'adieu'

Dispersing, as they go, with memories to linger or bring
Of them having attended . . . . yet another Wedding!!

(7.4)

A Young Prisoner's Remorse . . .
by Leo DSouza 16th Aug 2012 00.15 am

Today reflecting, sitting here in my Cell
How myself, I turned my life into Hell.
Looking back, through my inward eye
Of how those happy days I let slip by.
My siblings were all happy and gay
Then what made me this way?
Was it a streak of jealousy?
That lay dormant within me?
Or was it something I ask and at myself yell
Who knows? Will anyone tell?

My 1st small crime at 5 with my brother's bike
When through its tyres, I put a spike.
Everyone at home, since, looked at me with disdain
I couldn't control myself, but I too felt the pain.
I think from that day I drifted aloof
Just happy I was, over my head to have a roof.
As I grew, some wayward friends I had.
A little more control then, maybe I wouldn't have turned bad.
I don't blame my family, now thinking back
It's just the 'right attitude' that I lacked.

My brush with the Law, falling prey to drugs
Brought me face to face with hardened thugs.
I got out, swearing, never again to fall
To this life, but to strengthen my gall.
Leaving home to fend on my own
I Struggled, but resolved to reap only, what I had sown.
It was tough, if only my family knew
I was trying to mend . . . the good habits few
I know I hurt Dad and burst his bubble
By constantly getting into some trouble.
His dreams for me I badly shattered,
That day, when Jane's attacker I battered.
But I did it defending li'l sister Jane
For what he did to her, I felt the pain.

I've been 3 months now for me in this cell
At times the loneliness eats into me like Hell.
I think a lot of all you guys
And for all my deeds, ask myself . . . Why?
I'm put into a cell and in isolation kept
They've labeled me 'dangerous', for which I wept.
Mum you know I'm not like that
Even though I was a wayward brat.

Please explain to all at home I care
All my thoughts, in this Diary I share.
Please pray for me that they'll me forgive
And give me another chance . . . free to live.
Right now, that day is sure far away
I just mark my dark cell wall with chalk, for each passing day.
To GOD I often kneel and ask in prayer
Please God, give me again, just a few days with my family to share.

(7.5)

An Ode to a Train Driver . . .

Composed by Leo DSouza on Thursday, May 04, 2012 at 12:47pm.
(While travelling Jabalpur to Udaipur)

Dedicated to my Late Grandfather D.J. Nazareth attached to GIP, Before
nationalization, when they were responsible for their own engine. He always
kept his shining and was nicknamed . . . Bobby Dazzler. Dedicated also to all
the Drivers and their fraternity.

He leaves his home, kids and his wife
In his hands he has our Life.
Rarely faltering, his job on track, keeps him
He's always fit, never needing a Gym.

Alert Eyes and mind he must posses
Faltering on either, lands him in a mess.
The lights, Red, Orange & Green . . . he must be able to discern
Seeing when to stop or go, he's trained to learn.
Every day he is on the run
Even though . . . work for him is not all fun.

At destinations he goes to a Running Room to Rest
So next day, he restarts another day . . . full of zest.
In the morning they send him the Book called 'Dak'*
So he knows . . . on what train route he has to embark.
He then ensures he gets packed his Line Box
Lanterns, Green & Red flags, a uniform if needed and his Locks.

For any obstacle on the track, he blows his horn
Blowing it continuously . . . . till it is gone.
At times the obstinate and deliberate . . . just carry on there to lie
He's not to blame . . . when he overruns them, and they die.

His Rules to him are loud and clear
He cannot stop for anyone—even its one very dear.
No case against him, for rash and negligent driving can be slapped
Cos it 'twas not him but the victim that was zapped.

He's cursed & abused when trains run late
the reasons beyond his control are part of his fate.
It's often due to VIPs and Ministers, the delay
He, them, cant question, just silently obey.

It irks him when someone pulls the chain
The precious minutes lost, to trace the culprit and get an explain.
In spite of all odds, he's at the control
Heat, cold, or inclement weather alone he faces them all.

No AC for him, just a fan, all the while
Yet doggedly he's there . . . wearing a smile.
Transporting us . . . town by town, state by state, mile by mile.

Human error at times its toll it takes
Overworked when, a mistake he makes
No doubt . . . . It results in many lives lost
But, does anyone think . . . to him it happened . . . at what cost?

At times his alertness . . . an accident he averts
But, that's forgotten by higher-ups, who are twerts.
Look at a Rail map or reality on ground
One sees trains crisscrossing all day round

We need to stand up and his tribe Salute
Train travel without them, would never be so comfy and to everyone suit.

---

*Dak = Daily Roaster book for Running Staff in Railways.

(7.6)

.... and the Morning After!!
Composed by Leo DSouza on Sunday, August 5, 2012 at 3:28pm

. . . the mother gave birth
In the family there was so much mirth
All wanted to the hospital to troop
To express their joy as a group.
The husband was all up-beat
This really deserved . . . the best treat!!
Friends and Relatives a beeline made
To the Maternity Home, good tidings to bade.
There was so much Joy in the air
Like it was a big grand fancy fair!!
. . . They put little Sarah into School
The house grew silent like an ice cold pool.
There was no pattering of little feet
That made a sound itself so sweet.
Now Maggie felt so bored at home alone
No friends close by to chat or phone.
She just went about her Chores
Watching hours tick by . . . her spirit soars.
. . . Their little daughter the Nest has flown
to make a career of her own.
Maggie & Melvick again felt so alone
Home didn't look anymore like Home.
They separately, out the window would stare
Why they thought, is life so unfair?
Every evening eagerly waiting for the phone to ring
To their ears . . . her sweet voice it' would bring.
. . . She rang and broke the Good news
They felt joy and sorrow with feelings mixed
Planning how soon the date they could fix.
Their eyes would cloud in mist
Thinking how her phone calls & her they will Miss.
They got about busily making phone calls
To inform close relatives and friends . . . all
And then that night . . .

They got that call . . . it was a terrible Blast
Tearing thru the market, their darling baby away had passed.
. . . The funeral they felt now OLD and Cold
Gone was their baby, no more hopes to hold.
Their hopes of a grandchild faded from their lap
Dashed forever . . . . like a final clap.
Now they sit brooding, eyes always damp
This world being for them now, just a Transit Camp
. . . Their departing Coffins went out the door
Friends & Neighbours sat huddled in Sorrow.
They would miss them sitting on the lawn
Feeding pigeons early in the morn.
A Perfect Couple they had made
In Unison, Spontaneously, they all said.

(7.7)

Baby Days!! . . .

Composed by Leo DSouza. 12th august, 2013 14.32 hrs.
Emotions are not new, to a baby race,
As their eyes light up, recognizing a face.
Tiny fingers reaching out in space,
Or chubby legs, jerking in your face.

As days pass, their eyes dart around,
Focusing generally on anything, shaped round.
Glee – writ large in their, baby eyes,
Gurgling appreciation, bonding ties.

Distaste they show, spitting out undesired feeds,
Making Mothers cater to their whims and needs.
When a tantrum, they have to throw
It's a wonder, with whom, how they know.

To be carried brings them, great pleasure,
Don't grumble mamma, you said,' I'm your Treasure'!!.
To wake you up at the oddest hour, each night,
They've made it their Royal Birth right.

All night long, they choose to whimper, bawl or cry
As Mother sacrifices sleep, to keep them dry.
In the day, she hopes they'll sleep
But, 'Play times' then, so preparedness she has to keep.

They let out a yell, when people come and touch their cheek,
Or come too close, at them to peek.
Disdain & Disgust, they openly at some show,
Wondering why, such adults, that much don't know.

Now this man Papa, who seemed, seeing me, so proud!!,
Why do I hear him, grumbling aloud?
I enjoy waking him too, to walk the floor,
Till finally, I feel, to sleep, I must go.

Baby Days are lovely, oh yes! They are
If only, adults from us, stay far.
We enjoy our squeals and shouts
That make people, just run about.

Baby Days are lovely, oh yes!, they are
Why does growing up, that feeling mar?
Only a Mother knows, how far she can go,
No wonder, Most Mothers say,.. 'Thank you, Not any More'!

(7.8)

Bakers Knead.. Our Dough!!

Composed by Leo DSouza Saturday, September 1, 2012 at 5:01pm

A feeling so nice entering a Bakery
So many goodies you get to see.
The Pastries all laid out so fine
Everyone wishing, every piece was mine.
The Ginger biscuits brown and round
Every time you look, new things around are found.

The Macaroons face, in smiles, are split
The Cheese straws are delicious every bit.
Cookies in various flavors are sold
The Chocolate ones being good as gold.
The Cakes, your eyes, they do arrest
With beautiful icing flowers, neatly growing on their crest.
The Jam tarts neatly packed in a bag
Tongues of critics will stop to wag.
In the showcase lie Veg, Paneer* and mutton puffs
You can eat 2 or 3, it's still not enough.
For the Walnut and lemon Pie
Everyone clamors for and with each other vie.

The Cream Rolls they climb one atop the other
Cream packed tight, overflowing like lather.
Bread and Buns are a daily affair
They have to be . . . for them only we go there.
A variety of other goodies one will always find
Each one different and of its own kind.
The Bakery will always be my favorite spot
My eyes always taking in, the entire lot.
Whenever Inside there I trot.
Their every knead, I think I'll always need
'Cos it's as contagious as though you are hooked on weed!!
For their Dough, bakers knead your dough
Every time inside there you go.

---

*Paneer= Indian hung cheese.

(7.9)

Birds Eye View of a Railway Platform . . .
. . . . Composed by Leo DSouza

A Railway Platform is a place to see
Everyone rushing, very excitedly.
Porters jostling, between the crowds
Vendors peddling their wares with shouts.

Carts of Toys, and men with Tea
Children running, very gleefully.
Men in Coats of Black and Pants so white
Clutching reservation Charts, are the TT's of tonight

Loud speakers blare the arrival of Mumbai Mail
Suddenly, confusion prevails, like hit by a Gail!
A crowd surrounds the TT now
Each clamoring, seeking accommodation, somehow.

Que's of passengers, jostling each other at the door
Those alighting & those wanting to go.
To occupy their berths, everyone is very upbeat
As invariably someone's luggage is under another's seat.

Now on the platform at each Bogie window
For every 1 going, there's 4, the event to ensure
The Parcel Trolley approaches, laden to the top
Pushed by 4 men, hurrying, without knowing the meaning of Stop!

You better move out, 'cos they will grumble
Even bang you, and cause you to stumble
The Aroma of Samosa's* and Omlette's now drifts
Tickling your senses and your attention shifts

The Alms seeking troupe appear, choosing the time right
Either when you opened your purse, or taking a bite.
A mother with a half-clad kid clutching her gown
Another on her hip, as bogie to bogie, they go down.

A Book cart appears as a diversion indeed
Displaying books & Magazines, if you care to read.
The daily News and books of Fortune foretold
Film Mags for the star struck & Playboy, if you're bold.

The driver and Guard wave their Flags of Green
As soon as their' go signal', they have seen
The opposite way seems to move, the Platform
As the train pulls out, the station from.

The hawkers begin moving their carts to a platform new
And the whole process starts anew.
Newer Passengers, another Train
This happens all day . . . again and again.

---

*Samosa = Triangular Savory with vegetable filling

(7.10)

Bonds of Friendship..

by Leo DSouza on Thursday, December 29, 2011 at 4:47pm

Friendship is so lovely shared by one and all
No age or Barrier but enveloped by Big and Small
Toddlers in school just fall into the game
Sometimes without even knowing the others name.

Bonds are made as the years flit by
At times so strong . . . till the day they die
Partners you find . . . who from school did hold each other's hand
to end up at the Altar of God sharing a Golden Band

Years roll by and many drift apart I bet
while others hold fast never allowing in between anything to get.
By mail or Phone they kept in touch
sharing each other's joys, sorrows as much

God Blessed are those who honour such Friendship Bonds
Likening themselves in relation to a rivulet and pond
I have been lucky, to have so many Friends I treasure.
To be in touch with them always . . . is my Pleasure.

Fond memories I hold of every friend I make
Treasuring these till them, to my grave I take
Without them . . . so alone I would feel I think
They're to me as precious as to a girl . . . a mink.

To all the world I have just this to say
Build your Friendship Bonds and . . . . make them Stay.

(7.11)

'Counter Sales People'.
Composed by Leo DSouza Sunday, December 9, 2012 at 1:58am

As you walk into the shop, at you they first stare
Gauging you I'm sure, by what you wear.
Be it a shop that's small or in a Mall
The 'Stares' is common, they have it all.

Showing highest priced items first, they ensure they find,
Their 'Commissions' of-course, is also on their minds
What'll be, your purchasing Capacity?
'Cos they are 'born traders of this kind city.

Some are shrewd, unobtrusively, another item they bring
Hoping in case,. 'Bells of Interest' in you, they ring.
Some very 'effusive', trying everything to show
Just so 'something you buy', before you go.

There are others, who glare with Disdain
Thinking, I'm sure, you're in their neck, a Pain.
If they are Salesgirls, with whom you have to deal
There'll be some, who are eager, a 'Sale'' to seal

Others are busy, chatting or watching the guys
Or 'Passing' comments on customers, who didn't buy.
Many a Time, Ladies feel very insecure
As' Eyes' they feel, following them around the store.

Some Ogle, while others try their charms on girls
Hoping to strike a chord, for a whirl.
Pretty lasses too, to these guys, a beeline make
Enchanting them, with smiles, often fake,

Some entice him to offer a better bargain or price
Then later saying,' He's so cute and nice!!
The men look for counters 'Girl manned'
Pretending to buy, for their sister, a hair band.

164

Many a time, Men take a chance saying 'What the heck'!!
As they quietly steal a look down her neck.
Counter sales persons endure a lot from us
Some grumble, others work without a fuss.

At Big Malls they are hired generally to guide
But, often behind shelves, they're chatting or hide.
As a guide, they're supposed to offer Help
But, one's left searching, shelf to shelf.

Counter sales People have grown, into a unique breed
To cater to each individual shoppers' need.
Enduring working hours, so very long
Salary wise, it's a pittance, just a song,.

So when next you shop, treat them kind
Boost their Morale, don't curse, if you don't mind
'Cos just as for time, you are hard pressed
Think. Catering to various whims, they too are stressed,

(7.12)

Crossroads!!!
Composed by Leo DSouza Sunday, September 30, 2012 at 11:58pm

All thru Life we come to a Crossroad
When Joys and Miseries follow untold.
Hard Decisions everyone at one time take
For themselves and for their families sake.

Literally when driving too, one has to watch here
If others and your Life you hold dear.
The signal lights are there saying Ready, Go or Halt
But accidents do happen, when people do fault.

We are at Crossroads in Life, from the day we are born
Whether to smile or just to yawn
We discern early in life, the different Love from Mum and Dad.
Or when enough of my whimpering, they've had.

Early morning the Crossroads look so open and wide
No signal lights, only one's judgments to guide..
Criss-crossing traffic comes, a Free for all
Screeching Brakes, then a loud Bang, followed by a fall.

At Crossroads we are at Childhood too
Why our parents don't lavish Presents, like others do?
Why we cannot go out with our friend?
Why don't our Parents, sometime's Rules bend?

As the Sun begins to show its face
One sees Traffic cops on Crossroads, take their place.
An hour later, they're not there, definitely not
'Cos under a shady tree, is their favorite spot.

Then when we find hormones playing, in our lives havoc
Concentration's difficult, our thoughts do block.
At Crossroads regarding feelings for a Girl or boy
In our tender minds, thoughts we forever toy.

It's quite a hobby at Crossroads to stand and see
Vehicles of all kinds & sizes rushing speedily
2-Wheelers forever trying to jump the light
Instead of waiting, for the Green light.

At our workplace, to choose right from wrong
We just follow blindly where others throng
At Crossroads we are all the time
Am I doing Right? In this Life of mine?

Signals are not for them, think the cyclist
Brazenly moving when the light is Red, and being a pest
And when from Amber to Green change the light.
From extreme Left, they dart across to the Right!!

4-wheelers get away often with ear-plugs on
Cell phoning while driving, imagining they're each a Don!
The Cops meanwhile Soft-Target a Lady or a Girl
Because defaulting men, round their fingers they cannot twirl!

Family Life keeps one on Crossroads everyday
How to Please the wife & kids in every way!
Then when Age catches up on us
Crossroads of thoughts come up without a fuss.

In Life too when on Crossroads we do flop
Many will come to see, but to help, few will stop.
Many giving advice will be seen
Some even discouraging you to wait, for things to turn Green!

And when you stumble, crash and fall
To laugh at you, they'll even have the gall!
So when you reach the Crossroads of Life
Right decisions you must remember to take, to avoid strife..

And when you drive on the Road
At the Crossroad, Concentration is the key word.
Don't ever jump the signal light
Be it Morning, Noon or Night.

(7.13)

Dedicated to all Daughters . . . on behalf of all Fathers!
By Leo DSouza on Sunday, September 25, 2011 at 3:50pm

Daughters you make us Fathers heart swell with Pride,
Cos you're the next Best happening . . . . since our Bride!
Catering to your whims & fancies we would always go
Even if it's to stand on our head instead of toe!

Your Name brings A sparkle in our eye . . . people see
As we remember the chuckles & laughing loud in glee.
We recall the Hopping and skipping with those little feet
You're every move we cannot forget, that sound so sweet.

Clamouring for our attention . . . You would always be
Not wanting to be left out . . . yelling Me! Me! Me!
Our Joys you would equally be of, a part
Sharing it together from deep within your heart.

Our Troubles and worries . . . No matter if they were small
You would want to know and share them . . . One and all.
From a child to a teen . . . you were the apple of our eye
Quietly shedding a tear-if to u ever we had to say Bye

Maturing into a woman—we knew—you would go One Day
To another man . . . when . . . I DO . . . you would say
But whether with us or . . . in your husband's home
Our love for you will ever occupy . . . the Top of the Dome.

No power on earth can ever . . . severe this father—Daughter Bond
For we will always be for each other . . . LOVED AND FOND.

(7.14)

'Emotions'

Composed by Leo DSouza Sunday, December 9, 2012 at 1:10am

Emotions exist and vary in all of mankind
It's a common streak, you're sure to find
Some get sad, others want to sing
Anxiety and Hope, out it will bring.

When things don't go, the way we want
Out Bursts an emotion which, Control, you can't.
Since everyone goes thru the same
Some understand, Others don't, and that's a shame.

Love too is an emotion, shared by most
When for 2 it culminates, it's time to toast.
When this Emotion, Parents on Kids, they bestow
They do it naturally, without a show.

The Kids too shower it, on their toys
It doesn't matter if they are girls or Boys.
Growing, they find partners, with whom to share
Some hide it, Others on their sleeves do wear.

But, Loves only a part, there's also Anger and Hate
Balanced individuals learn to control, others just wait.
Few let it flow out in tears
Those with' Loving streaks' are called 'Dears'

Emotions sometimes erupt in Snarls or Smiles
In Life they follow you, every mile.
High flying Tempers, or a cool cool head
Man to these Emotions, are constantly wed.

To the young it's quite a battle
Coping with changes, they tend to prattle.
With Life, there'll always be 'Emotion'
It's Life's true and 'Unbreakable Portion'

(7.15)

EXAMS . . . for Students or Teachers . . . . ????

Composed By: Leonard DSouza Friday, May 18, 2012 at 2:12am
(Dedicated to All Teachers, Students and Parents, with a Clarion call to wake
up . . . to make a change)
(Being an Ex-teacher from St. Luke's. Solan . . . some of the sentiments expressed
are from personal experience)

EXAMS!!—The fever begins quite in advance
For some students, whose books, they've not even glanced.
It's a feeling that cannot be explained
While Teachers, setting papers, their minds are strained.

Students roam from pillar to post, for those missed notes
Teacher's burn mid-night oil, dinner consisting only, of soup and toast.
What questions to set—that's not too easy or tough
Wondering whether to write, students will have . . . time enough.

The classroom pranks—come to mind flitting by
Which question will they leave and which they'll try?
The smarter kids now draw up a study time-table
Putting away their DVD's, MP3's and T.V, Cable.

They now embark on a 'Study pilgrimage'
Aiming high is the aim, for the best percentage.
The weak willed, for 'Guess Questions', run
Even if it's all day . . . . Out in the sun.

The teacher meanwhile on which 'Q' to give a choice
'cos if with this they pass, he/she'll feel real nice.
In English, should it be just Nouns and Verbs
or do you think, it'll get on kids nerves?

Adjectives will be nice, Adverbs may be tough
But, then the syllabus has all this stuff.
The Guess 'Q's' have reduced the tension for some
but back of their mind, wondering . . . 'will they really come?'
They go to any lengths, just for a few tips and guesses in tit—bits,
Others, their answers, preparing on mini-mini chits.
In History, how many 'Q's on Babar & Akbar or Humayun?
In Geography, should it be on 'Climate' or 'Sand Dunes'?
Should 'The Law of Gravity' be asked in Physics?
Or in Math's.. To work out the cube root of three times 666.?

Now the days, only 7 are left, Exam fevers run high
Teachers are ready; papers are set . . . while students daily sigh.
Outside the Halls, heads buried still in books
Are scenes, across the world, not just seen but, is . . . in looks.

Exam halls open . . . students their desks occupy
Teachers with Answer books, as invigilators, now give a sigh
Their year's labor now stands the test
To weed out the weak and reward the Best.

Looking at the kids so worried and tense
Wondering, do these exams . . . really make any sense?
Should these kids, at their age, face this pressure?
Shouldn't they enjoy these times, and their days Treasure?

Will this System, ever change its pace
And help the kids and their Parents from running this Rat-Race?
Shouldn't it, now promote job-oriented courses
Or is this . . . benefiting 'big-wig's' and Minister's Purses?

Exams over, Teachers—Valuers they now become
Correcting Mistakes, and also enjoying the answers given by some.
Feeling sorry for marks to cut, yet not indulging to . . . freely give
The task is . . . the best they have to sieve.

171

Tabulating Marks—Report writing follows next
This to many, is worse that teaching the Text.
Report day comes—there's some in smiles and some in tears
Friend's greetings friends . . . all smiles and cheers.

Still others with crestfallen faces, hoping the ground, them, would swallow
Though it's too late, for their negligence, now to wallow.
Both Teachers & Students have their Test
Now awaiting the New Year to see . . . what the Govt's policy is next.

Hoping Policy makers, their grey cells, will use
To change our education, and into schooling pattern infuse
More Practical, Job-Oriented courses for all
Get rid of Institutions, which Politicians Control

Keep Schools and colleges run only by Educationists
Which will bring down.. Mounting fees . . . with Iron fists
No seats will be put "on SALE' anymore
These will be available as it was . . . before.
No students will have to seek a loan
No 'House Mortgage' will parents, to banks have to phone..

'Teachers' are said to 'mould the future's next gen'
This will happen, the education system changes . . . when.
Parents, Teachers, Students & Citizens . . . . unite for this 'Cause ',
It'll be for the benefit of everyone . . . . because.

(7.16)

'Fashion Trends'.

Composed by Leo DSouza. Monday, December 3, 2012 at 12:06am

Changing with the Times, is the Fashion Scene
What's 'New' today, the 'Oldies' had already seen.
A full circle completes the Fashion Trend
Yet, driving each older generation, round the bend.

Long Moons ago, Cowboy Hat and Jeans, were in Style
Ladies with flowing Gowns drove many a mile.
Gents trousers then, developed a pleat
While dresses shorter, just showed glimpses of ladies feet.

The Cowboy boots gave way to Ballroom shoes
'Damsels' flats changed to 'high heels' too.
Suits, from the double-breasted, to buttons three
Dresses shrunk, and stayed, till the knee.

By now the Cowboy hats, had long past gone
Suits changed colours from Black & Brown to Grey and Fawn.
Ladies haircuts, replaced the lovely long manes
Shoulder lengths & Perms, done with utmost pains.

Necklines dipped, and sleeves they got short
Blob Ear rings and necklaces, filled the slot
Bell bottomed pants, now came into vogue
Necklaces changed to something called 'Choke'

Men's Coat-tails disappeared, as the times, did change
Single or 2 slits, were the styles in range
The Drain pipe pants that came, shook up all
The low waist ones, you wondered, when they'd fall.

By now the Ladies, in their Mini's, appeared
Parents huffed & puffed, their daughter's safety feared.
Will powered dresses, brought many a Stare
Almost every girl, now, seemed 'out to dare'

The shoes too changed, the old ones went
Stilettos for Ladies, and chiseled toes for Gents.
Neck ties from broad, to narrow, then just 2 strings
This changing Fashion, such memories it brings.

With Necklines dipping low, and backs getting bare
For a change, men began to grow their Hair.
While some Ladies, to trousers did shift
Others skirts developed, a longer slit

These days, there's just 'Casuals' you see
Loose jackets & Shirts, just hanging free.
Boys pants, with 18 inch forks
They say, for them, "This Rocks'

Girls today have varied styles
Some lop sided dresses, hanging a mile
One shoulder bare
They even dare

Eye shadows that at times, frightens one
But, to them, it's style, and all the fun.
Boy's ear lobes, they sport an ear ring
Studs for some, for others, just a ring.

All said and done, as long as there's life
Youngsters will have Fashion, Elders the Strife.
So Long live Fashion, and it's changing Trends
And GOD save the Elders, being driven, round the bends.

(7.17)

Flight 264

Composed by Leo DSouza. Saturday, September 1, 2012 at 1:48am
(Dedicated to all 'Pilots' who Risk their Lives. Some even sacrificing theirs
for their Passengers on board whose safety they vowed to protect the day they
obtained their License to Fly)

It was a cold wintry night
Approaching, the Pilot saw the Airport beacon light
In a few minutes, he thought, he'd be getting ready to land
When came that shooting pain, in his left hand.

The Co-Pilot Murray decided back there he'd go, for one last stroll
As soon, they would land and on the tarmac roll.
His fiancée was there on Seat 6 B
He had strolled across, her to see.

Victor and Denise were returning from a trip abroad
Soon it'll be back to their hospital and ICU Ward.
This trip for them had been after 5 long years
While leaving they remembered from the ward, little Johnny's tears.
Now they pulled out their Rosaries in their hand
Praying, God will see they are ok and safely they land.

On Trevor and Mary's faces, of smiles, there were some traces
Envisioning the joy on their Grand children's faces
For each time they had made a plan
He had had trouble with his prostrate gland.
Now the flight seemed so out of hand . . . Are they going to crash?
Uncontrolled tears rolled down . . . all their dreams seemed to be dashed.

Jane turned to look on her finger, at the sapphire ring
Seeing it, what joy to her widowed mother, she thought, it would bring.
Roy her fiancée was to follow 2 days later
As he had one last party.. to cater
She now cursed her ill luck, why did she catch this flight 264
She too could have waited for 2 days more.

Robby and his sister Jane on Seat 15 & 16 A, seemed so cool
They were from holidays, returning to School.
Unaccompanied Minors in Flight 264's care
The Air Hostess', responsibility of the Airline would share.
With IPODS and Galaxy Tabs they were tuned in, with earplugs on
Unaware of the lurking Crash, when into oblivion they'll be gone.

Rekha and Sonam as Air hostesses, Flight 264 was their maiden flight
Nervous at first, but soon everything went right
Now suddenly Flight 264 was fast losing height
Oxygen Masks dropped . . . they saw Passengers in fright.
Rekha's thoughts to her 1 year daughter flew
Without her as Mom, what will she do?
Sonam was to be married next week
From No one, Solace could she seek.

Iqbal Suri sitting on seat 34 A
Looked out the window and at his wrist watch, mid air
A few seconds more, he thought, and then he would strike
Just like they did in Kandahar, similar like.
A Smile on his lips, eyes to Allah above
Then to his targeted passengers, this job he really did love.
The drop of Oxygen Masks, unnerved him now
Aborting Hijack plans . . . He prayed they'd land safe somehow
To Rahim his Boss he'll later explain
By hijacking now, nothing they would gain
For Death was imminent now for all on the plane.

For the Co-Pilot, it was his biggest test
Capt Sharma with a Heart attack was made to lie and rest
Quickly taking command, he contacted the ATC
Trying his best, the craft to keep steady
Switching on the Intercom, to 264's passengers he gave hope
Joking with them that he's smart and not a dope.
Appealing with the cabin Crew, to keep passengers Calm

While he tries Flight 264 to land, without any harm.
But deep inside, to his wife and family went his thoughts
How will Jyothi his wife pay installments, for the Flat and Car he bought?

Assuring the ATC he would take charge and land
But to keep 'Ambulance & Fire Brigade' ready on hand
From what he saw on newly installed CCTV, of the guy on 34 A
He alerted the Cops too, on landing, the hijacker too, to take care.
'First Aid' on landing to Capt Sharma he asked
Consoling himself for this glory of being 'Tragedy In-charge' he basked.

Now down below, the airstrip he saw, all lit
As flight 264 inched closer the ground, to hit.
He just hoped, in the dark, he shouldn't get a bird hit
Pulling the Throttle and Joystick, in his seat he did shift.
The Tarmac towards him was racing now
Screeching Tyres, then a Thump..He had landed . . . WOW!!

Deplaning Capt Sharma whose safety mattered most
Then the Passengers, lastly the crew—'the hosts'
Deplaning he got an applause from Officials and staff on Ground
For bringing in Flight 264 on the Tarmac, Safe and Sound!!

(7.18)

Glittering Stars . . . in the "SKY of FAME". (Part 1.).
Composed by Leo DSouza on Monday, May 14, 2012 at 10:39am
(This is dedicated to all the Stars of Yesteryears, their Famous Films and Lines
included in the Poem for posterity)

Looking up in the Star studded sky
like to all mortals, only twinkling stars did I spy.
A closer look at each one that night
I saw God's wonder, as he placed each on a star, glittering in their might.

God, for their brilliance played with them a game,
Then gave them a place, they won, in his, "SKY of FAME"
Charlton Heston was there on a studded stand
"I have only five words for you from my cold dead hands'
His words encrypted from the film, "BENHUR"
'Cos he was the man . . . without any fear.

God wondered how, Marlon Brando to use
His words, "I'm gonna make him an offer, he can't refuse"
From, "THE GODFATHER"—his famous Film
As he made him stand on a star..looking grim.

Clarke Gable was the star in-charge of the wind
For beautifully portraying Rhett Butler in.. "GONE WITH THE WIND"
"Frankly my dear, I don't give a damn" his famous words
Engraved on a star, where too sat, a pair of birds.

A beautiful star he allotted to 'MIDNIGHT LACE'S. Doris Day
With her words," Middle age is youth without levity and age without decay".
A corner, he gave ELVIS in the Sky
To use as his.. "BLUE HAWAI"
While he sang . . . "Love me Tender..Love me True.."
Awaiting his fans, to join him too.

He told Ricky Nelson, he'll see for him, what he can
Because Ricky was a "Travelling Man"
He suggested he should go and say . . . "Hello to Mary Lou"
Meanwhile he would find for him a Star too.

"THE LADY IN QUESTION", Rita Hayworth he dubbed
Her words, "All I wanted was just what everybody wants-you know to be loved"
Holding it he made her sit
Close to the 'Polar bear' from who's light, it lit.

"The world is not my Home', he heard Jim Reeves say
As he placed him near the enchanting..Doris Day.
From the Breeze he protected Marilyn Munroe and her skirt
So heavenly winds couldn't blow it up here, so she can flirt.
Though, "GENTLEMEN PREFER BLONDS" he placed J F K at the far end
in strife
While Jackie Onassis his Ex and now the Tycoon's wife
Sat watching them both . . . in this new life.

There was, Vivien Leigh from, "A STREET CAR NAMED DESIRE".
On a star a little higher
Saying, "I know I fib a good deal-after all a woman's charm is 50%..Illusion",
But happy now . . . from Hollywood's pollution.

John Wayne with his "STAGECOACH" horse still trot
He'd be given his horse and guns, he never thought.
His famous lines, "Life is tough, but it's tougher when you are stupid",
Still made him among the fairer sex.. their 'Cupid'

When placing, "SON OF PALEFACE" 'Bob Hope, he asked him his latest take
He said as before, "You know you're getting old, when the candles cost more than
the cake"

There were many more, he chose to place
In this Sky of Fame but, right now 'twas no space.
So when you next look at the sky above
Seek out your favorite stars that you love
Adding brilliance to the beautiful sky their name
In this God's creation . . . Sky of Fame"

(7.19)

Holiday Makers & Breakers!!

Composed by: Leo DSouza. Sunday, March 25, 2012 at 1:50am
(Dedicated to all those who land up on Friends & Relatives on"" A Holiday""!!)

We plan a Holiday . . . . on others we 'ourselves' impose,
Thinking.. 'How happy they'll be to see us . . . . we suppose.
Never once stopping to think.. What were their plans?
Were we really Welcome, or . . . depriving them of a Holiday to Silver Sands.

Your kids, you felt needed a 'break'
But, never stopped to ask John whether . . . he too planned his family to take
To a Beach or were they just staying back for our sake!

As 'Hosts' they now have to plan some extra meals
And you ask yourself . . . . so what . . . are those BIG DEALS!!
Ethel his wife, is now forced, early morning, to wear a Smile
To please you all by.. Going out that extra mile.

An outing or two, as Hosts, they have also to plan
Burdening their expenses more . . . 'Cos now it's a big clan!
The Gifts (for each) you feel compensated . . . that you took
But failed to notice them exchange . . . a queer look.
Blind to their feelings..the days relaxing, you enjoy
Never thinking . . . . for them . . . was it really a Joy!
For you the Fortnight seemed to have flown
But, poor hosts, silently in their rooms, you should've heard their 'groan'

To add further to their woes your train was running late
Though' it didn't make any difference to . . . you gait.
The Train, finally from the station, off it goes
Bringing an end to their 'fortnight' of woes!
Next day like you..they're back to the grind
Their Plans for a quite Holiday..have gone far behind
They now have to plan a Holiday for Next Year
Hoping, another relative or friend won't find them . . . 'Near and Dear'

(7.20)

Infatuation!!!

Composed by Leo DSouza on Friday, May 11, 2012 at 3:07pm
(Composed by Leo DSouza and Dedicated to all the young Restless Hearts!!

Infatuation ". . . it's not just a word that happened to me
It afflicted me ever since I was 3
He was there so strong and in my eyes . . . tall
No one in my mind, could touch him at all
Tall and strong . . . looking back then . . . he was all I had
Yes . . . . He was my one and only . . . favorite DAD.

In the School bus, Jim . . . he caught my eye
Sitting there looking so sweet and . . . Coy
Yes, He, me too saw, & to him I took a fancy
I longed to ride that bus, only him to see.

He was my 1st Crush those days
We teamed up always, in all our plays
I hid for him in my gym pocket . . . a toffee
He brought daily for me . . . . a lolly!
My small world around him I made revolve
Those days I thought . . . he was my only resolve.

Joey in middle school sang and strummed on stage
He was my new Idol, my hero . . . at that age
No guitarist or voice to him I'd compare
Against him—no one I'd allow anything to say
His looks & Smile; I felt were always on me
I pictured..at his side, I'll always be.

Herman I dated thru High School
We'd laugh, joke & with each other, play the fool.
To me he was my Mister Cool!!
Our feelings, we thought, for each other, was intense
Admonished & Advised by Parents, to "'Study" & have more sense"
We studied together and shared our Notes
Everyone around knew . . . on each other . . . we dote.

181

Years rolled by.. We went our separate ways
Occasional contact we made.. then . . . gaps of days.
Days to months, they quickly went by
I got used to it in time . . . though at first, I'd cry.

Infatuation is truly a cousin of 'Love bug'
Bites you once, but thru life, 'It', you lug
All generations have by it been bitten
At each stage—they too felt like us . . . 'a cuddly kitten'

We'd go to Parties but first making sure
The other's invited . . . . Otherwise . . . NO!!
We grew up and saw it was a part of life
With it's quota of smiles, tears and sometimes strife.
We now were settled having our own husband or wife
And children, whose similar feelings we could fathom
Not condemn them or leave them . . . at random

As Parents we're now alert, knowing and ready to guide
Showing them that, we stand there by their side.
'Cos "Infatuation's" not wrong . . . it's just a start
of a growing child who's unconscious, of his or her own restless Heart.

(7.21)

Joyful Splashes!!!
By Leonard DSouza on Thursday, July 26, 2012 at 12:59am

School Re-opening we associated always with Monsoon
'Cos heavy rains meant' holiday' for us . . . a boon.
This year Rains, too long, got delayed
Our Moods Morose . . . no jokes in class, us, could sway.
Then today, our prayers heard . . . it began to drizzle
All day we longed for a downpour . . . not this little by little
Dark clouds gathered . . . our eyes now focused outside
Every girl's smile, from ear to ear, was wide.
Imagining getting wet . . . soaked to the skin
Were fancy thoughts flitting thru our minds . . . us all stout or thin
In the break.. The drizzle increased its pace
Some took their chance and out did race
Other's wondering why the clock doesn't faster tick
So we could go out and be in the rain..Up to all the tricks.
Then just before the Final Bell
It poured, ringing to the Heat . . . its death knell
To us kids, this was the moment we waited for
Going home 'dry' in this weather would be such a 'bore'
So with the closing prayer . . . out we dashed
Into the pouring rain . . . enjoying every splash!
Such Bliss it was, as it poured and trickled down our heads

Soaking our uniforms, down to socks and kids
No Mom's or Dads around to pull us back
dry us well and off to bed. they'd us pack
So while some kicked off their shoes to wet their toes
The timid ones still hid behind classroom doors.
Ribbons opened, flying hair and belts open
Each one enjoying and one by one a friend roped in.
Hop-Scotch in the rain . . . Oh! such fun
We really enjoyed this carefree run

So Umbrellas, we didn't open . . . as to get wet was our Aim
For such pleasures..we felt there's no shame.
Playing Catching—cook.. 'twas fun in the rain
Holding hands and running forming a chain.
Some teachers seeing us thus . . . had on their face a smile
Thinking back, I'm sure, of their young days . . . all the while.
Rickshaw and Auto men were running around wild
Searching in this melee for their every child.

Girls with no cares today..just enjoying the Rain
For once we all were..just kids.. all over again!!
Rains didn't wash us off our feet
Instead, out in the open we all did meet.
No Cares of tomorrows running noses or fever crossed our minds
Just Excuses of how we got wet, for our parents, we had to find.
For now we just wanted to have our fun

Arms flaying..while dancing and in the rain to run
Such childhood pleasures, we'll never ever get
So all the consequences . . . we decided.. let's all forget
And enjoy now getting just . . . WET..WET . . . WET!!!!

(7.22)

K.B.C. A Game to Get . . .

(This a Poem on the TV Game on Indian TV adapted from "How to be a Millionaire)
Composed by Leo DSouza Friday, September 28, 2012 at 4:46pm

KBC has emerged for another time yet
Offering 5 Crores for people to get
13 Questions they have to answer
Asked by the Computer through, Amitabh Sir.

Help lines provided there are Four
Audience Poll, Phone a Friend and 2 more
Expert Advice and Double Dip
You still have to safely tread, or you'll slip.

Winners are those, who mostly use their brains
Having prepared and taken great pains
In this KBC, it's knowledge that wins
To see who, everyone sitting at home too, is on pins.

To keep viewers glued to their seats, sitting back
KBC offers the 'Ghar Baithe's'* One Lakh.
If they, to answer the 'Jackpot Question' do dare
There's an additional 2 lakhs, waiting there.

---

*Ghar Baithe= Sitting at Home

(7.23)

Life of a Clock . . .
Composed by Leo DSouza

I am a little Clock,
To tell you the Time of Day
And everywhere that people flock
They need me all the way.

I have two hands in front of my face
Round and round they move all day
Moving by seconds without a race
Non stop they move, all the way.

I have a Bell, which you can fix
For special moments, you want me to Ring
Only winding me up, does the trick
I set my brain, and as requested I Tring.

My Grandfather, in days gone by, he stood in the Hall
In every house, very tall and straight
Tunng, Tunng, and Tunng for every hour he'd call
And then for half an hour he'd wait.

His days were good, Halls were big
His gen next, didn't have such luck
His job, wherever standing, was just to tick.
And often, near him. Cob-webs, stuck.

Our Generation consists of Table clocks of varied designs
Or as a Fashion, wrist watches too
To our fate we just have to resign
Ticking away, with nothing else to do.

Today we have no spinning wheels at all
We're just quartz, with a Battery
We don't have to stand so tall
No Prominence, Respect or even Flattery!

We're just a clock on the wall
Hanging there so quiet and sublime
No given any respect at all
Instead blamed, saying, "There was no time'!!

Our kids & descendants have now gone digital
With figures flashing, on a screen
I'm sure, for us, it's not far till
We may never ever, again be seen!!

(7.24)

MOBILE PHONES—Sensations Subdued!!
by Leo DSouza. Tuesday, August 21, 2012 at 2:11am

When Landlines had become a bane to man
He sought an alternate to see if he can.
Mobiles History dates back to the early 1940's
To Reginald Fessenden's invention..that was Bulky.

They evolved from heavy & bulky to Thin and now Slim
In '56 Dr Cooper's 1st Hand held, he called Dr Engel, to speak to him.
Today we mobiles face so much stress
As we are now a part of humans dress.

Man he takes me everywhere he goes
Always keeping us charged on our non existing toes.
I hate it when he pockets me on his Hip
I often and sometimes succeed out and slip.

His wife on the other hand
is so difficult for me to understand.
She has a very funny quirk
Picks me up gently, as her hubby's off to work.

Piercing my eardrums with her shrill voice
as she chats with friends or her second choice!
From her I've heard all the gossip of the town
How Mrs. Sharma for the party wore Alka's gown.

While Rosie's dating every evening her neighbor Noel
Glad that I'm with her, for what happens, who can tell!
'Arun darling have you forgotten me'?
Whispered Julie, through me, so lovingly!

I wanted to yell back . . . "Dear Julie
Come and see he's now kissing Suzie"!!
'Bring the dough and tonight we'll go'
Conspired Mathew, planning a night out with Joe!

I was itching to tell his dad Bernard Gomes
'Cos this outing may ruin both homes!
Merlyn the 16 yr old out on her date
Clutching me tightly, my feelings too did satiate!!

I swore I'll be there to protect her tonight
For that I'll have to keep my eyes open wide.
I'll let my alarm go, if anything happens on the ride
But I doubt 'cos I'll be there right beside.

Johnny's pranks they give me so much pain
Pressing my buttons again and again.
I tell my circuit to skip a digit
As with his plans silently I go along with it.

Sadly we have a Voice box but cannot talk of our own
A message Pad on which we can't even send a tone.
I do have fun ringing, when it's a wrong number
Waking my owner from slumber, with a face as cool as a cucumber!

The situations that we see and share
Will make you with jealousy stare!
I lie in bed next to Mr. & Mrs. George's head
And watch his hands all over tread!

If only I told Mr. Iyer who his daughter Malati met today
I'd probably would have had to change my coat to Grey!
The Dirty jokes that show on my face
Didn't realise how progressed was this modern race.

189

Mohammed & Raju have used me to plan a heist
At the Regional Bank on the city's east
Come on somebody help me please
Pick me up and dial my keys.

My Circuit will do as I have it, told
to ring the Police and save The Regional Bank's Gold.
We mobiles just long that we could talk
or send our own messages, since No Talk!!

But then I tell myself very consolingly
That If I had to 'twould be like a World war 3
With what people do or see
Now that they all almost have, 3G.

(7.25)

Monkey Menace . . .

Composed by Leo DSouza Friday, November 9, 2012 at 2:46pm

If your garden is blessed with fruit trees
Be sure of regular visitors . . . the Monkeys!
They come, with a leader, in herds to raid
Even of Dog's barks or people, they are not afraid.

Plantains they love, but any fruit will do
They, the Garden, with destruction..askew.
They pick the ripe and raw, at their will
Until, they have, had their fill.

A mother with a kid, under her belly
Jumping branch to branch, without a melee
Sure footed are they, with their feet
In case of threat, they bare their teeth!

They also often, invade a house
Leaving the owners, with a grouse.
Adept are they, at opening even a latch
Kitchens they target, for their 'catch'!

Terror in some areas, they have spread
Making the housewife, often to see Red
As her days cooking, is all over the floor
Damaging her empty home, they had quite a go.

Tiled roofs they have ruined many
As they Hop or Jump, to their destiny
Temples, they very frequently haunt
Here, to eat, they get all they want.

On the way, to worship your deity, to save you from Hell
Clever hawkers, set up stalls, of groundnuts to sell.
As you feed the monkeys, and proceed to go
A few will follow, hoping to get more.

Even though very human, in behavior and looks
Man can't afford to be, in their bad books.
Even though they are Predecessors, of our Race
We've still got to take precautions, of this Monkey Menace!!

(7.26)

On Mother
A Poem conceptionalised as a Play with the Play script given below
(Composed by Leo Dsouza)

Mother cared for me from when I was born
Making beautiful clothes for me to adorn
She was like the sun that shone
Brightening my life every night and morn

As I grew she dressed me for school
Giving me a bath, to keep me clean and cool
Polishing my shoes and everyday clean socks
Taking great interest, preparing my tiffin box.

Checking & helping with my study
At the same time at home, being my buddy.
She encouraged me with my games too
Giving me important tips a few.

When in High School I had many a friend
Sometimes when they would drive me round the bend
I'd turn to Mother, 'cos she was my only Best Friend
Guiding me in my viewpoint from wrong to defend.

She taught me everything, a girl should know
Especially now, when to a Teen I grow.
No other in this world could ever become
Or take the place of my Darling Mom.

. . . .

Screen play for the above:

Scene opens with: Mother cradling her baby then stitching.
A girl with a cut-out of the Sun trots across the stage.

Scene shifts to Mother dressing a girl for school after she comes with a towel wrapped around, Then Mother combing her hair, polishing her shoes, offering clean socks.
Scene shifts to:—Mother making a tiffin.
Scene again shifts to:—Mother & Girl at table with books., talking then sharing a joke, telling a story.
Scene again shifts with both mother & daughter with badminton racquets and a Basketball, giving tips to the girl
Scene now shows: A group of friends sitting and chatting and arguing then leave. Girl turns to her Mother who listens and then explains.
Scene now opens with a young grown up, Mother talking about Movies (Film Magazine to be used). A Mobile too with Mother casually monitoring the calls made without causing a scene.

. . . .

(7.27)

My Camera & Me.
Composed by: Leo DSouza Thursday, October 25, 2012 at 12:03pm

I'll tell you a story of My Camera & Me
'Cos you know I always love Photography!
The 1st one for which I ever did wish
Was given to me by Uncle Fish.

Eight Snaps in all it would take
To develop them, all my pennies, I used to scrape!
Then 'Brownie', made in England was next
That came all the way from Sussex.

Photography was now my Hobby and a game
Its pictures were in a 1 x 1 inch frame.
Everywhere that I did go, he always came
Slung on my shoulder but, comfortable all the same

Cost of maintaining it was a costly affair
As D&P prices soared, day by day.
But, for capturing memories, Cost, didn't me scare
Brownie & Me would go everywhere.

Long years of Service, she did give
But, she didn't have very long to live.
One day at a Picnic, her lenses fell off
I was left, high & dry, like a standoff.

I searched for her lens under brambles, rocks and sand
For a replacement too, I tried, in every foreign land
But, Brownies production, had now been stopped
How I cursed the day, the lens had dropped.

'Instamatic' stepped in taking her place conveniently
Presented for my wedding, by Aunt Marie & Family.
With 4 flash bulbs, designed like a cube too
The Film in a cartridge was something new.

195

I clicked everything, Natures flowers and Trees
The Animals, Birds and even Bees
All in Natural colours, they looked so nice
Made me feel, as cool as Ice.

'Kodak' now introduced, a whole new Range
Capturing my interest, forcing a change
My photography had swelled, from Rolls one and two
Making the most of the roll, now of Thirty two!!

But soon Digital came and took over
No more trips to Studio Labs, I needed to hover!
For my daughter presented an 'Olympus' to me
Bought from her very first Salary.

Now freely anything I could click
It had provisions for Stills, Video and even a Movie Flick!
Then one day, my Olympus acted like a Jerk
He suddenly decided, no more, he wanted to work.

Now from FUJIFILM, FINEPIX came to my rescue
My daughter bought this one too.
With me My Camera was everywhere, you did look
Taking Pictures, to put on FACEBOOK!!

Events, Family Snaps and the lot
When occasions demanded . . . . so why not?
My pictures have taken my Camera and me
Into pages of News and 'History'

(7.28)

"Our Fast Changing World"
.Composed by Leo DSouza, on Wednesday, December 12, 2012 at 1:28am

The World is changing so very fast
Makes me wonder, how long it will last.
Earlier only Birds were know to fly
After' Wright Brothers', now it's possible for you and I.

'Ford' into this world, Automobiles they brought, you know
Today's line is leaving behind, even the Nano
Earlier single metallic roads sufficed, even though rough
Today even 8 lane smooth roads are not enough.

Studies in olden days, were just the 4 R's
'Subjects' today, are more than the hours.
In olden days, the Telephone was an unknown thing
When Land Lines came, they all had the same ring.

With multiple ring tones they come today
Without even looking, you know it's come from where.
Earlier you had to answer to know who that would be
Today, the screen flashes the name, on its caller id.

Blackberries for us, were gathered from the Trees
And 'Tablets' we took for Fever, cold or a sneeze.
Then days there were only bean and Pea Pods
Today they've devised even an I-Pod.

We only knew 'Fathers & Mothers' voice tone
Those days, kids came naturally, today, one can clone.
'Galaxy' was a gathering of a billion stars
Today,' Galaxy's are in the hands of children of ours.

It acts as a Phone, Music player, Computer, all rolled in one
Tomorrow it maybe a 'Cigarette lighter, Credit card or like a Vehicle Run.
Man may soon embed, under his skin
A Chip for enhanced memory, according to whim.

No VISAs for Travel, will man now need
Like 'StarTrek' Commands to a beaming machine feed.
Religion too was followed earlier, in Blind Faith
Today the Religious are questioned, and this they hate!

Grains & veggies sufficed, fulfilling mans need
Fertilizers boost output today, increased population to feed.
To cross Foreign lands earlier, man did swoon
Now man has pictures from Mars & Walked the Moon

Spectacles one wore when eyes were weak
Today,' Contacts' to see and beauty they seek

If Man could have his way
I'm sure he'd try to lengthen 'night and day'
Surely God's wondering, why he made man now
And planning to recall him, for a newer model somehow.

(7.29)

Rains.. For Kids a Sheer Delight!!
By Leo DSouza on Thursday, July 26, 2012 at 9:50am

Oh! What a pleasure 'twas to see yesterday
Kids of schools..out in the Rain..play
Uncaring of getting wet..Enjoying in utter Bliss
But well protected 'bags', I'm sure they had, for this.
Big or small they were no different
Enjoying Nagpur's 1st Heavy downpour . . . A God sent!!
Scenes of kids enjoying the rain..No money can buy
Unhindered by peers..They really did enjoy.
Joyous expressions on their faces was worth seeing
While grown-ups, under shelter, were seen fleeing.
No race to catch' Auto's' was there at all
Everyone wanting to enjoy this Rainfall.
While the Rain it continued with all its might
For Kids everywhere, I'm sure, it was sheer delight!!

(7.30)

Seen all on a Morning Walk !!
Composed by Leo DSouza on Monday, October 29, 2012 at 5:03pm

On a Morning walk, every Morn, with my Dog
Are Scenes, my brain records, and it does log.
Pot Bellied guys, brisk walking, to be trim
Buxom wives, half jogging, right behind him.

Joggers and walkers, the empty roads enjoy
It's nice to see, sometimes even, a young girl or boy.
One gets to breathe, the days fresh air
No Pollution is found, the Roads are bare.

The Early Birds, twittering and flying,
On open grounds, stray dogs, with each other vying.
Lone Ladies or in groups, clutching a stick, They catch
More to protect themselves, from a Chain-Snatch!

No Cops on duty, are seen, this early in the day
Maybe because, they know, at this time, there's no prey!
The Government sweepers are seen, rushing with their broom
As the roads they have to sweep, and groom.
Milk vans downloading, fresh packets, for the day
At various outlets, all along the way.
An army squad returning from a long exercise
Returning? Then you wonder what time did they rise?

Ladies learning to Drive, on an open ground
With professional agencies, or husbands, are found.
Few vehicles laden with veggies and fruits
All hurrying to far destinations, on various routes.

Auto's taking those arrived, by the morning express
Some village women too in rustic dress.
Tea stall vendors, selling their cuppa tea
Mostly at squares, doing business very briskly
Stranded 2-wheelers, having picked a flat
Early morning, they didn't bargain for that.
You also see some, with petrol tanks run dry
Still kicking with hope, they do try.
Among the walkers, there's also the slower ones, like me
Coupling their walks, with their pets 'morning glory'
Occasionally one comes across, a nasty old dog
Growling, his teeth he bares . . . the whole road he wants to hog.

The Sun too begins to show its face
Rising between trees and buildings, first his Rays.
Office goers that go far, for a bus they often race
Recalling our younger days brings a smile to our face.

(7.31)

'Sometimes'

Composed by Leo DSouza' Friday, November 30, 2012 at 12:51pm

Sometimes . . . . I sit and wonder
About Life and I begin to Ponder
Why is it . . . of things we are not sure?
Yet we long for more and more.

Sometime . . . . the past flit before one's eyes
Then we react, with smiles or sighs.
We see the Glories of the Past
And how they disappeared, so very fast.

Sometimes we wonder where we went wrong
Why good things, 'always', to us didn't belong.
How the joys of growing up, are a memory faint
With vivid colours, of it, our lives we paint.

Sometimes we see, Evil prospering over the good
When rightfully, the other way, it should.
Yet, it's the 'Have not's that wear the smile
And the 'Haves' sitting back, their time they while.

Sometimes . . . is a word so vague and unsure
Confusing one's mind . . . bringing a lure
More often than not, making people yearn
With Hope, driving frustration, more to earn.
Many a life is filled with . . . . SOMETIMES
Till Happiness, like a bell sounds its Chimes.

(7.32)

Summers In Nagpur
by Leo DSouza on Saturday, April 14, 2012 at 7:49pm

Our summers in Nagpur are known to the world over
Making it the hottest city, in this country ever.
Others shiver,' Visiting Nagpur', at this time to even think.
Transferred Officials here, their hearts just sink.

You'll see people well covered as they pass you by
Wrapped from top to toe, without a lie.
The Sun at this time of year, is scorching hot
One feels like . . . 'a chicken in a pot'

Whenever someone passes by and says a 'Hi'
You'd have to scratch your head & blink an eye
'Cos you can't make out boys from girls or gays
cos it was someone like a 'mummy' from Egyptian days.

You respond lest, they think you're in a slumber
Looking down, you note just their Vehicle number.
"Revelations" come to mind where tis said,' everyone will be known by his number.

The roads so hot on it, an egg you can fry
Don't believe? Try it then you'll utter..My! Oh! My!!
The crowds on the road you think they'll abate
But, No! Everyone's still rushing . . . as though they're late.

The Birds in the foliage are quiet, taking cover,
Just like Humans, in quiet gardens, you'll see, 'a couple lover'
From waterhole to waterhole, wild animals, in the forest roam,
Searching for water where, they'll rest and make a home
Wayside dogs in wet patches find their cool
While Humans, big and small, vie for the best Swimming pool

Packaged Water sellers thrive and try to make a quick buck
Adulterating and increasing their rates, just trying their luck
Juice Centers one finds dotting the street
Hand-carts, 2 wheelers quenching, parched throats demands, they try to meet.

Water Scarcity hits us, Taps run dry
Yet watering front of houses continue.. One wonders why.
This wetting house fronts continue from morn to morn
Illiterate or educated, to them it doesn't dawn
They're causing this scarcity and taps to run dry
Eventually they're the ones who'll suffer and cry
Wetting around their houses, the women derive a thrill
'To stop this' into them you cannot grill.

Common Train Travelers are the worst, facing the brunt
From ill kept coaches, boiling and steaming they grunt.
To add to their woes, the Railways they, little do
Packing the coaches like sardines instead of . . . the allotted 72.

The Doctors 'businesses' too at this time face a slump
so most of them, grab this chance on a holiday wagon to jump.
They' blow' their savings this time of the year
Before the monsoons bring it back . . . in top gear.

Green leafy veggies.. They become so scarce
if available, your purse strings, you've got to pull up, and brace
If ever we Napurians one day find ourselves in Hell
I'm sure, even Satan, will not hear us whimp and yell
For to this heat we are so used
Even 'Hells Flames' down there, may keep us coolly amused.

All said and done . . . This Nagpur, we will for nothing Trade
It's our home and for it . . . we were made
No other place such warm people you'll find
Extending HELP to any one of whatever kind
We love our seasons as they come and go
Gone used to our' Nagpur Summer's' we all are I'm sure.

(7.33)

The Best Age To Be.
Composed by Leo DSouza on Friday, September 14, 2012 at 10:41am

The Best age to be, say toddlers, is between 1 to 3
'cos that's when you are really carefree.
You can run around and laugh with glee
And everyone fusses on you and calls you, 'cutie'!!

No! said the 'Child' who's between 4, 5 and 6
Ours is the best, with each other we can freely mix.
Our Mom & Dad are there for problems to fix
While we can enjoy and get up to tricks.

Then there are the bigger ones from 7 to 10
Whose moods change now and then.
They like to feel big, in spite of being small
They feel theirs is the Best age of all.

Growing up years are the best says the 11's to 13's
'Cos some are nearing, the others already Teens.
They recognize the 'charms' of a girl or boy
'Cos that's on their mind, not some silly old toy.

The Teens from 14 to 19, for many it's a 1st love at that age
Their Life is now on a different page.
With hormones racing they have their own stress
For that' someone special' they just want to 'dress'.

Their Rooms become their special den
They make appearances only 'now and then'
The Parents from their rooms are 'Out of Bounds'
Even if, emanating from there are the 'weirdest sounds'!!

At 20 they're all planning their Bday of 21
'cos they feel their' childish days' they've now overrun.
This is the best age they feel and want to be
'Cos emerging ahead is 'the mystery world' they need to see.

Their parties consist of 'friends they wanna be with'
Not old fogies from the lot of 'kin and kith'
From 22 to 32, to adults they've matured into
They now have and want their Lives anew

'Clubbing and partying' which till now were Taboo
For them, it's a whole big world so new.
From 32 to 52 they have their kids of their own
They realize life's problems, which their Parents had known.

It's the Best age many of them feel
As Life has completed a Full Circle of the Wheel!!
50's and 60's they are now reaching the Retired Brink
They have to be careful what they eat and drink

For every little disorder there's a Pill
Skyrocketing their doctors Bill
Since they now have to take life very easy
Some sit Reading or just watching T.V.

This is the Best Age they all want to say
'Cos now their children have taken their worries away.
In the bracket of 60's to 80's for most they are . . . now the Head
Their own Parents, have long gone, resting in God's Bed.

They sit and watch with the same old pangs
Like their peers, their kids form, their own friends gangs!
80's to 100's . . . very few are around to sit and compare
By now they've lost their teeth, appetite and hair.

They just live and wait at 'God's Kingdom door'
'Cos they've lived a good life, and couldn't ask for more!

(7.34)

'Waiter's plight'
Composed by Leo DSouza. Sunday, December 9, 2012 at 4:01pm

A Restaurant looks so enticing, with tables well laid
Ambience & Decor, to varying taste are made.
Bright or dimly lit, to suit all moods
Their Menu's displaying, a variety of Foods.

Hovering around, are uniformed men we call 'waiters'
To serve all, Walk-in's, Executives or Daters!
It's about this clan, this is all about
Taking Orders, and for mistakes, get a shout.

Humble to the core, they are so trained
'Apologizing' for' nothing', just because, we are strained.
Mostly with a pleasing smile, they cajole you to try
The authentic Dish, accompanied with French fry.

With experience they know, what each dish contains
If uncertain, they call the Steward, using their brains.
So patient are they, when you take your time
Offering, while you decide, to bring 'A Soda and Lime'.

When the kids get restless, creating a din
They give them a smile, and strike a win.
Quickly they ask, 'Should Cold drinks' they bring
Knowing children, on this suggestion, their hopes they pin.

As they take Orders, suiting each Palate
Their own 'gastronomic juices' they keep on 'wait'.
Many a time, the delay, gets you in a flurry
But, depending on the Chef, they cannot hurry.

They suggest the 'Sweet Dish' in case you forgot
People agree, most often than not.
Deftly they clear the Tables, when you are done
Offering to 'Pack' a 'Leftover' for anyone.

207

To whom to give the Bill, they have brought
They had already gauged 'the host' from the lot.
Hovering close by as you check the Bill
Hoping you won't, a mistake find, they mentally 'Will'

Bringing Change or your card, close by they slip
Knowing it's 'bad manners,' showing eagerness, for the tip.
Quickly at the door, bidding you the time of Day
Entreating you, to come again, this way.

(7.35)

A Poet Goes Blank..

Composed by Leo DSouza Monday, August 20, 2012 at 9:41am

I got down Paper and Pen to write
Scribbled a few words, they didn't seem right
Crumpled, I threw it against the wall
Many more followed to lie with that crumpled ball.

I was by now in disarray and dismay
How come the rhymes not coming my way?
Topics I changed . . . to no better effect
Thinking each time . . . if not now . . . I'll be wrecked!

Restless for the First time I grew
for Completion of my 2nd Book . . . close, the deadline drew.
I looked around wondering what and how, to ease the pain
I walked, I ran, but all in vain.

Those poetic verses just me eluded
Thinking I'm going mad, kept myself secluded.
So overjoyed was I releasing the First
My readers, for more, began to thirst.

Accolades they came in many forms and flowers
A Tribute for my devotion and long long hours.
Printers & Publishers were clamoring for a Second
That's when I sat, my thoughts to beckon.

Alas! I thought what will I write
When nothing I have to put in black and white.
Dejected I felt, this is my end
Unless I pull myself, from round the bend.

Several days passed, time was drawing near
Rolled tobacco sticks & Pegs I turned to, out of fear
My room soon resembled a dingy bar
With Blue smoke filled, and cigarette butts near and far.

I often wandered at night disheveled, on the street
Hoping against hope, I'm not caught by cops on the beat.
I yearned and looked around for just any 'Prey'
That I could go back and write about today.

Night after Night, it would be the same
After all the praises, now 'twould be a shame!
Last night I decided, just one last try
To gather my thoughts, hoping they'll come by.

Was I becoming now a nervous wreck?
Then I decided . . . what the Heck!!
I'll tell the world openly what I feel
And to them . . . the truth I'll reveal.

Fearing now, whether they will leave my flank
But, they must know . . . . I'm a Poet gone Temporarily Blank!!

(7.36)

'Mobile Mummies'
Composed by Leo D.Souza. July 26, 2913 at 8.19 pm

These days it's not very clear,
And there's always a fear,
When on a 2 wheeler you see
Our Modern youth, like a 'Mobile Mummie'.

It's hard to understand, what the covering will serve,
A girl or boy to know, you're forced to find a curve!
These Mobile Mummies, would make an Egyptian confused too,
'Cos to see, such, only in the grave, they're used to.

Whoever it is, is equally driving rash!,
To go anywhere, they only believe, to make a dash!
They whizz past the Cops, who stand under a tree,
Waiting, a victim to challan*, or gain a cup of Tea.

When they pass me nodding a Hello,
I don't know whether, that's a friend or foe.
It's made me now, to memorize, a Vehicle Number
So I can recognize, if it's a Him or a Her.

The Cops too scratch their head, in utter wonder,
'Cos even the boys, have earrings in their ear.
They blow their whistle for all it's worth,
but these 'Mummies' escape, full of mirth.

There's a Law they say, disallowing 'Covering the Face',
Because the culprits cannot be caught or traced.
In summer, the excuse is Heat and Dust
Other seasons, I guess . . . their Face will Rust!!

---

*Challan = Traffic Violation Ticket

(7.37)

"The Newspaper"!!.
Composed by Leo DSouza Sept 22, 2012 at 4.14 pm

I'm plain to look, but have so many views
'Cos within my folds I hold the News.
My Front Page, everyday is a Craze
When I arrive, to see this, everyone does race.

For every inch of me . . . there's a Price
Thinking of it.. makes me feel nice.
I'm proud 'cos with the happenings mentioned in me
I too, go down in History.

There's not an incident in this whole wide world
That's not, through me gone unfurled.
For centuries my ancestors held sway
Enlightening people about happenings of their day.

I have brothers, sisters & relatives many
Some specialize, others reporting interesting things, any
Each of us have, our own pre planned pages
Some change, Others remain the same thru ages.

We have space dedicated to places far flung
As well as one devoted to the Young.
For the Aged to keep their minds alert
We give the 'Crossword', they have to find the word.

For Sports enthusiasts a section is allotted too
Just as crime is reported on page two.
The "'Have's" figure prominently on Page Three
A supplement for Entertainment is given FREE!

There's a page or two devoted to mini-ads
Advertising Vacancies, Sales and Fashion Fads!
If you need a Tutor, Plumber or a Coaching Class
Even Bathroom fittings, made of Brass..

There's never ever a place far to go
Through us, it's there daily, delivered at your door.

Now there are folks who for Market Trends do care
We offer them a page too, dealing in Stocks and Market Share.
We come with you, if you want, to take us
Ever willing we come by train, car or bus.
That's our life, we've learned to Live
Not asking for anything, but just to Give.

On Sundays for all there's a special treat
Dishes to Cook of all kinds, Veg, Fish and also Meat.
Everyone is keen to see our 'Middles'
While kids love the page with the Riddles.

When the Day is done and our News is now stale
We land up with the others, ready for Sale.
We lie in wait, for the Rag mans Cart
Back to the Paper Mills, A new Life to Start.

(7.38)

"Picnics".

Composed by Leo DSouza Nov 29,2012 at 1.35 am

'Picnics' are a Getaway
From the routines of everyday.
Planned by Family and friends
Tension filled lives, it definitely mends.

Young kids, about it, bubble with great joy
Be it a Girl or a Boy.
While youngsters plan, the games they'll play
Little oldies pack, the munchies for the way.

'Anglers' in the crowd, bring their hooks and line
The Romantic minded, seek solitude time.
Swimmers ensure to carry, their swimming gear
Adventurous, seek exploring places without fear.

Loners like me, take in the rustic scene
while photographers click, things you might not have seen.
Plant hunters search gardens and shoots
Preferring to get them, from the roots.

Culinary experts, on reaching, prepare the Tea
Then set up a makeshift kitchen, opening spices and ghee.
They later chop the chicken & clean the rice
The aroma filling, the air real nice.

Earlier the 'armature Chefs' go gather the wood
To start a fire, as best they could.
The Elders sit and play, a game of Cards
or form a group, for Dumb Charades'

There's 'Passing the Parcel' and 'Housie' for all
The 'wittiest' opting, the numbers to call.
Tipplers find the shade of a tree
Ideal for a Bar, clinking glasses & being, very 'Comfy"

So engrossed are all, just chilling out
To 'Go Home' . . . 'No'!! they let out a Shout!
Driving back, along the village bumpy road
Folk songs rent the air, making the journey, less bored.

Finally, everyone's back to the starting point
But, not before deciding, the when & where, for the next 'Picnic' joint!

(7.39)

Ode to an Indian Farmer.
Composed by LEO DSOUZA April 29, 2012 at 14.36 pm
(Inspired by my Holiday in Chota Havala* village in Udaipur(Rajasthan)

A Farmers a hardworking but . . . neglected lot
Bearing inclement weather, power-cuts and what not
Threats to lives & fields from wild animals they constantly face
fields trampled or even spoilt their crops of maize.
Sometimes their cattle the Panther's or Leopards pick
as they're often surrounded by mountains or jungles thick.

Doggedly yet . . . . they just go on
indirectly feeding us . . . . what they have sown.
Simple but hard life they always lead
Catering for themselves and . . . our need.
When one crop is all cut and done
on a new field . . . work already begun.

Not a produce from their field goes waste
Hay bundled for Sale before monsoon . . . storing they'd haste
The corn threshed and put in sacks
stored in a room 'cos, ... they have no racks.
Even with the cattle dung . . . fire cakes they make
Thus added income . . . . it would rake.

Their houses built mostly with mud and straw
So cool inside.. I felt and saw
with this hardy life . . . . SICK . . . they hardly get
Hence, no doctors . . . I saw or met.

Toiling thus, to their kids, just Naturally comes
Never hear them like urbanites say.."I'm feeling in the Dumps"
At night, all sleep mostly . . . open to the skies
No'Odomos'to ward off mosquitoes or flies
With Nature, they have learned to exist
No Urban life they know, ... or ever miss.

Little Gopi Ram, unlike 'Humpty Dumpty' had no wall
'Cos in villages they build no walls . . . trusting all
Every morn Gopi Ram had the Ox to feed
Comprising Hay, chara* and homegrown weed
Then the hand-pump next to switch on
So water could flow to the fields of corn

Rekha & Rani . . . the mother daughter duo
would brew the tea and for them pour
Father Ghasi Ram would be busy from the field uprooting weeds
while flitting around, birds big and small, picked their morning needs.

Gopi Ram's task next was to milk the cows
Sorting some for SALE and some for the house.
Then on his bicycle, with the cans, off he went
to the cities..full speed..and hell bent
so to each house he could deliver
Never grumbling..he'd do it.. day after day..like forever.

Returning home..he'd his school bag pack
with a copy. a slate and 2 roti's* he'd take.
Off to school..with his pals he'd tread
knowing that..'this alone' will bring his future bread.
Sitting on the ground under a tree
they'd study..maths and a little History.

Meanwhile back home Ghasi Ram the crops would tend
also securing fences which, wild animals, each night would bend.
Substituting Tractors for Ox he'd plough, another field
so a better crop of wheat it'll yield
Peacocks keeping him company would early morning, come
Helping him by picking & eating the insects some

No watch to guide, but just, the angle of the sun
Guided the farmer and his son.
By evening tide, Gopi Ram on return from school
wouldn't sit idle or drool
The evening Milk too was his chore
and about it . . . he'd dutifully go

217

Pure Ghee, the mother, she would churn
while other children, helping father turn by turn
To the market they never have to go
Everything's in their field..that's for sure.

I wish our life, like theirs, had an even pace
instead of this Mad Urban . . . rat race.
Yet, . . . many, on them look down
Simply because, they're not from 'Town"

I'd give everything, like them, to go and stay
in a village, ploughing and farming . . . day to day.
To all my Urban friends I plead
Respect your farmer, he caters to your 'Feed'
Just think, would you be able to live like him
without Laptop, mobikes, cars, mobiles or SIM?
Then . . .Thank the Lord . . . . for creating the likes of them.

---

*Chota Havala= Small Palace. * Chara = Cow feed. *Roti's=
unleavened bread.

Chapter VIII

Tragedies and Sagas

Friends, my all time favourite compositions are

'Tragedies and Sagas'. In this edition I have included

only a few under this category, as not many like

to read this type of poetry but seek light reading matter..

(8.1)

MURDER at HARMONY!!

Composed by Leo DSouza. Saturday, September 1, 2012 at 8:41pm

Ahmad quickly buried the knife
Seeing Sunita's body on the floor
Slowly the blood drained out her life
Now he was wondering where to go.

The Party last night, at 'Harmony' had carried on very late
Everyone having a lovely time
Sunita was told she'd be dropped . . . to just wait.
When he closed up to retire, everything seemed fine.

Morning's hangover made him move to the Refrigerator
That's when he spied her on the floor.
Who, he wondered could have, so much hated her?
He was determined to know more.

Evening had seen Alex, Ravi and Sunita have a drink
The Other Guests busy in a Pool game
Could either of them . . . . he began to think.
That it had to be Sunita . . . such a shame!!

Her throat was slit and signs of Rape
The Police were searching for a clue
In the corner by the door was her Cape
The Police said, he, was suspect too!!

Collecting evidence, questioning guests
The Police they were very thorough
Everyone called for fingerprint test
Obtaining vital clues about her.

Ahmad arrested and produced in court
While beneath Sunita's nails they found some pubic hair
DNC proved that Ahmad it was not
Even though his shirt had a tear.

John was about to fly out of town
The Investigations revealed their old affair.
From the craft they brought him down
Grilled, his confession raised their hair!!

He had lured Sunita to a private room, on a Pretext
Then he pushed her on the Bed.
For ditching him, he was vexed
As she scratched his manhood, he said.

Then with rage in a flash he stabbed her once
Getting up, to leave her to die.
But, rising, on him she did pounce
Threatening to scream, she did cry.

He then slit her throat and closed the door
Opened the window, to come by later.
Returning late, he dragged her till the fridge door
When footsteps he heard of a late retreating waiter.

Making his escape he drove back home
Showered and cleaned his shoes of the garden mud
Accepting fate, now, that out the truth had come
He just felt sorry for his old friend Ahmad

Nailed him were Old letters confiscated from John's residence
The Case dragged on for years so many
Ahmad got 3 years for destruction of evidence
John' got Death but, is still alive..It's so funny
The Media simply labeling it.. 'Murder at Harmony'.

(8.2)

Sweet Progressive Love.
Composed by: Leo DSouza Saturday, August 25, 2012 at 2:03am

John and Jane were neighbours before
Growing up together . . . . being next door.
They even shared a bus going to school
'No distractions' for both, was a family Rule.

Carefree Childhoods, to awkward teens, they both went thru
Happy Family lives was all they ever knew.
Socials and Outings, both families together often went
As good neighbours, years together they spent.

School days over, they moved to get a Degree
Often now, each other they didn't even see.
Engineering Degree his aim, he did pursue
She took Fashion designing, and learnt to sew.

The Fashion ladder up, she began to climb
Designing outfits, while the clock continued to chime.
Meanwhile Semesters he cleared, one by one
On his way, an Engineer to become.

Results came, he topped the class
"GLASSY" titled was her show, with Gowns of Beads and Glass
Both families overjoyed, decided to meet
Along with friends, who wanted 'both' to greet.

John the debonair, so happy and gay
Jane with long tresses, both looking a lovely pair.
That night they too, each other, differently saw
Feelings from 'cold storage' had begun to 'thaw'

Both saw each other in utter awe
And felt in their beings and hearts . . . a gnaw.
Unnoticed by doting parents, passed the night
Each with their feelings began to fight.

The next day over a cup of Coffee
Expressing themselves, hoping for a maybe
Days were now filled with a purpose new
Each longing for the evening's moments few

This was the beginning, just the start
Discovering a new found throb, in their heart.
From Coffee tables to Evening Drives
Their Love growing by bounds began to thrive.

The Stars and Moon for them, developed a new light
Bringing a twinkling future within sight.
Early morning walks in the light wet mist
Enjoying as the Breeze, her long soft tresses, they kissed.

Their Courting lasted for months so sweet
John had now completely swept her off her feet
In this World he was feeling Right on Top
So, on a moonlit night, the question he did Pop.

Both families' happiness knew no bounds
Preparedness & Planning now, were the only sounds.
Cards printed, posted all were gone
Greetings were pouring in, even on phone.

This morning the Church decorated with flowers
Time's flying, inching closer, pushing behind the hours
John and Jane have come,' I DO' to each other say
Please do come, You're invited too, today's their Wedding Day!!

(8.3)

The Lion's Growl.

Composed by Leo DSouza. July 13, 2013 at 1:18am
Grrr . . . . Grrr, Grrr I growled from my cage
Annoyed at being disturbed, showing my rage.
I was brought here, just a month back
Torn away from my Human friends, Peter and Jack.

Six months ago I was up for sale
In a pet shop known as 'Jungle Trail'.
Shut up in a cage so small
I couldn't walk or even crawl.

With Bow Wow and a meow . . . meow, as room mates
Oblivious of the mercenary, marking our tags with rates.
All day long 'visitors' would come stare and go
Some bold, others not wanting their timidity, to show.

This cruelty we just couldn't bear,
Gnawing at ourselves, tearing at times our hair.
For Mercy, we daily sent up a prayer
In our own animal way.

Peter & Jack one fair, the other tall and dark
Came in one day, bought me for a lark
My new home was fun, as I was Free
Roaming the flat, so abandonedly

My masters hugged and cuddled me so much
I had nothing wanting, as such.
But, I was growing fast, before their eye
I loved most my walks, under the open sky.

Then sadness crept into their eyes one day
'Goodbye' to me, they decided to say.
Some uniformed men came in Blue
To take me away from them, I knew,

I was now enjoying life in the open pen
Of-course youngsters are evil now and then.
I narrowed my eyes and at them, growl
Grrr . . . Grrrr. Grrr as towards them I prowl.

Then suddenly two figures, from the lawns arise
I thought they're familiar, someone I recognize,
One dressed in Jeans, the other in a sweater
I ran towards them . . . . My Jack and Peter!!

There were screams all around, as I leapt
Across the moat, while with Joy I wept.
Security drew their Guns, me to nail
As I bounded towards Peter & Jack, at the Guard Rail.

I licked their faces and round their neck put my paws
They were my only Family, because.
My heart with joy did abound
Then 2 shots dropped me to the ground.

Life fading, the last that I saw
Peter & Jack crying, each holding one paw.
GOD, Forgive those guards, they were not to know
It was only my Gratitude and Love, I did show.

(8.4)

When The Bride Answered . . . Loud and Clear..!!!
Composed by Leo DSouza Sunday, September 2, 2012 at 12:16am

'Cappuccino' it was where they met 3 years ago
She was that girl, in gay abandon, dressed in yellow
It was a Business meeting that he sat in
Yet his mind, her picture etched, has always been.

Edna's parents were anxious, Jim was a nice boy
She was now Senior Executive, yet marriage was no toy.
They had broached the subject, she just brushed it off
Glen her brother too, at marriage did scoff.

Errol met Edna 2 days after that chance encounter
They had got along well and he loved her banter.
Eight years her senior, he knew it would one day be an issue
Right now to mop up the spilt coffee, he used the tissue.

Edward and Mary her parents, rang Jim McCartney's home
Robert McCartney picked the call, with joy was overcome.
Lucy his wife, from the mantle shelf, a smile she shared
Robert she knew, for Jim, always cared.

The meeting with Errol whom Edna did call
Didn't go off well with Edward and Mary at all
They didn't succumb, just did tarry
How could they allow Edna, 8 years her senior, marry?

When Edna heard about Jim she flatly refused
but the situation, she couldn't diffuse
Time passed, she thought things had to cool
Neither Errol or Jim she wanted to Fool.

Then, Errol had to travel abroad on work
For courtesy sake, she met Jim, the meeting, unable to shirk
She noticed, he was coming over almost every other night
She didn't mind, as long as her parents thought it's all right.

Against her wishes, now her wedding was fixed
She was confused with feelings mixed
Errol got held up, wouldn't be back till next Monday
And her wedding was planned for next Sunday.

No amount of coaxing, explaining would help
She could scream, cry or yelp
Preparation in place, the wedding would go on
Errol flew in on Edna's . . . . SOS phone.

He met her that morning, whispered in her ear
The moment he got a chance to come near.
There was quite a scene at her house
He walked away; it seemed, like a mouse.

The guests took their places in the Church pew
The minutes for Church service, left . . . only few.
Jim arrived looking dashing in a suit of dark Blue
Everyone awaited Edna to put in an appearance too

The Priest came, with the delay, a bit perturbed
Behind his mind, hoping it won't happen, what he feared.
Then he sighed in relief, Edna's car was seen
Dressed in Lacy white, she looked a Queen!

The Service Started, it was time for the Vows with grace
In the front, the witnesses took their place.
'Will you take . . . . he said 'YES, I DO"
Smiles flashed while Cameras clicked too

The Mike into her hands, it next went.
For this "answer', in practice, 'months she spent'
The Priest asked . . . Will you . . . "NO she answered Loud and Clear."
'Sorry everyone, my pleas till now no one would ever hear'
'They gave us 'no chance' . . . . So let it be'
Then turning to Errol, said . . . "for me it's He"
And turning walked away, arm in arm, HAPPILY!!!.

(8.5)

Happyville Town
Composed by Leo DSouza. July 22,2013 at 02.35 am

Old Mrs. Fernandez, with Ruth and Kate,
Had just gone out the front Gate.
The lights were on in the Park,
But the streets were quiet and dark.

Uncle Peter had just returned from work,
Checking each car door . . . that was his daily quirk.
In the distance, the wind whistled and blew,
Was it good or an 'Omen', ... no one knew.

Mr. Smith was out with his walking stick,
Showing Jane and John a magic trick.
The dogs were chasing one another
Running after them, was Mark their brother.

'Where's my soup'.. 'twas time for Henry to ask
Before laying plates for dinner, that was my last task.
Bringing the newspaper, he sat in his rocking chair
He too commented on the cool, outside air..

My favourite program CSI, was on the Telly,
'It had reached a turning point', was saying Nellie.
Henry, settled in with his soup to drink'
'twas then I heard something fall . . . . in the kitchen sink.

Was it the whistling wind, that's come this way, so soon??
I wondered, watching Henry, picking up his spoon..
I walked across to close the window,
and securely latched even the door.

The water quivered too in my cup,
I looked at it, wondering, what's up?
Did I by mistake, bang the table?
From my place, surely, I was not able.

The glasses on their racks did clink
Surely. at this hour. no one's having a drink.
By now the Spoons and Ladle's too began to swing,
It sounded like, they had begun to sing,

Just then, down below, some Sirens Sounded,
Who, I wondered now was being hounded?
Voices outside, told me, somethings amiss
Womanly Instinct, made me investigate this.

The Tables rocked, the pictures went askew,
Something was serious, we now definitely knew.
Evacuating decisions we now had to make
We were in the midst of an Earthquake,

Suddenly our world was Topsy-Turvy,
Escape we just had to, and in a hurry.
The Earth Shook, our Houses trembled
Before we knew it, . . . a beam just crumbled,

We jumped 2 steps at a time, the stairs
Saving ourselves only, no other cares.
Our neighbours were in real big trouble.
They were trapped below their house Rubble.

Out in the street, Cars and Trees were lying like ballast
Worst than last year's Hurricane' Pearly', that had then hit us.
Half broken will powers, fully broken Homes,
Strewn far and Wide, Rooftops, Bricks and stones.

Mr. Smith was lying face down, still gripping his walking stick
Staring at dead bodies, was making me sick.
Mrs. Fernandez, Ruth and Kate, were lying in a heap
Seeing them Jane and John began to weep.

The Earthquake had measured 9.8 on the Richter Scale,
Fear writ on survivors faces, left them pale.
Children were sole survivors, in many places,
Bleak future encrypted, on everyone's faces.

Relief Shelters sprang up everywhere,
From affluent to Refugee, we were there,
Living on Dole outs, & Government Aid,
The Dead outnumbered the living, it was said.

Next day, in the Silent calm we crept
For loved ones and Dead, we silently wept.
We had to put this quake behind us now,
Rebuild our lives, Life to go on, somehow.

The Scars that showed on each one's face
Will be etched forever, resembling a brand new Race..
There'll never be, for us, another town 'Happyville'
For that day, our happiness forever, the Earthquake, did kill.

(8.6)

'Tragedy at Sea'.
Composed by Leo DSouza June 30,2013 at 10.37 am

I saw a ship a wrecking
Getting wrecked on the rough, rough sea.
The Storm at them was mocking
As I looked aghast, from 'Silver's' Cabin B

Faint yells and screams they came
Over gusty winds, so strong
Nature seemed playing with them, a game
The climate had gone gone . . . all wrong!

Water gushing on the tilting deck
Slipping and sliding, people going overboard
From my vantage, only words came . . . 'OH! HECK!!
Mind racing yet, how they to safety, could be towed.

Weighty Luggage being dumped I could see
Just to Balance and save precious lives
Why, I wondered, this fury had to be
As again the ship took another of its nosedives.

Still waving, clamouring, full of Hope!
Frightened, terror filled people, yell and shout
wondering with the situation how to cope
'Hoping hearts' with no iota of doubt.

The Radar Mast was the First to go
Snapping and putting the vessel in turmoil
Crewmen scuttling now frantically, to and fro
as harder realizing, they have to toil.

The giant waves tossed them over and over,
Till just a wreck was.. 'that Might'
Lives snuffed out, like a plucked clover
As slowly she inclined and sank out of sight.

Aghast was I, with others from our ship
witnessing a tragedy of humanity gone
Terror paleing even the hardened lip
'Unimaginable' it was, when the sun rose, next morn.

Chapter IX

My Country I Know

In this Chapter I have given a vivid account of My Country as I have known it, having grown up here, seeing my friends celebrate the various and diverse 'Festivals', witnessed numerous 'Elections', seen some 'Absurd Laws' enacted, known and read about a plethora of 'Prime Ministers" and functioning of 'Varied Presidents' and finally seeing its 'Modification'.

(9.1)

2012 . . . The Year that we knew (A Saga of events)!!
Composed by Leo DSouza. Thursday, January 3, 2013 at 1:13am

It was the year 2012, so full of strife
Political unrest, hampering Common Mans life.
Crime rates, they were on the rise
In India, Petrol only saw an upward price.

Obama in the U.S. was elected again
While in India, Mamta Banerjee lost the Train!
We lost great luminaries of Tinsel Town
Rajesh Khanna who, wore the 1st Super Hero Crown.

Achala Sachdev, Joy Mukherjee, Yash Chopra and Dara Singh
Sitar Maestro Pt. Ravi Shankar & Mehadi Hassan, the Gazal King.
On A.K.Hangal's death, people asked,'Itna Sannata Kyon hai Bhai?'
Then Jaspal Bhatti's car went 'Ulta Pulta' & he did die.

Internationally, Whitney Huston to whose songs many would swoon
Even Neil Armstrong, who walked the moon.
Two days before the end of 2012
India's ex PM, I K Gujral went, he was PM no: 12.

6th February marked Queen Elizabeth's Diamond Jubilee
No other Monarch ruled as long as she.
Mumbai's Central & Harbor line went out of gear
In Kurla, a Fire in April destroyed its signal this year.

Natural Calamities occurred now and then
Taking lives, like a Typhoon killing all of 1067.
While London saw and hosted the Summer Olympics
July end in India, 630 Million had to depend for light, on Candlesticks

On August 6th Man's 'Curiosity' landed on Mars
Though Mallaya's Kingfisher, couldn't take off from Airports of ours.
Oct 24-30th Hurricane Sandy killed 209, spreading Fear
In the Caribbean, Bahamas, U.S. and Canada.

In Tokyo, worlds highest 634 meters, self supporting Tower opened in May
While the Century's 2nd and last Solar Transit, we saw that day.
Marriages broke down in many Celebrity's homes
Example we had of Tom Cruise and Katie Holmes.

Chris Gayle celebrating triumph over Sri Lanka, danced Gangum Style
The Dance itself getting noticed by Guinness Book, after a while.
The Indian Govt jumped from Fuel to Fire and cut our Gas
Bringing demonstrations on streets, enmass.

The world was stunned when Donna Summer did die
And when at Last, Sachin decided to Retire, but only from ODI
On 18th Nov Balasaheb's Funeral brought Mumbai to a grinding Halt
2 Teen girls arrested, for commenting on FB about it, their only fault.

For Ajmal Kasab, on 21st Nov, it was Doomsday
Bringing to an end . . . all the Biryani, in Jail, he ate away.
Anna Hazare's fight against Corruption took India by Storm
Kejriwal riding piggy back on him, broke away, a political party to form.

Dr Varghese Kurien of the White Revolution passed away on 11/9
While Kejriwal, accused Robert Vadra of Corruption, giving him a rough time.
In Sports the fastest man declared was Usain Bolt
Winning a 'double double' and 'double triple' we are told.

In Gujarat, Modi had a thumping victory
Couldn't get all the seats, though he did try
On the PM's seat now, he has set his eye
But the BJP are weary, everyone knows why.

Nitin Gadkari says he will not leave his crown
Which is making many in the party, to frown
He's trying his best to cover up very cleverly
The Scam that broke about his baby 'Purti'

Tony Grieg's wicket was the last to fall
Now we'll miss his commentary . . . Ball to Ball.
For 12.12.12 there was everywhere a great hype
Everyone clamoring, for those moments to swipe.

235

The World was predicted, on 21st Dec to end
Everyone tried all ways, themselves to mend
Apprehension was writ large, on many a face
Wondering about how the end will be of this Race.

Boarding a Bus, 23 yr old 'Damini' didn't know it'll end in her Rape
The Brutality of the Act left the nation and World Agape.
On 29th Dec, just 3 days before 2012 could end
She gave up her fight, GOD to her, his Mercy did send.

Finally like every year 2012 too, we saw run through
Everyone Somber, in Damini's grief, awaited the New Year too.
From the embers of the bonfires of the year gone by
Rose the Hopes and Wishes of every Man, Woman, Girl or Boy.

Silently and Majestically, She came in like a Queen
Gliding lightheartedly was OUR NEW YEAR 2013!!

(9.2)

Some Absurd Laws!!
by Leo DSouza JUNE 19,2011 AT 2.42 AM.

These are often made without a thought
by Grey haired guys . . . just because for Independence they fought.
Absurdity . . . most of them are called
no wonder, all rise up & they get mauled!

Boys a Bike at 16 they can ride
as a 'Learner'—so long as a Senior is beside.
No matter if he, the signs, can't read
'cos on the roads-they're themselves missing—Yes Indeed!!

At 18, They hardly turn to toys from their paper boats
when Politicians say-Remember me! . . . cos now u can Vote!
They still are groping and going thru tremendous Strife
Then they're told . . . You're 21 . . . you can take a Wife.

How sad . . . his wedding day he'll remember for Life
Cos beside him he would have a wife but, Cannot drink . . . . till 25!!
By then, maybe he'll have to tow along, a kid or two
Wondering, What more the Govt by then . . . won't let him do!

Long live our Absurd Laws!!
That will always be . . . . Full of Flaws!!

(9.3)

ANNA HAZARE-Biography and LOKPAL BILL!!
—by Leo DSouza on Thursday, August 25, 2011 at 10:25am

Born Kisan Bapat Baburao Hazare on 15 Jan 1940
he grew to make 'fighting for Justice' his forte.
Raised by a childless aunt in Mumbai
he sure is one helluva guy.
Recruited into the Army in 1963 as a driver
Driving uniformed men of valour!
To a rank of 'Sepoy'* he did rise
Taking VRS in '78 . . . now developing his village he set his eyes.
To a drought prone village-he began 'conservation of water',
Having all the time..being Free and a bachelor.
In '95 he unearthed the 'scam of grabbing land'
from Agriculturist..and formed a band
to form 'Bhrashtachar Virodhi *Jan in 1991
Roping in the 'corrupt'.. one by one.
In '97 he moved the RTI which was passed in 1993
Benefiting us citizens . . . including you and me.

A self proclaimed crusader for injustices is he
picking on anything resembling an anomaly
Fighting' injustices', himself he took upon
'Going on Fast' for which..a robe he did adorn.
Though 'ideas' of his were 'good and right'
Bulldozing the Govt he thought was his birthright.
When 'Opposition'..the Govt they could not topple,
with Jan Lokpal Bill to him they trooped..on the double!

But when the Public with him, began to flow
It made them 'jittery' and very Sore.
If his Bill was accepted and Passed by this Govt ours
most of them would've been found 'behind bars'
A joint meeting of Govt and Opposition—did they call
Both the 'Bills 'got rejected..by one and all.
Though the end of this— we've still got to see.
All that the Movement's done so far . . . . is create 'History'

25th August.. The PM and Opposition requested Anna to end his fast
but determined he is he says to make it last.

In Negotiations he wants 3 items to be included
Include Lower Bureaucracy, Citizens charter and Lok Ayukta state wise he
concluded
Start discussions in parliament tomorrow was his contend
To this . . . give written assurance . . . if my fast I hv to end.
Agitation he says he will continue..even though he ends his fast
Until the Lok Pal Bill is done and passed.

---

*Sepoy = Armyman from the ranks. * Brashtachar Virodhi: Against
Corruption

(9.4)

Corruption—Thy Name is India!!
by Leo DSouza Wednesday, June 15, 2011 at 7:02pm

Corruption's a part in an Indian's life
If u don't participate—you're in strife.
Into any Govt office as you go
From the Peon to the officer . . . it's all in a row
You object to 'give'—you're in a stew
And left standing all day . . . . in a queue.

On the roads—the cop's you find . . . under a tree
Waiting for the bait . . . not one or two..But three.
Politicians their voices against it . . . they often raise
For a common man . . . its part of a race.

Schools/colleges as a 'donation' . . . they ask
For Parents, from where to shell out . . . . is a task.
In Delhi University . . . it's such a clout
100% for admissions today . . . is the Cut-out.

Job seekers . . . Interviews they easily crack
But when a cut is asked . . . . to zero you are back.
Daily needs . . . Veggies and fruits are soaring high
Blaming the inclement weather, sunny days or cloudy sky

Tuition Classes . . . are now the Norms of the day
to score that 100% they'll help they say.
12 months and 8 periods a day they find is 'short', the course to cover
But, in 3 months tuitions . . . they do it however!

Sadhu's and Sant's begin . . . to drive it out . . . a Fast

Garnering Public support with one or other Farce.
Themselves declare their Assts . . . In India or Abroad
Getting it from where? Surely not from 'GOD'!!

Where and when this will end . . . everyone asks
Hands tied we are . . . no choice but, in it we bask
Ready on someone or other we willingly throw the Blame
Little realizing . . . for India.. it's a shame!!

(9.5)

Elections..
Composed by Leo DSouza Friday, November 9, 2012 at 3:23pm

To Many, Elections are, the beginning to an end
Of a Govt that, during it's tenure, did not mend.
To some it's time, to stuff their Purse
Others still feel, it's a Curse!

The Common man with promises, each party tries, to woo
Later, it doesn't matter, what they really do.
The country on the whole, is put in turmoil
Normal movements on roads, they vow to spoil.

The fever starts, when candidates, seek a ticket
If denied, then they plan a picket.
College students and Urchins are Politicians 1st choice
As empty vessels, generally make the most noise!

Freebies are given, left right and center
Eyes focused on 'Madam Vote', just to win her.
From 10 kgs rice to a coloured T.V.
Enticing a vote from young, & from the house, the Lady!

From every party leader, promises flow galore
Touring Constituencies, they generally would ignore.
Defacing walls, with Posters, more and more
But once voted, you, they do not know.

Crores they spend, from Business houses that donate
Local leaders woo you, and even become your Mate!
They defame each other, across the Globe
Though they are all clothed, with the same Robe!

Election Fever grips one and all
Trying to vote out the Govt, and make it fall.
With results declared, we wait with bated breathe
When newer Crooks come in, the future we dread!

Now the Prices, they soon begin to soar
As citizens voices, they begin to Roar!
The newly elected, begin Victory to Toast
No Choice, we've got, but to bear this, another 5 years at most

(9.6)

India's Golden Years!!
By Leo DSouza on Saturday, November 12, 2011 at 7:09pm

A Band of Freedom Fighters in 1947,
Took over Power . . . The British, from our land were driven.
Youth, elders, sportspersons and writers . . . they were ONE
Playing their part till . . . . Freedom was WON.

As the years rolled by . . . Statesmen changed,
New Indian Heads took over . . . . things began to change.
Food began to get scarce . . . . other essentials too.
Poverty crept in for the poor . . . . the rich, richer still grew.
Adulteration and scarcity was to people nothing new

A Common man just struggled to 'live'
While the elite had . . . so much but . . . . not to' give'
The Elders and Freedom Fighters were soon things of the past
If you wanted 'Justice' it was always . . . 'STRIKE' or "Fast"

Lawlessness became the order of the day
In India too . . . . many surfaced as . . . 'Gay'
CANCER and AIDS one couldn't just shrug
As youths 'indulge' because of . . . DRUGS.

Politicians didn't require their usual . . . Bread and Jam
They've made enough from one or other . . . 'SCAM'
Changing names of Road, Cities, airports and stations each day
Is how the 'Tax payers 'money is gradually blown away?

Oh! India when will your Glory return to Shine
Or are all Indians content to have our second name . . . 'CRIME'
50 Golden years have passed . . . . such a Shame!!
Nothing 'Concrete's 'done . . . . who's to Blame?

It's time we wake up and bring back . . . . 'OUR HINDUSTAN"
From what it's now commonly world over called . . . . 'SCAMISTAN"

(This was composed a few years ago)

(9.7)

"Our Prime Ministers"..

(History . . . . In Verse).-by Leo DSouza. On Wednesday, August 1, 2012 at 4:46pm

From last 65 years since Independence we've seen
Prime Ministers.. so many that have been.
We had one softer than the petals of the rose he wore
Another Tall in his ideas yet, short in stature
One with the guts and will of steel
A farmer too . . . and for them he did feel.
Some came with just a desire to be PM
Others through default..but, we can't blame them

For Politics that stepped in . . . and the problems that they did create
We as citizens have become only . . . . spectators of late.
There's on each so much to tell
as each incident of theirs . . . rings a bell

A brief sketch or picture of each I'll paint for you
Giving each for whatever they did their . . . . due.
Jawaharlal Nehru on 15th August 1947 was the 1st to be sworn in
Receiving India's Independence . . . in the presence of Lord Mountbatten

An apt post for the one who, our Freedom's struggle fought
He deserved the job, is what everyone thought.
Loved by all and mostly the country's children by far
Lovingly referred to by them as their . . . . Cha—Cha.

For 18yrs,6 months he was at the Helm
Loved by all countrymen and he too cared for them.
During his reign, in 1964, we had the Chinese Aggression
Defeating them raised our Indian Army's Impression.

His signature was the red button hole rose he wore
When he died..his gardener swore, never more that rose he'd grow.
Lal Bahadur Shastri, replaced Nehru to become the 2nd PM next
'Jai Jawan-Jai Kisan' was his slogan in text.

Becoming PM he was compared and put to test
In his 16 months . . . he proved to be the best.
To his credit was the 'Green Revolution'
which, was his top most mission

Cease fire talks with truant Pakistan, was held in Tashkent
Negotiated & Cajoled in our favour . . . he signed the Agreement
But of a massive heart attack, from this world . . . same night he went.
Our Interim/Acting PM was the erstwhile G L Nanda
as the Nation without a PM was thrown asunder.

Indira Gandhi got elected the 3rd PM on 24th Jan 1966
She started re-building an Empire . . . with solid bricks
With an Iron rod . . . India around she twirled
2012 records show, She was longest serving Woman PM in the world!

She had many 1st to her name, including the Indo-Pak war of 1971
She gave Bangladesh it's freedom but, opposition against her, rose up as one.
Morarji Desai the 4th PM routed her out in 1977 on a Janata Ticket
But, he was already on a sticky wicket.

The 1st PM he was, for Peace talks with Pak conferred,' Order of Pakistan'
He had to go for his 'Urine Therapy' few could Digest or understand.
A Prestigious issue now . . . the PM's Post was made
When Charan Singh the 5th PM came in . . . a farmer by trade.

Lasting 5 months 17 days without attending a single Lok Sabha Session
as Indira withdrew Congress support . . . thus ending his mission.
Indira Gandhi now swept the Polls, as the 6th PM was re-elected
But foolishness to 'Rule by Decree'', she EMERGENCY selected

With "Operation Blue Star' Terrorism she targeted
To end up . . . . by her own body guards, on her lawns . . . . Assassinated.
Her son Rajiv Gandhi as the 7th PM . . . . India forward took
for the Army, modern weapons he began to look.

'Bofor's' guns he procured but, ended being named in a kickback scam
No one knows the truth till date . . . how much was true or how much just sham.
Under him India developed IT and Education

India now began to be feared as a developing Nation.

Bofor's Kickback scam took its toll
In '89 elections Rajiv lost the Polls.
V P Singh succeeded him as PM to be next, he came
Implementing Mandal's Commissions Reservation bill, he thought he'd frame

But, widespread riots . . . Indian students were all up in flames.
For him it spelt . . . . the end of the game.
Chandrasekhar took over as 9th PM, having long eyed the post
Alas! for him, 'twas not a ride, as he thought, on a roller coast.

Congress withdrew support after Rajiv's Assassination in Tamil Nad
Having got caught in a human Bomb . . . . shard.
Riding High now on the Sympathy wave
The Congress now brought P V Narashimha Rao, themselves to save

He continued fighting Terrorism and for the TADA Act, bid
At this time Advani began his 'Rath Yatra', in a bid
To sway some community, and got demolished the Babri Masjid.
Advani went scot free,
PV Narashimha Rao 'twas who had to flee.

Atal Bihari Vajpayee came in with a hung parliament
But Packing . . . lacking majority, in 13 days he went.
H D Devagowda the next PM always seemed a misfit
Though he tried to do his little bit

For the 1st time a Chinese Premier visited India
All thought Indo-China's strained relations were over by far
Introducing President's rule in Gujarat.. it spelt his doom
Under his feet..the grass was cut very soon.

I K Gujral the gentleman PM now took the seat
He was always dressed so very neat.
But then in just one year his Govt too fell
The BJP winning elections . . . rang the bell.
A.B Vajpayee they'd bring back . . . all could tell

During his regime we saw 'The Parliament Attack'
Terrorism had swung his ugly head back
'Gujarat Violence just came erupting by
'Flight IC 814 got hijacked, the terrorist to Kandahar, were allowed to fly

Irony of it all, for these very issues, the BJP attacked the Congress
When actually, in their regime, created was, this mess
Sonia Gandhi led the Congress to a huge victory
Man Mohan Singh was put up as PM and not she
To outsmart the Opposition, who were in her bonnet, like a bee.

Man Mohan 1st revoked POTA and introduced RTI
That benefited common people like you and I.
But Ministers from all ranks and file
Got into scams of every sort, wiping away from citizens. their smile.

Now Anna Hazare has made a farce of going on indefinite Fast
To get Jan Lokpal Bill, to HIS liking, making Corruption.. something of the past
The Congress got out of every tight corner till now we have seen
All Eyes will be glued and focused on Elections of 2014.

(9.8)

Our Varied Presidents!!
by Leonard DSouza on Sunday, July 29, 2012 at 4:34pm

India's Presidents all people so politically mature
All Controversies and strife's . . . they do endure.
Each one in spite of their individual personality
Adorned the Neutral Role to lead this Great Country.

Dr Rajendra Prasad to be the First, he was Chosen
after Independence, the country's care on his shoulders were laden.
A great Statesman, hailing from Bihar and son of the soil
He governed well and had long hours in Office to toil.

The Learned Dr S Radhakrishnan, from Chennai, was next on the seat
A great orator & Philosopher, none other could match or beat.
A great educationist he was all the way
so, his birthday, on his death, was named . . . 'Teachers Day'

Hyderabad's son, Dr Zakir Husain was elected next
An orphan at 14 yrs, he rose to be the Best.
Religious and very devout man to GOD was he
Got down to pray one day and . . . died on his knees.

V.V. Giri was elevated as the Fourth President
Of Berhampur, now Orissa, he was a resident.
The only living President, Indian Post honoured with a Stamp
He was the 2nd of 12 children . . . his home resembled a Camp.

Mohammed Hidyautullah, hailing from Nagpur, the next, made us feel nice
Alas! He was only Acting President for 35 days, then elected Vice.
Fakruddin Ali Ahmad the 5th President rule was from 1974 to 1977
Hailed from Delhi and a professional lawyer even

During his reign,' Emergency' he pronounced
A move that saw flak and the world denounced
But, looking back at those days, today
India had straightened up . . . in a big Big way.

So mysterious was his death and so sudden
India was stunned and everyone saddened.
At this stage the vice President took charge that was B.D.Jatti
The only man till date holding office of V.P. and President simultaneously

A stop-gap arrangement that just had to be
Till our 6th President elected was N S Reddy.
Another Record!! The only President elected.. 'Unopposed'!
And the youngest to head India for this Post.

Giani Zail Singh the 7th, hailed from Faridkot
He was to the Nehru-Gandhi family . . . a devout.
From a humble beginning of a carpenters son
He had the Post of President . . . elections won.

R. Venkataraman became the President No: 8
He worked with 4 Prime Ministers..A Record to date!
Had the distinction of appointing 3 of them
He came in when Rajiv Gandhi was P.M. then.

After his term, we had Dr Shankar Dayal Sharma of M.P.
Whose 'Teddy bear walk' was loved and enjoyable to see.
He was another learned man and well read
His last few month saw him getting sick, sicker and then Dead.

Dr K R Narayanan from Kerala, the 10th we had
His rule from 1977 to 2002 was good not bad.
Since we had for President experienced the South
We continued to elect from Rameshwaram to further their clout.

Our 11th President elected was Dr A P J Kalam the Scientist
India's head was now a 'Missile Technologist
Loved by Opposition and all, but by children the best.
The 12th and First Lady chosen as his successor Pratibha Patil
But, her husband's criminal cases bothered her and all, still.

Unfortunately for her, some Ministers in some or other Scam had a hand
She too fell prey, planning a house for retirement on Army land.
Our 13th President elected on 25th July 2012 was Pranab Mukherjee
Whose sister, from young, him in Presidents seat dreamt to see.

Being well read and very knowledgeable
To test, how from this inflation, to pull us out he will be able.
With his diverse experience in the political field
Will he stand his ground in decisions . . . or will he to pressures . . . yield?

(9.9)

The Nagpur We Remember!!!
by Leo DSouza on Saturday, July 21, 2012 at 12:25am

Nagpur of Old..Still brings back vivid memories
Bringing before our eyes . . . old Glories.
Our Railway Station Majestically stood out
Bereft of Tea-stalls, Auto's and ticket touts.

No Cars & Scooters crowding the parking lot
Passengers arriving comfortably..not witnessing brawls and bouts.
Yes, Tonga's were there . . . . forget the smells, a pretty sight
Seeing Carriages with horses brown, black or white.

Our Roads were narrow yet, to walk..plenty of space
Unhindered by rashly driven cars to crush you & away race.
Going to K.P. Ground for Children was always a delight
With Ayah's* in tow, to play, but returning before night.

A live Band at the Bandstand, music played
Children enjoyed, danced and swayed.
Early Morning, you'd find bullock-carts on the road
Keeping to the left, carrying their marketable loads.

Teenagers following to flick an Orange or Mango too
The Cart-men being aware were ever watchful too.
Single Storey houses and sprawling bungalows existed then
The city was silent . . . . with hardly a din.

All roads were kept neat and clean
Citizens throwing garbage or plastics was . . . . never seen.
The city was small, not so many Lay-outs
Ambazari & Telenkhadi gardens were our only Resorts,
But beautifully maintained and famous 'Picnic' spots.

Shops in Sadar and Buldi had verandahs with little railings too
'Twas here, while parents shopped, to sit . . . . we'd love to.
Beyond Buldi there was only the old airport
Enroute, vast & dense forest was all, to see, we got.

For Cycles, Dynamo's was the Craze
Rickshaws with kerosene lamps lit the ways.
Wickered lamps served as Street lights
Otherwise too, no one ventured out at nights.
Every evening each lamp-post a man climbed to light
And no one grumbled, "It's not Bright"!!

Boys and Girls organized on cycles 'Paper Chases'
Picking chits with instructions and messages at various places
Every 'Cycle' had to be Registered with a 'Billa'*
While every house was prefixed or suffixed with 'Villa'

Few Clubs did exist but not any Pubs
Every house owned 'metal buckets' and 'big Oval tubs'
Punkhas* existed as there were no electric fans
"Punkha wallahs was a chore, mostly for a man.

'Khus Tatties*' on windows and doors were seen everywhere
Govt Buildings & Houses who, the heat couldn't bear
Every Square, on a round cement platform, stood a traffic cop
Directing traffic with painted boards of 'GO' or 'STOP'

There were mobikes borne night patrol cops too I recall
'Cos I was once on a cycle caught . . . for not having headlights at all.
Being a visitor and young I was let off
No bribes asked, but, Rules explained with a stern warning, let off.

Railways ran shuttles to neighbouring Ajni and back
For us kids & many it was 'Thrills on a Track'
Berrow* trees with almost every house was dotted
Still, other's trees were raided when, loaded ones we spotted.

Hockey & Football in Schools were favourite games
Unlike todays cricket and, loved by both boys and dames.
Low parapet walls were seen everywhere
'Twas one too at 'Ashokas' & Indian Coffee House square

Only in Railways, Banks and Empress Mills, existed jobs
Or in small offices and some small shops
Vendors with baskets of fruit & Veggies came to the door
Very few to Phule Market' did go.

Milkmen on bicycles & cans delivered your milk at dawn
In selected Areas, there was the Army Dairy—cart by a horse drawn.
But, those were Good ole days of The Nagpur we remember
Almost Everything was Routine every year..January to December.

Glossary: *Auto's = a small affordable public transport commonly called Autorickshas.*
Tonga's:= a horse driven cart that was used for Public transport.
Billa:= A metal token of brass with a registration number engraved
*Ayah's= Nanny. *Pankha = Cloth fan made of Cloth and bamboo*
*suspended from the roof. *Pankha wallah—Man used to physically pull the rope,*
back and forth when the (Pankha) had to be used
**Khas Tatties= Frameof bamboo and twigs from the Khus(Poppy) plant.* Berrow=*
Summer Berries.

(9.10)

India's Modifications.
Composed by Leo DSouza Tuesday 17th Dec,2013

With Scams & corruption rampant every day,
India looked for someone new to 'show the way'
Securing their coffers, by pulling the grass
Politicians befooled citizens, making hay, showing their class.

Opposition were quick on their feet,
The Ruling party, planning to defeat.
A powerful Orator, the opposition had found,
Plotting & planning, to win the Assembly round.

Everytime he opined, or gave a quote
Distorting History or facts, didn't matter, he needed the Vote.
The Ruling family, he found a 'soft' Target
As spiraling went prices in the market.

A New party emerged, with 'A Broom'
Hoping to clean sweep the Political Room.
The Ruling Govt was routed to the core
Bringing them victory 0 to 4.

Now in the Capital none, a clear majority got,
Everyone wondered..Will there be a Govt: or not?
With a lot of seats but, ... Just short of 6
Found the Hopefuls too, in a fix.

The emerging group too, faced the same fate
Refusing to Allie the main contenders as mate.
Bidding for time, keeping the Nation on Wait!
Hoping against hope for a knock at their Gate.

Invoking President's Rule would be the next option now,
Leaving the country in the lurch somehow.
To save face, the new Hopeful may slide into the groove
That they can govern, they'll want to prove.

Unqualified supporters & infighting with their Guruji*
How long, if they do, we'll have to see.
Their allies, whoever, will now lay out the Rug
Only to topple them maybe later, by pulling the Plug.

As predicted, they threw in the towel
Because other parties didn't vote their way, in the Lok Pal*.

---

*Guruji= Mentor or leader.. * Lok Pal = A legislation aiming to give power to the people too.

(9.11)

A Prime Ministers Woes—A Satirical Verse
(From his point of view)
Composed by Leo Dsouza in lighter vein

I've always envied the seat of the P.M.
Envying those free flights and Perks accorded to them.
I swore 'one day' that seat will be mine.
Then with Party workers, we could drink and dine.

Great that day 'twas when my party won,
I thought, 'now's our day, we'll have fun'
My short lived joy turned sour and full of anxiety,
'Cos I was 'Dependent' without a 'Clear Majority'.

My friend egged me on, the challenge to face,
Who knew? Every step Intake, would bring disgrace.
I have two buxom ladies, who give me a treat
Threatening every day, to pull the rug, beneath my feet.

With the Past Regime I thought, gone were the Scams
Little did I know, my Party too, brought a lot of shams.
As my Cabinate began to shake, bit by bit,
I turned to my poetry, to save me, with my wit.

When the 'Red ladies'(Onions), from the market went out
I quickly blamed it on the drought.
But when those soft girls(Tomatoes and eyeless Potatoes followed cue
Lucky me, I fell back on the 'untimely rain and Dew'

I bounced back with a nuclear blast,
I survived, but knew this won't for long last.
I found myself alone, to face the brunt,
My party for me, was now defunct.

Trains began colliding rapidly, one after another
How many people could I reach out to, and call 'brother'
Disgust was writ large on my face
I decided 'Enough'! I'll not compete another race.

Then our neighbours to play Cricket
While a western Lion, proved to be a slippery wicket.
Of ruining a pitch, I never expected or knew
I just remembered Shakespeare's 'Taming of the Shrew'

My friend, with folded hands the Lion met
While I was fuming and writhing inside yet.
From the Lion, an assurance, we quickly drew
Knowing that later, something new will stew.

Then an atrocity on a missionary brought me pains
I knew then, for life, I'd be haunted by the Staines.
These communities Votes I knew I lost forever
I must make good, I thought, I must be clever.

The PWD taught me when building bridges, create diversions
So for the rest of my PM days, I'll make that my mission.
So to see my neighbours by bus, I did make History
But for what I went, to me, is still a mystery.

So cold was my counterpart I noticed with grief,
I was in half a mind to make my visit brief.
When my neighbours 3 chiefs absented from the 'Welcome Row'
I then sadly remembered the one i removed, now.

My neighbours no excuses made
But their chiefs, another neighbour farewell bade.
I swore I'll never again be so sinister
And never ever to again be Prime Minister.

With shattered dreams, a broken heart, that will never mend
I'm now looking forward, for this Term to end.

(9.12)

Our Commissions and Govt's Today!!
Composed by Leo DSouza Sept 13, 2012 at 01.35 am

Fodder, Coffins, CWC, 3G, Coalgate are some Scams that Arose
Erupting after Commission Reports, make an Expose.
Firstly why were they allowed to flow over the brink?
Did any right minded citizen, stop to think?

The Heads of all such Commissions, why did they let it be
when, as ordinary citizens, it's happening they could see?
Or as Head of Commissions do they feel great
When their delayed Reports, months and years later, arouse such hate?

Political Heads too must be brought to task
for disrupting Parliament, For this, did we Vote for them we ask!!
For a Common mans strike it's . . . "No work No Pay"
Then why doesn't that apply to Parliamentarians too, today?

Walkouts in Parliament MUST be Constitutionally Banned
And those remaining, to Pass Bills, must be given a Free Hand.
'No Freebies' for the 'Walkouts' should be allowed
Parliament will then function without a 'Walkout'
When for every penny that they have to 'shug'
They'll realise, this country, they cannot 'thug'

For all 'Acts' they find 'Old' they conveniently' Repeal'
But to amend out outdated Constitution, they do not feel.
Or is it that they don't want to take the pains
Maybe because for that, they realize, we require people with Brains!!

The Commissions & Reports derive conclusions on calculations produce
Creating hulabuloos and losses only which they have deduced.
Hypothetical Losses deduced that might have been
From ground realities, the attention, away they wean
Example, in the Coalgate scam we see, from land that's not even'Mined'
'Calculated Losses' the Commission managed to find.

The CAG and Commissions have proved that to date
their 'Fault Finding' erupts, only when, for Commissions, they are paid.
Can we ask What Control has the CAG put in place
to block such happenings or tried to trace?

Why do fingers point to only the Government in Power
when, other 'Prior Governments' ruled too similarly, by far.
Every new Government comes with a Vendetta
Instead of trying to Rule & Govern better.

The 1st year when to Power they come
Inauguration Programmes each one accepts some
The following 2 years they amass their wealth
Not openly of course but, by deception and stealth!!
Of the One year that's left of the remaining 3
They Raise their Hands, Petrol Prices and their own Salary!!

With 2 years left for them of their Rule
They shift away from their Manifesto, trying the public to fool.
Now it's time to sling on Rivals, the mud
With everyone doing it, it's like a flood!!

The Election commission has got to wean
the Corrupt out, and keep only those Clean.
Only then we can hope for this to Stop
Otherwise Government after Government, come and flop!!

Chapter X

Emotional Floods

Using my imaginative Characters to talk

I hope to stir a chord deep within my readers

So that they can feel their own emotions erupt into

a world of 'Fulfilment'.

(10.1)

A Last Plaintive Prayer to GOD . . .

Composed by Leo DSouza Monday, September 17, 2012 at 11:02am

You Gave me Everything Lord, so Thank you I must
In Life I Think I've reached my crust.
Because of The Wake-up Call you gave, I've started the Acts
sorting things for family to face realities and facts.
So when I am gone, they just fit in place
None can cheat or them displace.
For the little I struggled for them to save
I've 'willed' it well, so there's no fighting when I'm in my grave.

I've updated the Bank Pass Books
so they don't have to rely on other crooks
I've showed them where to pay the Electric & water Bill
I'm doing it still, while they get a hang of it till
From where the groceries and milk to bring
The telephone payments where to make, so it continues to ring.
The Investment and House papers all properly filed
My friends list with whom I've reconciled.

Lord, when I'm gone away
Please help my dependant wife, who for now I'll just name 'A'
Give her the strength to live each day
Dry the tears and her strength let it be
as she'll be left to look after the kids who, are our family.

At times Relatives I know, didn't approve my actions, as right
But Lord you know I always stood for what's right.
White-washing and Hypocrisy I just couldn't stand
in my life, family, workplace or motherland.
The 'brunt' from these actions, save them Lord
So they are comfortable with People and YOU their GOD.

For my shattered children, please don't spoil their Dreams
Open for them avenues with the Best Schemes.
To Live and Choose their lives, freedom to them, I always gave
Let it Continue Lord, even as I lie in my grave.

Of them all my daughter is the stronger one
who'll shoulder responsibilities and from them will not run.
Give her the strength, as she's sensitive too,
for the decisions she can't take, but for those few
where, she's hesitant, be her Guide
Walk with her always, side by side.

My Son he always feels ambushed
but takes on responsibilities when he's pushed
He has great talents, that I've seen
Bless and Forgive him Lord, for the wrongs that may have been.
For his confidence, your Help is needed, to restore
So Help him Lord, day to day, so he can make it grow.
Bestowing in him a Loving nature, we Thank you for
Just give him directions where and how to go.

These children which with Love you gave us will always be
yours. We tried our best so very willingly
True Values of life in them to install
Even if, around them, they ever face a stone wall.

They question this, 'cos in today's world they see 'Falshood' win
They find the 'good' and 'Honest' are looked down upon as sin.
So Lord, I'm penning down my journals Final Page
'Take care of them, as I begin my life's journey's last stage.
to the Promised Land, where I want to be
So forgive my faults, till that day I see
YOU unite my family, in YOUR KINGDOM with me.

(10.2)

A Note from Charlie . . . to family and friends.
By Leo DSouza on Thursday, June 21, 2012 at 10:27am

Hi folks, I'm happy here so don't worry about me
I've met both Dad's and also Mum Gertie
Gran'pa Tony keeps enquiring about Karen and Dan
While my Dads in Joseph's workshop . . . a Handy man

Mum's given charge of 'Fashion' and 'Snacks
Frying 'Patties' still and introducing' Low Backs'.
Uncle Georgie still pushing 'Tomco Sales' & looking for papers to keep
While U. Mervyn's feeling sorry, about Sachins score he couldn't get a peek.

Uncle Fish, Georgie Rocque and I compare notes on the C.I.
How we did M/C. shows . . . them both and I.
There's a Mini Train in Eden, where U. Edwin's the Guard
So, he's always 'shunting' between room and the yard.

Half of Nagpur . . . . seems to be here
So many most of you know and to you are Dear.
Mervyn Scott, still sings,' She wears my Ring'
while Joe Dem, sits in a corner, nurturing his drink.

Val from 3V and Errol DSouza are now best of friends
Marie Lobo still narrates a lot of News Trends.
Fr. Alfie remembers his 'Ball curry and Yellow rice'
Phillip Dalgado and Avy Athayde say . . . here it's very nice.

U. Eddie Coutinho is here with his Pacha Pach
I can go on to say . . . there's so so Much
Fr. Lawrie got 2 Arthur's (Gregory and Fernandez) with Muriel to form a
CHORAL group
While Joe Pitts organizes an AI Social with 'Dinner and Soup'

U. Vivian's given charge of Heaven's Shares
While Percy Gregory takes care of those, fond of 'Dares'.
Shirley Bastian & Sally to train the young were given
as God feels . . . soon . . . Hi-Tech . . . he'll need also in Heaven.

While on Earth we thought, in Heaven there's limited Space
but, believe me there's enough, for 3 times Earth's race.
So Many Religious are here but, like others treated alike
They're made to walk . . . No Cars, Scooty's or Motorbikes.
God censures them every Sunday for, what on earth they did
About Scriptures, why their own versions they spread.

He questions them, what they did for the needy and Poor
And why so often they were rude, and showed people the Door.
Blaise, he said, come Charlie let's start the Whist
We'll ask Joe Pitts for players from the C.I. List

Dad's brothers Augustine, Marcus too I met
A. Mary and U Alex I haven't bumped into yet.
God's invited 'ITC' and 'Babu Lal' to open a Stall
'Cos they've been responsible here . . . to send us all.
His only condition every pack and bottle will be 'permanently sealed'
He wants to give us only the pleasure but, not to temptation yield.

A 4 Wheeler he gave me he called 'Souzoto'
No Camera's allowed here, so sorry no Photo.
So While I Tour around and meet some more
relatives and friends, I was too young to know
I'll say bye for now and don't for me cry
Just 'Thank God', he didn't let me 'suffer, linger and die'

(10.3)

A Short Tour To The Land Above.
by Leo DSouza on Monday, June 25, 2012 at 8:59pm
(Dedicated to some Friends who now Rest In Peace)

A few years ago when I had my Heart By-Pass
God gave me a Short Stay Wild Card Entry, HIS Kingdom to survey and Pass.
When Young we were told after Life, there was Heaven, Hell and Purgatory
But Friends, believe me, that's all absurdity.
It's Just EARTH that's a Reality
For here one faces his own Hell or Purgatory
Paying for wrongs weighed with equality.

IT's here only we pay for all our earthly needs
Even suffering for all our wrongful deeds.
On my Wild Card Tour to the Land Beyond, I saw
So many faces I knew and those, we prayed for.

I saw Innocent Pereira with his Sax
After blowing out Music galore . . . now likes to relax.
Eric DSilva the stalwart from the Catholic Club
His brother Jackie, at last Shoulders they rub.
Edmund DSouza moves around, still narrating about KIM
From Rudyard Kipling . . . that's how every Aloysian remembers him.
The dashing Vaiter Murray with his Jive
are memories of him all Jabalpurians on, still thrive.

Uncle Isadore playing cards like in the Club every morn
He found Aunty Helen who'd left him earlier and gone.
Meeting Aunty Ruby Lobo from Denning Road was no Mystery
Also seeing Ozzie Fernandez (Fundo) catching up with History.
Georgie DSilva the heavy body but, light hearted soul
Driving Cars & Shikar was always his goal.
Dennis Alvarez my friend, who'd, joined the Army
A Knock-out in the ring sent him back to his family.

E P O Sullivan or 'Sulla' as he was commonly called
brought memories of his 'Vinegar soaked Canes' now thrown out or sold.
Cuthbert Collaco at all funerals asked . . . who's next?
But when he was called . . . he was out of Text.
George Nazareth who, successfully ran the Fancy Fete
Finally came home . . . . his Maker he met.

Vincent & Agnes D'Sa are united now
Their son Henry seen with his Uncle Maxie in tow.
I saw the Sequieras Anthon & his Parents from Ranjhi
Fr Tundhyil the Ex Parish Priest of St Thomas Church too I did see.
Ronnie Tobin still sings' O Ropra Nobis' up here
As all the angels gather round and Cheer.

Stephen Vyse regrets he didn't say Goodbye
when he locked his room that night and quietly in bed did lie.
Peta Gurdialsingh gave me a smile saying, Hi Leo
I had to go . . . God just gave the excuse of 'Polio'
Lionel Collaco the Joker and debonair guy
jokingly said he still can't understand, he had to come here this early why!
Capturing the scenes of Eden was Alban Gregory, on canvas
also making portraits of Arun Peters & Edwina Dick as they did pass.

Young Deepak Johar rose from the Grotto, from Our Lady's Feet
And with Brian Tellis, their creator they did meet.
Bishop Dubbleman from under the old Cathedral he crept
As everyone for dear Fr Dicky Bent's loss truly wept.
The loving and caring dear old Aunty Wood
To forget her even if anyone tried . . . they, how could?
Uncle Polycarp Lobo from Ridge Road he went
His gun going off . . . by accident.

Since my Wild card tour had inclusions of a few that were new
I'm sure, but not deliberate, I've forgotten a few.
My records didn't have many after 2009
I just scanned the new entrants list . . . as it was time
I had to return to this Earth of yours and mine
I noticed Romeo Ambrose's name the last in line
so kept a message for him to update me with Names after Two double O Nine
So, on my next tour.. that list I'll visit line by line.

Meanwhile if anyone finds familiar Names not here
Send them in . . . . Your requests to I'll try to, to adhere.

(10.4)

Broken Dreams . . .

Composed by: Leo DSouza on Saturday, May 12, 2012 at 2:24am
(Dedicated to those struggling Single Mom's.)

He came into my Life
I believed everything he said
Agreeing to be 'His wife'
And then we were wed

Our Happy days lasted barely a year
Then things began to change
I felt like in a Mire
His 'interest' now had a new range.

Everything I did, it pleased him never
His mother or sister, he said, did it better
I was expected always to be the giver
Fall in step with others, to the letter.

My thoughts & feelings it didn't matter
I was only expected to adjust
Not get hurt, with about me, the chatter
Just smile, not let my anger, Burst.

I cried alone in my room most nights
Wondering where had I gone wrong
No solution for me, seemed in sight
Broken I was the day my Michelle was born

He didn't even bother at the hospital to call
Leaving me in that condition . . . a week ago he'd gone
No news since then . . . nothing at all
I was left with lingering memories though brief
Wallowing in my sorrow, every night and Morn

I sobbed that day when my baby's letter to him . . . came back
'Unopened', with. "LEFT..Forward address unknown"
I quietly hid it . . . from her . . . . in my rack
Didn't even tell her . . . from there too he has flown.

I had to pull up my socks and turn a new leaf
Now for my new baby girl, forgetting my grief
Every night my Pillow, my hugs would get
And yet . . . every morning. the pillow would be soaking wet

The hurt inside was way down deep, every new morn,
My Broken Dreams . . . . all lay Shattered
My life looked so forlorn
I was worse than a woman battered.

And now with Michelle in this world, I was alone
I struggled in the days and months
As they dragged by . . . one by one
Running low too on only my funds.
Giving up, I had almost done.

Years have gone . . . my Michelle grown
She's the apple of my eye
My shattered dreams in a corner I have thrown
Feelings I have but . . . cannot trust another guy.

He doesn't care . . . his heart doesn't melt
We're just a two-some now
She's grown and understands how I felt
Though I never told her . . . . he left us . . . . how.
After all she's still her father's child
A fact I don't want from her, to rob.
One day I'll tell her . . . making it mild
It will be for me . . . the biggest painful job.
Till then, undaunted I'll just go on
Pouring on her.. All my love
Holding and cuddling her..Every night and morn.
She's to be and forever will be . . . . MY DOVE!

(10.5)

A Tribute to a Brother

(dedicated to my brother CHARLES DSOUZA who passed away on 2nd June 2012
Composed by: Leo DSouza on Wednesday, June 6, 2012 at 5:43pm

For the first 10 years of my life I was the King
Till Mum n Dad whispered, to me, A Brother they'll bring
It didn't register in my mind then, what it meant
But, my little mind in turmoil . . . my days were spent.

Then that day, in Mum's arms wrapped, you came
I knew then . . . now my life will not be the same.
Already planning in my mind..The games that we'd share
Attracted to you, in Awe . . . I would stand and stare.
Your Pink little fingers and wriggling li'l toes
Amused us all . . . and as the saying goes,

'You were a bundle of Joy' making everyone Happy
Even though, now and then, you'd wet your Nappy.
Your toddling days we all did enjoy by far
Even watching you make' wooden blocks' your 'car'
Imaginary roads . . . on our floor you'd make
Swerving or overtaking cars . . . was your favorite take.

To launch you on my shoulders when, you up I threw
You went right over . . . I saw you flew
'Twas not on purpose, 'cos it surprised me too
The fall broke your li'l arm but, it hurt me too.
To crawl around, in plaster, still you went
With a Tak-Tak-Tak still, you were hell bent.

This 'Tak-Tak-Tak . . . Your favorite' phrase' . . . . it became
Explaining & narrating incidents,' was there, all the same.
When you began to talk, you were so cute
With a 'dudoo bottle' clenched in your mouth, you were a beaut.

You asked for "Kugger' in a Cup and Kokker
(Meaning . . . Sugar in a Cup and Saucer)
To make you give up the bottle . . . for us it was a treat,
Till one day, a COW, did the feat

You walked in saying . . . . 'Mama, cow took baba dudoo bottle'
Your expression made us laugh and want to giggle.
To school on my 'cycle', you, I'd take double
So sweetly you sat those 7 miles, without any trouble

Some Pranks of mine . . . The brunt, you silently bore
Once dropping you across the road, I still recall it so
We grew up understanding each other's whims and wants'
Strengthening our' Brotherly bond' even when facing other's taunt's.
We were there for each other, holding each other in awe
you, the outgoing Debonair..Surrounded by Gals galore

Quietly I watched you grow to become a man of fun
Carving a niche for yourself as M.C.—to perfection your job was done.
Thermocol Sculpting with you was a 3D Art, you loved so much
Many a Centerpiece carved with themes..You, no one, could ever touch!

Your calm composure . . . . in all strides of life
took you places..Solving at work—place or home a strife.
This composure . . . endeared you to one and all
Never letting the other feel . . . he was going to fall.

Your Driving Passion . . . Drove you many a mile
No matter the distance, you covered it with deft and a smile.
No distance too great . . . you loved to be at the wheel
Discomfort as Passengers . . . no one ever did feel

Your 'Care' for others . . . it stood out, always, first.
Taking things calmly . . . be it 'family matters' or friends..Outbursts.
Not wanting to give trouble to others, you always swore
You did it too that day..Maneuvering your Qualis so

your family's lives you saved . . . Sacrificing, your own
Leaving us, your family, for you, to forever mourn.
Though gone . . . you will not be forgotten by us ever

A Husband, A Father, In-law, Uncle & Nephew & 'A BROTHER
FOREVER'

(10.6)

Blind Existence!!

by Leo DSouza on Sunday, July 22, 2012 at 8:36pm

Every Birth to Parents is such a Joy
Whether the child is a girl or boy.
Earlier a girl child born . . . . was considered a curse
Education has slowly . . . . made it less worse.
Joey's parents too were overjoyed on his birth
Celebrations were galore . . . . all were full of mirth.
Friends and Relatives flocked as usual . . . to see Joey that's me
To quote them,' what a cute, Chweeet little Baby'!
I turned my head each time they moved, left or right
Instinctively I knew from that first night
that something for me was, . . . 'just not all right'
Celebrations ended . . . guests and relatives had all gone
I knew I was not the 'lucky kid' born.
Days went to months..Mum's voice I followed everywhere
She was so loving . . . looking after my every care.
One day Dad brought home a 'winding merry-go-around'
I was attracted, turning my head, hearing its sound
Aunty Kavita my neighbours Mom, gave me a rattle
Each time it slipped, finding it, for me was a battle.
I fought alone, no one, I could tell
I could only recognize the sound of its bell.
I don't blame Mum and Dad, how could they know
I could identify them only, from their voices so.

A Clap to the left and I would turn
Fingers flicking to my right, Left and Right..I learnt.
My Check-up due, so to the Doctors, one day we went
'Twas raining heavy, so dad an auto sent.
The Doctor, pulled my arms and knocked my knees
A Stethoscope to my chest to check if there was any wheeze
A' Ting' sound to both my ears he made
Using a torch, my eyes repeatedly flickering motions made.
'Tsch Tsch' I heard & turned to him with a smile

To compose himself . . . he took quite a while.
Some shuffling of feet & Scraping of chairs I heard
We had moved to his Chamber & awaited his diagnostic word
He took his time but, was very gentle and kind
In breaking the news to them . . . . 'I was Born Blind' !!
I felt mother clutch me to her chest
Dad's arms around us both . . . it felt the Best.
Slowly their steps retreated towards home
My instincts told me . . . they were sad and forlorn.
All that night Mum's warm tears I felt trickle down my cheek
Dad's attitude too, I sensed was dejected and meek.
Days that followed, me, to various hospitals they took
So every Doctor could give me a second look.
When all said . . . 'Nothing can be done . . . you've come too late'
They accepted me, as I was; now this was my future fate.
My parents stood and helped me all along the way, like a game
To recognize things by sounds and told me its name.
Shaking the bottle, I soon learnt the sound meant Milk
Mum's soft cool dress, I recognized as Silk.
The Air overhead with a twirling sound
Was the 'Fan', they said, going round and round.
A soft 'thump' they said was my gift . . . a Ball
When I banged into something hard . . . They called it a wall.
I grew and friends followed the usual school trail
I kept pace with them, learning every same thing in Braille
With equal gusto, I played, all the games
Discerning sounds, to the goal accurately I could aim.
On the streets, my white stick showed me the way
I didn't like or want 'Pity' but, conquered each day
Movies I enjoyed..My ears replaced my lack of sight
I learned all tunes & Songs with equal delight.
A Special friend also taught me to dance
On stage..No one, my disability knew.. without a second glance.

I Passed School.... topping the Merit List
That clouded my Parents eyes.... with Mist.
With head held high to University I could go
To follow a path and open for me,' Knowledge' more!
An IAS Officer was my dream and ultimate aim
To reach it.. accepted challenges, as they came.
Believe me; it's not easy to exist when one is blind
Many a person I met that were very unkind.
If a Child nudged or pushed, that I'd understand
But, these were people, same age or older, from my motherland.
Pushed, abused & made fun of.... 'for being blind'!
As though I had a choice... my sight to find.
My strength I drew from people like these
Whose sole aim in life was,' selfishness' and to disabled tease.
They had sight but could not see
What was good for them was equally good for me.
I at least knew day from night without my sight
While they needed alarms to ring, or sun to shine with all it's might.
With the rustle of the leaves from the trees
I discerned wind from breeze.
Birds twittering spoke to me of Joy or Fear
I could even smell Rain & tell whether it's far or near.
Some Luxuries like driving, I know I'll never learn
But who cares, as long as GOD gave me the power to discern
Good from bad... and I have no regrets in life
For though Blind..I've seen more of the world and strife.
God Bless My Parents, for teaching me, 'not to give up on life'
The World has made me a 'Man of Sustenance'
Seeing More.. Than living a life of mere... 'Blind Existence'!!

On Blind Existence: Audrey Coutinho D'Souza A very moving poem Leo . . .

(10.7)

but, she's not my child!!.
Composed by Leo DSouza 2nd May 2012, at 1:51pm
(Dedicated to the abused kids of this world.)

Lying there, on the hospital bed, reading a book
Wearing a smile & that far away look
Recalling that so awful day
Mum walking thru the door . . . happy and gay

'Zaap' . . . the sound of the slap . . . still ringing in her ears
Dad so furious and unsober, having topped his Whiskey with Beers.
Her mum's pleas . . . 'it's not what you see'
Falling on deaf ears of . . . . her hubby.

Another ringing Rap & Mum falling silently
His muttering so clear to her . . . still a child
. . . . 'But she's not my child'!

Her own walk out of the door . . . feeling so alone
Feeling of not 'accepted' . . . in her own home
Then telling Uncle Hari . . . from next door
To see Mum..lying unconscious on the floor
. . . . His words, . . . "but she's not my child", made a dent
Though she couldn't fathom then, what it meant.

Sixteen year ago . . . . it was that day
When they were a threesome family, so happy and gay.

She visualized, basking in the shade of the gulmohar tree
Watching two sparrows take care, 'another's baby!!
Mother sparrow squeaking but ever so mild
To them, never once thinking . . . . "but she's not my child"!

Also noisily cawing flew the crows
Calling for 'support' against the cat's tours,
Climbing the tree . . . headed for their nest
Daily being quite a pest!

Looking down at her nest, mother crow blew her top
Seeing baby Raven, taken . . . . frustrated, not being able to stop
Yet painfully she cawed . . . . but never said
 . . . . "But she was not my child " . . . 'good she's dead'

Then there was Mamma Puss who passed away, leaving two kits
Too small to know, they went hungrily to Dog Julie's tits
Suckling, which she allowed, along with her four
Sprucing them all equally, behind the door
Poor Julie too, adopted them, with her lot
But never ever . . . . "they're not mine or thought".

Then that day . . . Jim and Jane had gone to Court
Dad Jim accusing mum Jane of being a flirt
Their lawyers argued left and right throwing accusations wild
With 'mud slinging' both ways about, (me), 'the poor child'

Where's Mother now . . . from the hospital bed, she wondering kept
Still with Dad or . . . . had she . . . . too left.?
Solace in reading . . . she always found
As it took away her worries and frown.

Why had Dad.. acted so strange & unkind
A million questions, raced always thru her mind.
Resolved she was, from the hospital, when she goes
She'd put behind her . . . . all her woes.
She'd pick her life and move onward now
Until, from this earth . . . . she takes a bow.

" . . . But She's not my child" . . . still brings back the tears
For what the World will hold for her . . . she has those fears.

279

(10.8)

Charlie . . . A Month Without You.
By Leo DSouza on Monday, July 2, 2012 at 12:38am
(Dedicated to my Brother Charlie . . . . with emotions from a loving family)

30 Days have gone they seemed just yesterday
When the News came . . . I didn't know what to say
I asked God why He didn't hear my prayers for you
He just whispered,' Amy . . . He's my son, and I need him too.!
Charlie, you were such a good Son-in-law
Not talking much, but, to my needs and comfort you saw.
You made me so comfortable in your Home
Never ever made me feel at all alone.
Secretly I admired how well you cared
For my daughter Andrea and the kids you both shared.
Your handiwork with Thermocol were pieces of art
Done with dedication, straight from your heart.
Being an Art & Craft Teacher myself, I couldn't match any of those
you were 'matchless' without a lie, to say it goes.
I cannot believe, since you left, a month has gone by
Just thinking of you, tears roll down my eye
As your wife now alone . . . each night myself to sleep . . . I cry.
You know the reason, I won't spell out . . . . 'Why'
I know I have to be the strength for the kids . . . so I'll try
So used to your frequent tours, that I still feel
And imagine you're coming in, and the crunch on gravel, your wheel.
I miss your sitting at the table with the papers, every morn
Recall also your Joy when each Child was born.
I miss your banter and the good times we shared
So engrossed with work were you, still, for us, you cared.
We miss those Sunday lunches that you made
Like their taste . . . those memories, will never fade.
Those Bar-be-cue days and the parties we threw
You setting the place with Music and the Bar too

Are things that now, we are going to miss
Your JIM REEVES rightly said,' Memories are made of This!!
Every moment, seconds right through my life
I'm going to miss you & till my last breath, will still be your wife.
Papa there's just one prayer I say each morn
I'm glad God made me your First born.
From you I learnt so many things in life
to face all situations, through fun days and strife.
Your Talent in art into my veins did seep
Thank you papa . . . your memory too I'll always keep.

You gave Mervyn and me a Wedding so grand
Everything that day had that . . . 'Charlie Brand'
I was so happy for the time spent with us that Friday night
Fresh memories linger of your Car departing Saturday morn, till out of sight
The 'Shocking News' I didn't believe on Saturday night
And wished I had not 'let you go' but to you held on tight.
But don't worry Papa . . . I'm sure God knows best
Why he put us through such misery and Test.
I'll try to be the support to mamma, like you
And help out the best . . . for Alyssa and Rue.
Papa I still can't believe, you're not there
Owain and I treasure those moments with you, we did share.
Thank you Papa, for me, what all you've done
For giving me a childhood, so full of fun.
Seeing me through my higher education in the U.K, too
I'll never let down both Mamma and you.
Had we known, this trip . . . YOU . . . from us 'twould take
We would have remained home & this trip'd forsake.
If only Papa, you, to us a sign gave or made a yelp
We would have got in time . . . medical help.
Instead you drove on, not wanting us to alarm
Little did we realize you drove in pain & not with your usual Charm.
We thank you Papa for driving us off the road to safety
but, if only, we didn't have,' your death to see'
The 'courage in adversity', you instilled in us all
Stood us good then, to make arrangements and Mamma to call.
In spite of my tears, I tried my grief not, to Ruella show
Even though the doctor had told me,' you were no more'.

Though I was born second.. for you I was second to none
Even now I'll strive to be the best . . . like you had done.
With a heavy heart I'll be leaving Nagpur and India again
but you know, for strength and I know, I'll have with me Owain.
Papa I was the youngest of your daughters three

But, you gave off your love to us equally.
In a corner of your heart, for me you had a soft spot
For all your goodness to me . . . that I'll never blot.
Being the youngest, many times you let me have fun
At Times even if my studies were not done.
I miss you Papa lots and every moment of the day
I don't have words to express and what to say.
I always enjoyed, on a drive, going with you
and to every 'Picnic' spot, that we all went to.
To me you were my 'Hero' and 'Star'
and to you I'll always be close . . . . not far.
How I wish, when I graduated, you were here
I know you're smiling, that smile, Papa dear
With Charlene & Alyssa, for Mamma, I'll be there,
Helping her cope with life and together we'll share
All the work . . . as though you're still there.
Dear Charlie, as an elder brother living next door
It broke my already damaged heart . . . to see you go.
I also want you to know
That day you went . . . you had no Foe
Everyone came in shock, even the boys from the Basti* next door.
That day before you left . . . I thought I heard you call
Jumping out of bed, around fivesh, I recall
That when I opened my front door
I saw you loading your Van and getting ready to go
Little realizing.. in a few days.. You'd be 'no more'
Maybe that was God's way of giving me a glance
of you . . . without telling me . . . there won't be another chance.
It's unbelievable 30 days flew so fast
Leaving us with Memories only of the Past.
Even now, when, every car door slam, I hear
I think it's you and your footsteps coming near
But, when that Gate latch doesn't click

I know then, my imagination is on me, playing a trick.
Then I hear another horn Beep
and wonder why, whoever, in front of the gate their scooter did keep.
But no! it's not you I then realize . . . in pain
you won't be backing you car to that gate . . . ever again.
At times we may not have agreed on something's I know
But, deep inside we had no place for Hate, but only Love' twould grow.
Charlie on the lighter side . . . now that you are in Heaven
Fear not, God's kept me to look after, 'the interests of a son and "Seven
women"!!
And now that it's been 'A Month Without YOU'
We'll all keep hoping and praying . . . . till we all join you, one day, too.

(10.9)

Chosen & Wanted Kids

by Leo DSouza on Sunday, August 12, 2012 at 12:59pm

Thousands of children in Homes are up for Takes
Parents killed in Accidents, floods and quakes.
At times kids get lost in Crowds, or accidents so freak
Their future alone in a 'Home' is so very bleak.
They need love and a home of their own
A Place to Live, they can call home!

Man's 1st aim, when he stands on his feet
Life's expectations, he wants to meet
He saves for a Home and longs for a family
So marries to live hopefully & contentedly.
If, they can't have a child for reasons some
They look to see how this to overcome.
From Pillar to Post they look for a solution . . . .
Then someone suggests 'Adoption'

'Adoption' once was a word taboo
Society's thoughts have since, radically changed too.
Children Get Homes, Parents . . . a Child
That's putting it so very Mild.
Elders must break social barriers to adopt
After all, GOD gave man a heart so loving and soft.
If they adopt, the child's Love is worth all the Gold
'Cos They not others, will be there when they are alone and old.

So many Couples want to be a Mum and DAD
But only few kids are lucky, that's sad!
Those bold enough, realise it's not that bad
They now have their child or they never would have had.
Adopted or 'Chosen & Wanted' Kids have reason to rejoice
For to their Fosters, they were their 1st Choice.

But Kids must be told early, not left too late
Or they may, their new found Parents . . . Hate.
'cos remarks made by Society, from the old school of thought,
Have not realized, the misery they have brought.

'Chosen & Wanted' Children bring to a Home sunshine and Joy
It's the same whether Girl or Boy.
The Parents over them always dote
Happiness enters the Lives of both.
They're bestowed with extra love 'cos they were 'chosen'
'Natural Born' would never logically understand the reason.
Once installed, Parents replace the title' adopted' with, 'Mine',
That's the reason in their lives, they find Bright Sunshine!!

GOD Bless both the Parents and their new found joy
There's no more time to brood, just to enjoy
So if your 'chosen & wanted', just Thank the Lord
'cos you're special to your Parents and God.
Make them special in your lives too
You're from the Land of the 'Chosen Few'

(10.10)

Don't Cry Mummy, Dont Cry!!
By Leonard DSouza Monday, April 23, 2012 at 12:32pm

Mummy I'm free from all that pain & in Heaven now,
It was very painful yet, I smiled somehow
Didn't want you or Daddy to feel sad
But, Mummy, it was very very painful and bad
So, Don't Cry Mummy, don't cry.

Just say Thanks to Uncle Dr Sen.
He was so gentle with me, the Nurses when
Gave me injections mornings and nights
He only, understood my weak plight.
So, don't cry Mummy, don't cry.

I recall when I was small, I was not knowing
It was the stages of my growing
What else was there I could do
I cried, 'cos around . . . . I couldn't find you
But now, Don't Cry Mummy don't cry.

I often cried, troubling for my bottle or feed
I cried for every lil thing, that I'd need
I cried even for my rattle and toys
I'm sure you'll understand Mum; I did it like other small boys.
Now don't you cry Mummy, don't cry.

Those days I cried, troubling you even for a bath too
To comb my hair, or put on my shoe
I was little and always wanted to play
But pleading of you now, don't cry Mummy, please don't cry.

It was then when I was ten
I thought that Home was like a Den
Don't do this—don't do that!
But Mummy Pl understand, I didn't want to do Hindi or Math
I now understand, that's what, made you cry
But now, don't cry mummy, don't cry.

I wasn't around to be a Teen
God called me, I think, for what he'd seen
I'm Sorry Mummy, for that day I died
Looking from above I saw . . . how much you cried
But now please Don't Cry Mummy, don't cry.

God led me here—into the gates of Heaven
There's lots of little children, like me, even
So don't Cry Mummy, don't cry
Just hold back those tears . . . please try.

When Dad beat me some days . . . I didn't mind
In other ways, he was always so kind
God had a Choice-'twas either me or Dad he said, that Day
He chose me, dear Mummy, to let Dad with Sarah, Joe and you Stay.
So, Don't Cry Mummy, don't cry.

Tell Dad, I still love him too
As with Jesus I kneel, praying, for him and you.
A lovely Father, in him, to me, Jesus gave
You'll did for me, the Best and gave
I love those words, "Wonderful Son", on my grave.
But now, don't Cry Mummy, don't cry.

Mum I often heard the sounds of Dad and you fight
But, I was too little to understand your plight
I always saw Dad going, in Cards his luck to try
And then wanted but couldn't say, "Don't Cry, mummy don't cry.

My Guardian Angel she still comes each day
Still guarding over me . . . and to play
Lots of little kids are here happy and gay
We sit together—for our Mummies and Daddies, we pray.
So, Don't Cry Mummy, don't cry.

Up here in Heaven, I met Granddad
We sit; he tells me stories of you and Dad
Grandma, dear Mum is . . . . Here too
But, no longer does she sew.
We don't have time to be Sorry or even try
So don't Cry, Mummy, don't cry.

One day strolling down Eden when
I met 'Nosey' old Aunty Jen
She's changed too Mum, not what we thought
From the trees beyond, some flowers for me, she brought.
She knelt with me, and prayed for you
So, you'll be Happy, in whatever you do.
So, Don't Cry Mummy, don't cry.

Thank you Mum for the Candles on my grave you lit
From up here, I see them getting smaller, bit by bit.
Those flowers you brought, so nice did smell
With everyone praising you Mum, my heart does swell.
I love them very much tell Sarah and Joe
Though I'm not there with them . . . . to grow.
I'm sure they are . . . not naughty like I,
So, Don't Cry Mummy, Don't Cry.

Up here it's so quiet and so calm
Ah! Mum, I also met Uncle John who died, from across our farm
He's not as cranky as he used to be
'Cos now, we are all . . . A Big Family!
So, Don't Cry Mummy don't cry.

Eden here, is always in full bloom
Watered by the 'Tears shed' from Earth, in Gloom
The lawns here are soft and oh so green
Everything around here-unlike Earth—is so so clean.
Even here Mummy we have a Big 'B'
Only here it's called, "Jesus' Big Book "Accountability"
Each day Jesus Opens it & decides who to call
From Earth below, Old, Young or Small.
So, Don't Cry for me Mummy, don't Cry.

My life there was short but . . . . here it's not
I'm here for Eternity . . . that's saying a lot.
Oh! Mummy I saw Jesus at Fr. Michael . . . shout
For on Earth, only Preaching but, practicing it not.
He kept him with other Fathers and Sisters, in the Yard
HE calls 'Purgatory', to improve and be sorry . . . with an Angel Guard.
I asked Jesus . . . He said he chose them to be First
But they let others die of 'Hunger and Thirst
These others he calls them one by one, in
For cursing' such religious' . . . He didn't consider . . . A SIN.
So Don't Cry Mummy, don't cry.

There's so much to say but not to-night
A message for those on Earth-'Just do what is Right'
Now Don't Cry Mummy, Please don't Cry
I'm here with Jesus . . . being a Good Boy!!

(10.11.)

Fulfillment.
Composed by Leo DSouza. on Wednesday, October 27, 2010 at 1:31am

These are feelings that surface when the kids have grown
Even more so when—the nest they have flown.
Memories linger of yonder years—when
Their comfort meant more than—your own sleepless nites, then.
Alarms being set—for bottle feeds
Changing wet nappies and other deeds.

Getting them ready and leaving for school,
At times, shamming stomach ache-you, they'd try to fool.
A bitter pill offered- . . . . soon did the trick
They chose school . . . . rather than be sick!

Years flitted by-they were Trend Setters . . . 2-wheeler borne!
Tension gripping us— till they were safely home.
Cafe' Coffee Day & Malls . . . . soon were their jaunts
We . . . expected to meet all their wants!
Multiplexes drained us—yet, repeatedly them . . . . we gave
Questioning ourselves . . . . Didn't we stint ourselves—and for them did save?

Dates!! . . . . Brought hidden fears—that what IF
Underlying fears lingered we felt like . . . . on edge of a cliff!!
With hope . . . deep down knowing nothing'll go wrong
And when the tides had gone . . . . We loved the surf
Enjoying Family chats . . . on our familiar turf.

The Nest . . . now they have flown
And we are alone
Dwelling on memories with feelings of Joy
Of giving our Best to them alike girl or boy.
Fulfillment tightens around our hearts—like a band
Knowing—what all we did—today they before the world can stand!
We ponder back of how the years went by . . . .
Turmoil's and strife that at times . . . . almost made us cry.
Their success in life-has blossomed for us,
Into fruitful fulfillment, after all we did fuss.
Glistening eyes of ours . . . . are not of woe . . . . but Joy
A Mission accomplished but . . . . here, still to guide!
We now lie back and bask . . . . thru the remaining days
Looking out now, for the familiar footsteps at the door.
Anxious that, they'd come just as in the morning, they did go!!

(10.12)

"It's Cold Out Here".
Composed by Leo DSouza
Saturday, December 15, 2012 at 1:08pm

To all Friends and relatives, getting ready for X'Mas
This year's celebrations, like others, I'm going to miss.
Lying here with friends, we feel so alone
Oh! How we wish we were at Home.

It's so dark and cold out here
How we wish, you all were near.
I'm talking about this Cold and Dingy hole
Which, on earth was our final goal.

All around this resting place, traffic whizzes by
While this season, Carol voices, rent the sky.
I know all will be getting ready, with Fun and Cheer
Just want you to know,' its cold out here'!

Quiet and desolate, we lie in this yard
With just a caretaker, but no guard.
The Cold wind blows, but doesn't save
Those Flowers, now dried, put on our grave.

An eerie feeling fills this place, every night
We're in the dark, with just no light.
Up there at least, we could enjoy a beer
But, today you know,' It's cold out here'!

Occasionally a good soul puts a candle light
On this, or some other Grave, so white.
I appreciate your prayers, and that silent Tear
But really, 'It's cold out here'!

For X'Mas, A Mass for us here, so nice it would be
This 'yard' would see too, faces so' Merry'
The air would fill this place with Christmas Cheer
We wouldn't have to say,' It's cold and lonely out here'!

For us on X'Mas Night
GOD promised, to shine the Stars so Bright
And to make the Leaves of trees, like Buntings quiver
Though bringing the Cold, but being dead, we wouldn't shiver.

How nice we'd feel, to be in the midst of, so much Cheer
out here'!!

(10.13)

Lingering Memories
by Leo DSouza Saturday, April 21, 2012 at 2:20pm

Memories of walking green fields, running wild
But, under watchful eyes of Mum n Dad nearby.
Watching Butterflies go flitting by
Myself—hurting on a stone—beginning to cry
But always holding hands strolling, was Mum n Dad nearby
With 'li'l brother Nathan in his baby pram
What lovely days they were—out in the farm
As we crossed green green fields or ran
On the way to . . . . see my Gracy Nan.

Memories flit by as the years did pass
From bright green to dark then brown went the grass.
Like me, the Butterflies too, did fly
But they, searching better pastures— not like I.

Passing School— where I wonder . . . did the years go
Just carrying me onward in their flow.
Memories of crying when 'Fluffy' my cat had died
From keeping another—from then on—I shied.

With Scanty rain one year . . . and Dad's crops failed
In spite of heavy debts-he warded off being jailed.
On the table served those days was just dried bread
For us kids.. 'We're full-you all eat' . . . Mum n Dad often said
Tears roll down my cheeks, just thinking back
Their Sacrifices . . . so there's always something for us..On the rack.

Like and from Mum, I learnt to stitch and sew
Making gowns, dresses and some money too
No 'Call centers' then, for us to make a fast buck
We just depended on our Fate and Luck.
My adolescent days flitted by—I think back and frown
How 'Happy' they made me feel that day . . . walking the aisle with Jimmy Brown.

Robert and Nancy our 'Lil two we now had
With Jimmy's well paying job..Days were not so bad.
Things had improved, and financially too.. For Dad
So at home too all were glad.

Nathan had grown . . . . an Air Squadron he had joined
Doing well was he, while we, Tense with no Peace of mind.
He was the First to go . . . . way Beyond
Fighting, saving our country with those colours . . . he had freshly donned.
Our hearts dropped that day . . . seeing 2 Officers at our Door
Speaking to Dad . . . . and then Mum fall to the floor.

He looked so peaceful lying in his casket
Reminding me of pictures of 'Moses in a Basket'
The 21 gun Salute boomed, the Bugles blew
Nathan had gone beyond to a land . . . so new.
Slowly we watched his Casket..lowered down and in
Bidding him 'farewell', memories just flooding in.

My Jimmy, a month later at his work, an accident met
In hospital, in a Coma he lay..gasping for breath
Struggling thus for a week..he peacefully moved on
Leaving me and the kids, all shattered and forlorn

Mum took to Bed after that day
Tears streaking down constantly . . . she'd her Rosary Pray.
Dad ploughed on . . . hiding his grief
We'd see him often, quietly, wiping his eyes, very brief.
He got a stroke one day.. that brought us gloom
Both laid up now . . . it sure spelled doom
With kids, I moved in . . . . with them to stay
Doing everything untiringly . . . day after day

The grass outside, I compared to a coloured Clown
Sometimes green, then wet and back to brown
When and how seasons changed..I had no time to see
Accepting fate . . . and what had to be.

To-day walking behind their Coffins I recall
Those yonder years, of us 'Happy all'
During the dim midnight light, a sudden 'Call' they got together
Just like they met . . . . they moved on Forever.

Truly 'orphaned' now I feel, with Greenfields all around
But, Silence hitting me, no Mum and Dad's sound
A handful of dust & a rose on their Coffins I throw,
I'm left all alone now . . . . to watch my children grow.

(10.14)

Love, Betrayal & Conquered Life
—by Leonard DSouza. Sunday, April 22, 2012 at 12:50pm

The Lights were dim—the music Loud
Each Couple to themselves on a No: 9 Cloud
It was here I cast my eyes on him
So handsome, tall and soldierly trim

Our eyes too met—in spite of lights so dim
'Twas the beginning of our relationship
In life . . . what it gave or took, it's up's and dips

Dating was never so beautiful, we felt
Into his arms each time we met—I'd melt.
So tender—so pure & magical was our love
We felt made for each other, like a glove.

Then, one day—she came—into our life
I didn't know—so confident I was, being his wife.
Befriending her—I did seeing her so alone
Asking her to treat this, as her Home.

Every outing we went Ted & I invited her too
little realizing—the harm to us—she'd do
His work I thought was keeping him late
Longing to hear the click—of the gate.

Her absence—I didn't connect to Ted being late
How'd I know—it was a clandestine 'date'
Unaware of things going on—behind my back
My faith in Ted, it didn't lack.
I was jolted one day, out of my blue
When I was alerted by my neighbour Sue.

They were seen, she said, at the Mall
Behaving so freely, just having a ball.
When confronted-Ted denied & passed it off
Blaming neighbours gossip—he gave it a laugh.

Seeds of doubt, that were now sown
I secretly spied for facts—I had not known
She was leaving town, one day she said
But that night, I was alone in bed.
His Tour came up suddenly—I was told
That's when I found missing—all my Gold.

I braced myself now, for a big inevitable shock
When 5 days later at my front door, I heard a knock.
They came, they said, to 'gently' break the news to me
Little did they know, of what I'd gone thru—the misery.

I was now alone
He was gone
I cried that night & for many a day
How my 'happiness' could be taken away.

In man and the world I had lost all trust
To pull myself out—I thought, I MUST.
Putting 'things' behind me, now I went
Sorting my life—alone my days to spend.

Securing a job, I busied myself
Not wanting,-'in the 'Past', to dwell
Success came to me—now I was at the top
My job meant so much—I won't let it flop.

New recruitments we were doing one day
Both men and women crowded our Office bay.
A shock I got—seeing him walk to the door
What, I wondered, was he doing here on my office floor?

In front of the Panel, there he was
Broken now, I could see and inwardly, knew the cause.
Hardening my heart—I left the Panel to decide
He glanced up & saw me—his eyes went wide

I thought I saw on his lips—a light quiver
To take him back—I decided—I'll never.
He begged, almost cried, for the job to be considered
'Age' went against him, the Panel thought—he was 'weathered'
Seeing his back recede—as he went
I could see he was a man so . . . 'spent'
That night as I lay back in my covers
I thought of those days of ours-, as lovers.
But, things were not dull now for me—but bright
I had now 6 months back—met my Mr. Right.

A month later, ... Bob and I were one
Had . . . . suffered betrayal but now conquered Life and . . . Won!!

(10.15)

The House is Quiet . . . there's no crowd!!.

Composed by Leo DSouza on Tuesday, September 11, 2012 at 12:15am
(This is composed in memory of Charlie my brother on his 53rd Bday today
11.09.2012 . . . . The 1st Bday after he passed on)(Personal & Exclusive
Copyright)

The House is Quiet, There's no crowd
Silence is covered in a shroud
The Compound is not lit
We didn't think it fit
The Bar too runs dry
As thinking of you, tears fill our eye

The mind recalls the music you played
But today, we are all dismayed.
Memories of you greeting all
Everyone both Big and small
Each Bday Party of yours so different was the food
Putting everyone in an eatable mood.
For the drinkers there was always a blend
Drink of one's choice, you in an element to send.

Today we just bow our heads and Pray
God Keeps you in his kingdom..to stay.
Who all are praying . . . . why do you wonder?
It's the family & also Althea & Karen who've come from Down under
So Rest in Peace Dear Charlie we pray
As we Think of you very especially Today.

(10.16)

Two Little Arms!!!
Composed by Dominic Leonard DSouza.
Wednesday, June 15, 2011 at 12:50am

It was two little arms around me that day
As her mother's coffin was lowered down to rest and stay
They clung to me . . . . not loosening their grip
For no other for her was there . . . . in Life's long trip.
Each passing day . . . . love shone covering that tiny face
Bringing back memories to me . . . . Of her mother Grace.

Each Night I just found around me . . . . two little arms

Her every need I now had to fulfill
Without letting her feel the loss, though my heart was smarting still.
My life she now took over . . . with not a second to spare
Rushing home from work, I knew she was always there.
After every achievement . . . there were around me..Those same two little arms.
Years soon began to pass . . . she grew up before my eyes
We shared all joys, sorrows and sighs!
A bouncy girl in school she was . . . topping the class
Excelling in things . . . . soon school did pass.
She blossomed thru adolescence, and a young woman she was now
Soon those two little arms would be gone..to make a vow.

A Beautiful bride she did make
As from me the shackles . . . . I thought she'd break
But before embarking on her new wedded life
She came back to hug me with those Two little arms.

Years rolled by and I became frail and weak
With no one to do things for.. Or to speak
The Doc thought that she should come to be
With me before it's too late . . . and I would not her see
As I felt my life ebbing away . . . I could faintly from my bed
See her wipe those tears..I taught her not to shed
Then Two Little arms I felt . . . . Wrapped around me

Her final gift . . . my grand-daughters it was, that I did see.
Before the original Two little arms..a final Farewell to me did bid
I continued my journey knowing there would always be
Two Little arms . . . . to hug and caress her now—her daughter Betty.

Chapter XI

Social Awakening

Firmly believing that every writer should use his or her talents to spread some good messages through their works, so we can conscientiously make a change in our surroundings and also hope, to change the lives and habits of our co-habitats. I have tried in my own small way to do this to make people aware about 'Cleanliness' about injustices to our 'Labour Class' and also the honourable and dignified work done by a "Garbage man".

(11.1)

Labour Class . . .

..(Dedicated to the Labourers' all over the world)..
by: Leo DSouza on Wednesday, May 16, 2012 at 10:33am

Every country to them are prone,
as they form the Nation's back-bone.
In developing countries, they come so cheap
The rich, on their toils, fortunes reap.

They are generally exploited to the core
Each day, numbers increasing, more and more.
In our poor country like India one will find
All age groups, engaged in labor, of every kind.

At tea kiosks, young boys you, they serve
'Child Labor's' banned—yet, owners have the nerve
Cleaning utensils at Restaurants they will be
Where at least 2 square meals is a guarantee.

Working from dawn to dusk without a murmur
Yet, smiling you'll find them, working with fervor.
With their meager earnings that the owners to them dole
Many houses are run, they are, the bread earner, sole.

It's illegal to hire minor's the Govt says
Yet they have, for them, to earn, no avenues or ways.
Every factory, its production, to them owes
Though their Labour's profit's, in the owners pocket, goes

With their sweat and toil, Skyscrapers, they raise
In these Flats & Mansions, the moneyed class stays.
Not educated, but building plans they, accurately follow
Raising Pillars and centering & what's where to go.

Have anyone to their homes and shanties been?
Tin sheets & Plastic bags for roofs and doors of green
Overflowing stagnant drains in front are glaring facts
Colonies of their own . . . along railway tracks.

Parents pack Tiffin's of chapattis, chilies and salt
That's all they can afford—and that's not their fault
Leaving their kids, even babies at times they move to the site
Coming home, to their 'day orphaned' kids, late at night.

These children fall prey to the cities devils
They're found smoking and gambling lured by evils.
They are, our little slum dog millionaire's
Learning to exist in spite of all odds and everyone's stares.

Take any sphere of life on earth
It's the workers role that stands out first.
Road building, dams and Townships too
The workers expertise beats us.. me and you.
But what do they get in return
Poor pay, shanty homes and no fuel to burn.
Contaminated water to bathe and drink
But to Development, they're our important link.
'Cos without them, we are like, 'A pen without any ink'.

The Branded clothes that the elite vie to wear
Comes from their daughters & wives, toiling at times, all day.
In packing industries, all size boxes, they all day pack
Then to the storerooms carry them, on their back.

Mobiles and electronic gadgets that the markets flood
Are assembled by them, with their sweat and blood.
Vehicles that we, so proudly on the road do drive,
It's just the pleasure, on your face, on which they thrive.

Their dreams they have long forgotten to dream
But by their hard work, others enjoy the Cream.
When will these people be given their rightful due?
It has to be done and begun by . . . me and you.
We got to rise and take up their cause
And Press the Govt to protect them with proper laws.

Come folks, it's time for them we begin to speak
Hold their hands; lead them Step by Step . . . . to the peak.

On: *LABOUR CLASS*

Chanella Cubbins this should be published . . . for all of India to read. it is so beautifully written and paints such a real picture Leo. It's almost as if you were watching it all happen as u wrote it. I think this one needs to be published to make ppl aware.

Chanella Cubbins Yeessss!!!!!!! I am so happy Leo. You know you don't just write a bunch of flowery words . . . . you write what is real in this world. YOU make a difference Leo . . . . u give people something to think about . . . food for thought. And hopefully your words will help change the way people live for the better. God bless Leo . . . . I hope and pray u help make this world a better place. :)

Zoe Alvares Yes you have to publish, it gives such a vivid picture. We see it happening everywhere and for most it's become the norm . . . . but to read it in verse like this in black and white, it hits you . . . . it's so essential that people read this and think and act

(11.2)

The Garbage Man—
Composed by Leo DSouza Wednesday, August 22, 2012 at 1:14pm

Everyday this man comes in his Van
He's known as the cities, Garbage man
Collecting Garbage door to door
Taking it to the cities outskirts, he does go.

He does his job without any distaste
Even though he collects all the waste.
Coming daily, Hail, Rain or Storm
He collects the garbage and then, he is gone.

Because of him our roads remain clean
He picks the rubbish wherever it's seen.
But did you ever stop to think
How he works with the stink?

People don't care or try
To separate the wet from the dry
They should to their children show
Never to spill or throw garbage on the floor.

Even from Complexes and Flats people throw
Uncaringly, their garbage down below.
Sweeping personal garbage on the road is a common sight
Which often leads to many a neighbours fight!!

Would any of you dare to do?
The work he does for me and you?
So let us all Respect this man
Even though he's called, 'THE GARBAGE MAN "!!!

(11.3)

Save Those Precious Drops!!

... Composed by Leo DSouza Sept 10, 2012 5.10 pm

In Life, man must know, nothing is Free
Even the water that flows into the sea.
GOD gave us this Planet filled with things we need
But, it is being misused by Man's own greed!!

Even the Air we breathe, it seems so Free
But, for it's purity our Thanks must go to the Trees.
We see man Splashing Water without a care
He doesn't fathom, it's fast becoming so Rare!
The kids right from school have to be taught
To Waste Water . . . . They MUST NOT!!

Every morning around us we see, Women sprinkling their Yard
Little realizing, for others, to get even a bucket is, so so hard.
Save those Precious Drops is all we plead
Shortage of Water, will one day our Pockets Bleed.
It will be a sad sad sight
For want of water, there'll be many a fight.

Already States in India and countries are fighting to Share
'GOD given waters', meant to flow everywhere.
Rivers GOD gave to make land fertile
Yet we see fights, why in a state, it's flowing an extra mile!!

In villages and Farms when their wells run dry
They'll blame the Govt and make an outcry!!
instead of educating their masses, the reasons to save water, and why,
You see maids in a house, let the taps just flow
While with only a bucket, they're mopping the floor.
They wash with running water vessels and clothes
Instead of learning how the taps to close.

When kids want water, they take a full glass
Drink half and throw the rest . . . . Alas!!
If only Man could save those precious drops
we will have plenty for ourselves and our crops.

There has to be a massive education thrust
If these bad habits we have to bust.
In an era when, Man has touched Moon and Mars, it's sad
That we've for ourselves made this Water Crisis so very bad!

(11.4)

"Oh! Cut Not Us Trees"!!
Composed by Leo DSouza Sept 10, 2012 at 12.43 am

Oh! Cut not us trees, just let us live
We have so much for you to give.
When Temperatures rise up and soar
The Rippling of our leaves, control it so.
Making the atmosphere around us, not unpleasant any more
and making it an even flow.

Oh! Cut not us Trees, let us live
We have so much for you to give.
Our roots they hold your soil so firm
The same soil that's cared for by even the worm
Our roots, if they don't say a word
With the rains, your soil it will erode.

Oh! Cut not us trees, let us live
We have so much for you to give.
Destroying will bring out the fury of nature
Sweeping elements, reducing Earth's stature.
By destroying us, the seasons go in turmoil
Weather changes and everything begins to spoil.

Oh! Cut not us trees, let us live
For we have so much for you to give.
Thus cry not only trees but, every other element
Trying to change destructive man who's Hell bent.
The Flood waters over the earth's surface will freely flow
Unhindered taking everything in its flow

Oh! Cut not us Trees, let us live
We have so much for you to give.
Destroying by his actions, this Universe
If not stopped, for himself he's making it worse!
So take heed when you hear that plaintive cry
And Save our Planet earth for You and I

(11.5)

PLIGHT of a GIRL CHILD!!
Composed by Leo DSouza July 5,2013 at 02.20am

'It's a Girl', morosely the Nurse did announce,
to the relatives, on her as they did pounce
Emerging from the delivery Room
Immediately, joy vanished, setting a pall of gloom.

I couldn't fathom, what had happened, I was too young
Didn't know, as curses, for the girl child, they flung.
When I went in with Ma, I saw Aunty too cry
Telling someone.. 'It's sad, as Anil wanted a Boy'!!

My Mom and I were the only few maybe
That went, Mother and Child, to see.
Anil was the new baby's father
Who, chose the 'Bar' than see his wife rather.

To take them home even, her parents were called
'cos with the baby's coming, her life snowballed.
She was ill treated & abused, as though the fault was hers
They showed no pity, just threats and jeers,

The baby, with no fault, neglected, was she
Her life like Mothers was all misery.
At her birth, no fanfare or merriment was found
She was ignored, whenever around.

Anything she needed, was given second thought
Mostly ignored or seldom bought.
No Plans for school they made for her
'What's the USE' they'd discuss and confer.

As I grew, neglected and unwanted I felt
but, Lived in 'Hope', their hearts to melt.
Towards Grandparents I would run excitedly
with anything new, then stop short, after steps three.

311

My father, I loved in spite of this
He cared I knew, but lived in ignorant bliss.
Nurtured by his parents, with superstitious beliefs
Little realizing, the scar on me, it leaves.

Mother toiled hard, stinted and saved
With dreams of a future, for me, she paved.
Against In laws, she took a stand and broke the rule,
Determined as she was, she sent me to school.

Each day in school, alone, I would weep in pain
The reasons to no one, could I explain.
Just resolved that 'Mother's sacrifice' won't be in vain.
To school I'll go, sunshine, hail or rain.

My youth I spent, with no friends or toys
Now in College, I made friends with Girls and boys.
Around me I found I was not the only one
There were other girls too, with no sunshine or fun.

Why I questioned myself, does this happen here?
when Headlines scream out of 'Progressive India'
'Children' I feel don't need to school . . . . go
It's their Parents who have to learn much more.

Didn't Grandpa ever think..that once Grandma was a female too?
And Gran-ma, Am I different . . . from you?
It's GOD that gives a Daughter or Son
This 'Atrocities on woman' abroad, is just not done.

Only here 'Abortion' and 'female infanticide' is found
Is this India's progress on the ground?
When sons settle down, Parents are unaware
That what happens to them, is the least of his care.

It's then the daughter that comes up front
Doing everything for them, though she got the 'Brunt'
of their 'wrath', for being 'a girl child'
But what helped was, being humble and mild.

The salt of my tears all dried up now
To care for them I've taken a vow
I often sit recalling all of my past plight
As a Girl child, being denied even my birth right'

From this a lesson I give to everyone
Accept a 'Girl' as you do your son
'Girls' or 'Boys' . . . . God Created them all . . . . everyone..!!

(11.6)

Secrets in Waste.
Composed by Leo DSouza.August 23,2012 at 08.42 am

When the food is not to your taste
Don't you simply throw it out as waste?
Your dumping ground is your garbage bin
and you turn back home with a contended grin!

But did you know with your haste
You're life story too . . . lies with your waste?
Your old romances come to be known
from the 'love notes' you tore and thought carefully thrown!

From those old and discarded pair of shoes
you're obviously saying you've got modern new ones to use.
By the number of bottles your hubby throws
speaks of his 'subdued' woes!

Some people unmindfully throw old broken glass
'uncaring for others safety' they show their 'class'!
At times the bins full of clippings of trees and grass
telling us your gardeners, your garden trimmed enmass.

There are some that 'don't give' but 'throw food'
the world surmises, when eating, they lost their mood.
When in the bin, a broken plate you get
It tells us that now you have an incomplete dinner set!!

When many eggshells to the bin, a step they make,
Signals go out . . . that you have baked a cake!!
When daily your your dustbin is full to the brim
Tells us, you're a strict homemaker and very grim.

With the 3-4 packets of cigarette packets you daily throw
A heavy smoker you are we now all know.
But when there are assorted things thrown carefree
It explains itself . . . you are on a Spring Cleaning Spree.

Those kiddies books that you've just sold
tells us, your kids have now grown old.
When old text and note books, in your bin are found
You're neighbours know, your children, to the next level are bound.

The old contraceptive or packets that you throw
speak of your active sex life of the night before!
When perhaps the dust blower finds your rings
You're getting 'careless' a message it brings.

So next time be careful what you throw out
Your Dustbin 'waste speaks' & the world of you, knows all about.

(11.7)

Girls Deserve a 'YES' and a 'NOD'
Composed by Leo DSouza Sept3[rd], 2012 at 5.17 pm

When he met her . . . love bells had rung
They were two beings, so very young
Meeting everyday on the sly
Parents their whereabouts, shouldn't know Where or Why!!
Their pangs of love and temptations grew
Consequences of their actions they never knew.
Tripti continued living in utter bliss
Believing in Anil's intentions, that led to this.

Ruchika and Sohail were married over a year
Needing that job, pregnancy she did fear.
Sohail of her did take every care
But on his mind, was a family heir.
Succumbing to family pressures, they just fell prey
How Ruchika, when she knew, cursed that day.

Simon and Sandra well settled in life
Sandra to him was a doting wife.
With a good job, at work, Simon faced no trouble
Together they made a perfect couple.
Their Honeymoon they enjoyed to the hilt
Feelings got stronger, moods never did wilt.
Radiant and Glowing their love was always found
They made the most loving pair in town

When Tripti one day found somethings amiss
Confiding in Anil, she told him of this.
He lost his cool and began to shout
Asking her what was this all about?
Shocked she could only at him stare
After everything . . . now how could he dare?
He stomped out the door and from her life
He couldn't accept responsibilities of a wife!!

Sohail when he knew he comforted her
Explaining things will soon, jobwise, work out for Ruchika.
Taking leave to the Gynaec they did go
So that they could Confirm and learn more.
Sex determination test, the gynaec refused to do
As the Law forbade it too.

Sandra was overjoyed when an inkling she had
Excited she was to tell Simon, he's becoming a Dad.
Today in her step, there was an extra bounce
Fears of motherhood, she was determined to trounce.
Thinking, in the Office, she would have to take care
Planning even the Clothes she would now have to wear.

Determined Tripti with this she would go through
As a Single Mother, she would join the band too.
As the date began to approach
Various obstacles she had to broach
Undaunted she was with no Parents support
But she was determined, not to abort.
She met Ruchika and Sohail at Dr Sood's
Silently she envied their joyous mood.
When they heard about her plight
They bonded with her at first sight.

Ruchika delivered a baby girl
Sohail's world now began to whirl
Crestfallen and aloof, happy he was not
Who wanted a girl? Now he wished, she did Abort.
This suddeen change in him, got her perplexed
He kept away on some or other pretext.

Sandra & Simon's turn was also due
Both of their parents down they flew
Anxious moments, they passed that day
Hoping Mother and Child will be okay.

317

Tripti too was blessed with a girl
The baby beside her, lying in a curl
Radiant she was so full of joy
It didn't matter to her, it was not a boy.

Sandra soon gave birth to a pair of twins
The First was healthy, the second girl was thin
But their double happines shone from within.
Simon overjoyed, kept his cell busy
Telling the world the good news, he was in a dizzy.

Tripti on her daughter began to dote
Now, she was Mother and Father to her, both.
With determination she brought her up well
She had no Father, no one could tell.

Ruchika's inlaws were a troublesome lot
Ill treating her, every opportunity, they got.
For them, nothing mattered, but a boy
Ignoring the child, not even a toy.
Packed her off to her mothers, to stay
For a Girl child, this price, she was made to pay.

Years passed, Anil lay dying with no remorse
Tripti took her daughter to see him because
He was her dad after all
At the funeral, clutching her daughter, let a teardrop fall.

Sohail had now grayed with years
Alone now, parents dead, his sorrow brought on the tears.
Clutching his daughter Meena to his chest
Telling Ruchika, she did well and won the Test.

The Twins by now had matured and grown
To the states they had flown
Simon & Sandra felt truly Blessed
Accepting God's gifts, years ago, was their biggest Invest.

From this all couples should take a cue
For a 'Girl Child' is a blessing too
If perchance they had resorted to Female Foeticide
Today they would have had their faces to hide.
A 'Girl' is also a gift from GOD
So when the time comes, Give the Girl Child a 'Yes' and a 'Nod'

(11.8)

Things KIDS Need to Know!
Composed by Leonard DSouzaAug 8, 2012 at 11:55 am

Kids from the moment you get up in the morn
to brush your teeth, wash your face, to rid that yawn
Remember there are some things you have to know
As you, in the world, have to grow..

Settle your Bed—hang and fold your clothes
Make sure to the right place your shoe goes
Your study table should always be neat
Remember it's your 'Knowledge Seat'!!

'PLEASE' and 'THANK YOU' to say for the Bread
and for passing the 'Cheese Spread'
Make it a 'Habit' and your 'Cup of Tea'
'Cos outside it wont always be your 'Family'

Even when you go to College or School
Don't ever forget this Golden Rule.
Bidding time to Elders, doesn't make you Small
Instead you'll be liked and cared by all.

When you are travelling in a Bus
An empty seat, offer the Lady, without a Fuss
In Restuarants, Picture Halls everywhere
Remember 'Ladies First' to get the Chair.

Protect and Respect the Feminine kind everywhere
Doesn't matter if your friends at you, laugh or stare.
From the attention that you get, they will burn
and by your example they will learn.

If you are a girl, don't make fun of a Boy
Like you, he too is Human, not a Toy!
Make friends and mix freely with the males
Use your head, don't just into their arms.. sail!!

It doesn't matter if your Good and others Bad
It shows the upbringing that they had.
Given a choice would you prefer that?
And Scarred for life being called a BRAT!!

Don't bully the juniors in schools, Colleges or from your Block
It's with 'adulation' they look to you and 'flock'
Be respectful at all times to your Elders
in trouble times, they will be your defenders.

Ever wondered why long Merit Lists exists for Board Exams?
'cos they're the ones, from the Leaked Papers Scam!
So Beware, keep far from these types
they're actually Moral-less, living on mere hypes.

Don't ever let MORALS in LIFE, take a back seat
In Life for every Struggle is followed with a Treat!!
So Kids, the Right Path you have to Follow
In the long run, you'll Prosper, instead of a life that's Hollow.!!

Chapter XII

Tributes in Verse

In this Chapter I have paid personal tributes to people

who I remember in things they have done, impacts they

have created around us and as salutations

paid with Love and Respect, to them as

People and on their Special Occasions.

(12.1)

Numbers That Guide!!

Composed specially for Niece Bianca by: Leo D'Souza

A number is said to guide one's life,
Seeing People through Happiness and Strife.
Though No; 1 is yours Now, always and before
For you it's really 3 and 2 not less, not more,
I derived this from the verse below,
As I saw you from an infant grow.
Read along and you will see,
It's a fact, not just, made up by me.
I remember you, when you were 3
Flipping around, like a busy bee.
You were one among the smart few,
I noticed it, when you were merely 2.
The years kept on rolling by,
You grew up smarter, cuter and shy.
Before our eyes, you turned into a young lass,
Carrying yourself well, with dignity and class!
Trophies came to you in a row,
Merely entering ensured, to you it would go.
Besides a photographic memory, that you had,
Art and acting too, for you was a fad!!
Your Marriage date too added upto 3
When you became 2 you see.
This number destined your profession also
I'm sure you couldn't ask for more!
While 'these numbers' we, so proudly display,
Because they are entrusted to your care!
For us they are a 'set', brushed up like 'dears'
While for you <u>today</u>, they make up your 'Years'!!

(12.2)

Milestones of Love . . .
Composed by: Leo DSouza on 2nd Oct, 2013.

It's another Milestone you have reached,
As one by one, the earlier ones you breached.
Looking back, I'm sure, you'll recall,
The long gone years of fun and all.

Your schooling days and the fun you had,
Almost driving Peers & Teachers mad!!
Going thru 'Adolescent days' with an enigmatic smile,
Capturing maidens hearts . . . . mile after mile!!

Then in your very flamboyant style,
As you took your wife, down the aisle.
Also to fatherhood, as you moved on,
The day that your son, to you both, was born.

Your mates envied your frame, so proper and trim,
Jokingly asking your wife,' Don't you feed him?'
You even prospered, in the work you did,
Worries if any, you didn't show, just hid.

Soon you were a father, twice over, seen,
As the second son, came on the scene.
The Wify and you now were so thrilled,
Your 'Cup of Joy' to the brim, now filled.

Today, I'm sure, with Joy you recall
As each 'Milestone of Love', you crossed them all.
From Husband, Dad, Father-in-law to Grand Dad,
A share of everyone, you've truly had!

Inviting me for today, though you said, "No Gift",
With this composition, I thought, I'd your 'Spirit lift'!
Joining with Relatives & Friends to say,' YOU we Love'
As you Beam with 'God's Blessings from above'

(12.3)

His Spouse, The Poet and ICU.
Composed by Leo DSouza. Sunday, August 26, 2012 at 1:07am
(A True Life story of this poet)

Have any of you been to an ICU ward?
This author hopes not . . . . He prays to God!
Unless, this also happens to you
Only then you're welcome to ICU!!!

32 years ago, while their relatives battled for life
'Twas there he met, who then, would become his future wife.
Of all the Crazy places they met in Mayo's Hospital's ICU
When their thoughts were,' will they pull through?'

He had flown from Delhi to be with his Dad
Who, a heart attack he had, just had.
God's ways so mysterious I must say
Her Grand Uncle, to ICU was admitted the next day.

His future Father-in-law there 1st he met
Though there was 'nothing in the air' as yet!
His Father-in-law was a very jovial guy
Who, cottoned on to him, then . . . He didn't know why!!
Looking back now He can make a guess
Was He happy about it . . . now He can say,' YES".

His daughter he said was arriving 2 mornings later
And asked Him, if he could go and meet her.
Excited he was, his imagination ran amok
He couldn't believe this new found LUCK!!
Her Mum that evening, as Grim as could be
Stomped down her foot said, "No Let it be'!!
Throwing daggers at him for opening, to a stranger, his gob
Boomed . . . "I've put someone else on the job"!
Disappointed I was, my Luck I did blame
Golden Opportunity had gone, of meeting this dame!

That evening she came in a skirt of tomato pink
Bobbed cut curly hair..which all the more made him Think!
Deep down, his heart began to sway
Though this' dame' not a word to him, did she say.
Just a cute smile everyday he got
Making him what he really was here for . . . He forgot!!
Her younger sis so cute with a twinkle in her left eye
To break the ice thru her tried..he said did I
Like all damsels she was fighting . . . hard to get
But determined, in his own way was he yet.
With his emotions to control he had to fight
For he knew, this ICU, brought him,' Love at 1st Sight'.

It was X'Mas week, at the hospital's ICU he was holed
to take them to the dances, his brother he had told!
He couldn't go, even if he chose
'cos in Delhi left behind, were all his clothes.!!
He had flown down with just the clothes on his back
How could he have known, a beauty in his life, would come smack!!

Returning to Delhi after his dad returned home for rest
Thoughts of her haunted him like a pest.
Funny how, when really they hardly spoke
Was this real, or was this on him a Joke?
He wrote to her Dad permission to correspond if he may
When he got the reply,' YES', it made his day.

Everyday his letters they went by post
The postman in Delhi, had become his 'Host'
He took a transfer, returned for good back here
She had become for him, so very dear!
They decided their Romance from Paper sheaf's no longer to tarry
And set a date, with each other to Marry.
Making Plans of when to say 'I DO"
Preparing guest lists limiting it to very few.
For this there were genuine reasons too
His Uncle had died; her Granma was on deathbed too.

Breaking all traditions, taking everyone off guard
Their reception was held, not in a hall but, in her green backyard.
Their Backdrop was the Old Chikoo Tree
Like a fairy tale. for all to see.

Now friends this story is so very true
'Cos my Wife and I, are the couple from ICU
Committed all our lives to each other to only say,' I SEE YOU"!!!

(12.4)

With LOVE from Above!!
by Leo DSouza on Thursday, June 21, 2012 at 9:51am

I Love you Guys even though I'm not around
I enjoyed my short stay there on the ground.
Dear Andrea, Sorry I didn't call that night
I drove like Hell—hoping to be home so I might
at least say Bye . . . before I left
But in spite of my driving, which I did with deft
The pain was too much . . . I couldn't wait
God too was waiting for me.. at the gate.
I saved the kids.. the last and least I could for them do
Ensuring they'll be there.. to be with you.

Charlene & Mervyn I enjoyed that last night's stay
but Sweetheart, I had to leave.. and be on my way.
Alyssa & Owain. I was waiting to see you guys
Your 'happiness' I saw that day.. in your eyes.
Thank you Owain for all you did for me to revive
But God's plan was not for me to survive.
I'm sorry I won't be physically there around
when you decide to settle down.
My Blessings to you from above I'll give
Just go back, work well and happily live.

Mum Amy, I won't be there to drive you to Church
but, a way out, I'm sure Andrea, will search
Andrea I'm gonna miss you and everything we shared
We had no secrets between us..everything we bared
For my Office yarns I won't have anyone to share
But then there's now no Office.. so why do I care?

Rue, I didn't forget you but, for the last, I on purpose kept
you saw me slipping away that day, as towards the Lord I leapt.
I'm counting on you my little pet
Don't give up . . . for you . . . I'm still there yet.
You'll be thinking of Gran'ma and Mum I know
Don't worry, for them God will open another door.
There'll always be Audrey & Leo next door I know
Just take care of yourselves, is all I ask
Each go about doing sincerely your Job and Task
I'll be praying for you and patiently
waiting, when together, united again we'll be.
Oh! By the way God presented me a 4 wheeler he named for me 'Souzoto'
Now you know, I couldn't have asked for more.
Bye then I'll say to one and all
Just do what's right.. and await your final Call.

(12.5)

Lines in Tribute to JOE PITTS . . .
(Dedicated to the memory of Mr. Joe Pitts—Ex Secretary of Catholic Institute
and President of A.I. –
Nagpur)
by Leo DSouza on Wednesday, June 13, 2012 at 10:31am

A Black bag under his arm
With Solar-Toupee, everyone he'd charm
Soft Spoken he was in his ways
Cycling everyone knew him . . . nights and days.

The C.I. to him was like a personal fiefdom
Organizing many an event full of frolic and fun.
Table-Tennis, Flag-Whist, Cricket & Football were events few
And sections that flourished in his time we knew.

His Name became synonymous with the Catholic Institute
He cannot be forgotten by the old or the youth
He held the reign for many a long year
A watchful eye he had for everything..far and near.

No youth could with him dodge their age
He'd corner them . . . like a tiger in a cage
Single handedly he'd do almost everything
Ensuring to Members, he'd enjoyment bring.

A pleasure to work with him, it was for all
No' Infighting' ever, there was anyone can recall
Be it a 'Social','X'Mas Functions' or a 'Ball'
He was there long after the last man left the Hall.

A Multitasking guy, he was for sure
Guiding even the Anglo-Indians, collecting Subs, door to door.
Knowing the financial status of many an A.I. folk
Recommending Aid ONLY for Deserving, he kept tightly round his yoke.
Only the poorest A.I. Kids he would ensure
Received Educational—Aid, and more.

Thin and frail was his outward look
Yet, no nonsense, from anyone . . . he'd brook.
As the years went rolling by
He chose to fade away from Public Eye
His Sharp Memory, the strongest Asset, was failing in bits
Bringing tears to all.. 'Cos 'twas not the guy we knew as JOE PITTS.

GOD Grant him now Eternal Rest in his Kingdom above
for all the Good he did, for Friends and Relatives . . . . with Love.

(12.6)

Tribute to my Godmother Aunty Antonette
(Composed by Leo DSouza on 11th Sept, 2012)

90 Years to this day
There was merriment all the way
At the 'DSilva' house in Soccolvado, Assagaon Bardez they say
As baby Antonette was born that day.
Her Birth on Saturday 16th Sept 1922
Coincided with the Turks chasing The Greeks from Asia too.

Of her early youth & life not much can I say
'Cos it was before my time and day!
Being in Goa for all, walking a lot it meant
For Antonette today that walking has proved God sent.
'Cos when people half her age are down with aches and pains
She's up and about, summer, winter or rains.

She entered our family on 9th Feb 1948
When she took and made my Uncle George her mate.
It was not long after that date
To carry me, she didn't have long to wait.
At an age when I couldn't ever bother
At the Baptismal Font, she became my GODMOTHER!!

Now U. George at TOMCO worked, while she kept home
Even finding spare time for Religious Charity to Roam.
Joining Legions of Mary and the Sodality which were a prayerful group
Forming themselves into also a spiritual and Helpful troupe.
Visiting the poor, praying for & with the sick
The religious Fervor, made her life tick.

Because of the Miles we were not so close
But, whenever we met, of her love, she gave me my dose.
Like Sachin there . . . . Going on and on . . . she bats
Keeping her company all day are her Cats!!

Her home years ago was a refuge always for a neighboring kid
Aubrey, Gavin & others in and out they would flit.
Even for us at times, if to cycle to Khamaria, we did not feel
She would open her home and give us a meal.

So devout and strong was she in her faith
Church meant being on time not like most . . . . Late!!
She propagated the Bible specially the line, 'Love Thy Neighbor'
That was quickly picked up and followed by Marie her daughter!!
Daryl in Nagpur found and married a girl Rita Domingo
So when Ramon wanted a wife, she told him where to go!!
While Dominic is busy all day with the Church work and Club
Amelia she educated, so into the young minds of students, Lessons she can rub.

Very few, like me are fortunate at 63
To have their Godmothers at 90 and still there to see.
A few aches and pains, but still quite mobile
We pray to God He Spares her to touch the 100 mile!!
And I'm sure V. George too from above will agree and Smile.

(12.7)

Tribute to the Jubilarians (Chris & Kat)
Composed on26th May 2009. by Leo DSouza at 1:26am

'Twas 25 years ago, . . . 1984 to be exact
When 2 people vowed their love and decided to sign a pact.
'For better or worse, for richer for poorer and until death did them apart
They relied not on any one but . . . . feelings of their heart.

A charming couple they made, walking down the aisle
Hand in hand then—with intent to cover many a mile.
Together they stuck it out through thick and thin
Not all roses along the way—hardships too were in their bin.

Their joys we shared but, to themselves the troubles they kept
Consoling & using each other's shoulder if ever they wept.
Blessed with Amanda, their Joys knew no bounds
They were now three to do everywhere the rounds.

House hopping and making 'home' was their aim
Exploring avenues they were always game
To begin this journey—in Aurangabad they did land
Struggling all the way—sometimes even in sinking sand.

To Mumbai a land of plenty their feet did they plant
With wishes 'Double fold", GOD their prayers HE did grant
Literally, a handful now, Kath she was always kept busy
House chores—three kids—she handled everything in a dizzy!

They partied and kept for friends always . . . Open their Door
Many made a habit to visit Mumbai— more and more.
The kids they grew up cute and sweet
To watch them grow was always a Treat!

Both Grandparents always did dote on the 'Three'
Showering love and doing everything—for FREE
Chris's sights were focused now on Dubai
And very soon—there, . . . he did fly.

To Kath and the girls Nagpur was now home
Biding time here till he could say 'Come'
True 'Nagpurians' that they were for sure
Like Santa they'd come back —every December

Their Company everyone loved to have around
Evenings were filled with musical sounds.
Even though, we them, I'm sure sometimes did 'bug'
For us all . . . they always had a loving hug.

Ever helpful were both Chris and Kath to all
Harbouring no ills for anyone, big or small.
Today distance the only thing that's kept them far
But no one has of them bad thoughts to mar.

To me they have very special been
Likewise interest in our family—they were always keen.
To my aid they came.. When my heart . . . did flip
Stood by us, didn't let our spirits ever dip.

These were, of them, sweet memories down the years
For us they will always be—. . . 'Dears'
On this grand landmark in their lives, our wishes unfold
God's Blessings always, for Silver to turn to Gold.

May they as a family prosper and thrive
Begetting all that they for, did strive.
God Bless the Gregory's both big and small
Keep them as they are . . . "Lovable" to all.

Now as I grow old . . . poetic thoughts are a bit slow
Forgive me if anything above has hurt you so.
Just remember us in your prayers—night and day
AS "CONGRATULATIONS' to end . . . I say.

Now Kath this I wish to add:
Their flitting . . . . has still not ended.. Dubai was not their last
To New Zealand they migrated . . . putting Dubai into their Past.
Here they decided to settle down, even bought a house
Scenic NZ was all good . . . but Job wise 'interest' to Chris did not arouse.

To Dubai back, he decided to go . . . leaving the girls there but taking Kath in tow
Dubai too had changed . . . . Salaries and jobs became scarce.. with pay now low
So towards Baharain and better avenues they did find
Flitting between New Zealand-Baharain-India—to keep family ties bind

The 'kids' are 'young ladies' now . . . . making heads turn
And when they pass . . . . many a guy says WOW!!!
Kath & Chris . . . . they still are Trim, slim and kept their figure
No traces of the greying.unless with Dye, they cleverly it . . . do cover!

All the Best Kath and Chris and your 3 Gs
I couldn't stop myself . . . to add the verses . . . these.

(12.8)

Saluting Ex-Nagpurians as I Remember Them.
Composed by Leo DSouza. June 26,2012 at 12.41 am.
(Composed as a Sequel to;'A Note from Charlie to Family & Friends' and this is
dedicated to Nagpur Friends who are resting in Peace)

On 23rd October 2008 during my By-Pass
God gave me A Wild Card Entry to HIS Kingdom for a Short Visitor's Pass
So on a tour to the land far far beyond
'Tt was a pleasure meeting folks memories of whom, were so very fond.

In 'Christmas Spirit' Rupert Murze a paploo he had won
While Mary his wife now joined him, her work here . . . having been done.
With his signature Scarf around his neck was Alfie DSouza
And Hector's both.. one my neighbour, the other the Airline Engineer.

Bishop Bhai too was there in his Purple Cape
while Tony Pinto still clutching his Video tape.
Jose DSouza without eggs . . . couldn't make his Easter Chicks
while Aunt Sophie still cutting the Beef and a vegetable mix.

Uncle Caraciol Menezes with his towel around his shoulders strolled
early morn, like then, to pick up The Hitavada for stories it told.
Marie & Irene Athayde from their veranda still they look
at Alice & Mabel D'cunha with a parasol and book.

Aunt Beryl's lined up Plumbers, Masons, Carpenters and all
as Uncle Cajetan still cares for beneficiaries of Vincent De Paul
Aunt Lucy Lobo has her recipe of her favourite sweet
While Willie Baptist wonders why he crossed, that day, the street.

Louie Gregory wears his Blue Ribbon & Medal of Legion of Mary
helping Wild Card Visitors like me . . . our loads to carry.
His brother Iggy enjoys up here quite a clout
armed with Printing experience and a Left Jab in a boxing bout.
Alex Fletcher & his mum Milicint too were there
Alex as usual arranging, for Whist, the Tables and Chairs
The one that's having quite a Ball
is none other than our young and handsome Ryan Paul.

Babush Almeida & Ajay Krishna are in their prime
seeing them brought memories . . . of good ole times.
Along the poolside. close by were Clarence & Maryann Vyland, as they quietly
sip
the Cool Cool drink they got that day, on the Ship.

Fr John Anthony keeps wondering about his past
saying, 'Lastly' during sermons but, they would forever last
Fr Francis, the Lords Estate, charge he's now been given again
As Fr Stephen Moniz rue's being hounded by Wolves and the terrible pain.

The stately Fr Macarios walks along the evergreen paths
watching Sir Kenny and Jackie Collaco..one with English the other Maths.
Prisca Braganza from above lovingly watches over her boys
while Uncle Romulus & A Antoinette think about Stanley and Joy.

Aunt Mary Mitchell still treasures her box
containing everything she had, even her handkies and socks.
Two more brothers the Lancelots..Joe and Gerry formed a pack
Joe reminiscing of those days on the railyway track

Gerry being roped in by the 'Patni's for a share too in Gods Land
Hoping like in SFS property, someone up there too, will lend a hand.
Bishop Sylvester came up from the land of caves . . . Aurangabad
he wanted to be there longer . . . for that he felt sad.

The Rebeiro's here were a perfect pair
Joe went ahead to prepare the way so A Sarah could come and share.
God found Austin Nazareth the perfect man
to Edit, Review his Kingdom's very own 'SPAN'.

Dudlee Magee went Down under to come up above
to meet Daphne his wife, and true true love.

I tried to meet requests of many who called in
for a sequel but, omissions I'm sure there could have bin
So just give me a call and I will see
If there's a need to make a Season Three!!

(12.9)

Devotees Plight—
Composed by Leo DSouza June 27,2013 at 03.04 am

(This Poem is dedicated to the memory of our 5 IAF Personnel who sacrificed their life saving the life of the stranded at Uttarkhand* and other regions thereabout : Namely: DARREL CASTELLINO., FLT. LT. KAPOOR,; FLT LT: Praveen, Sergent Sudhakar, & JWO A K Singh . . . May they RIP.)

The trains were packed, with crowds no lull,
Devotees rushing, No thoughts to mull.
They came in flocks from far and near,
As always they did . . . . year after year.
Braving inclement weather, on they trudged,
Climbing summits, their faith didn't budge,

Frolic & Gaiety, out shadowed the sultry sky,
To understand the reason—none needed to ask,.Why?
Long Queue's wound themselves like crawling snakes
As upward they slithered over rocks and glades.

One destination, they all had in mind,
Peace & Tranquillity at God's feet to find.
Old and young in hordes they came
anywhere one looked . . . the scene looked the same.

Along the way were patches of pitched tents,
Old Parents, boys, girls, women and gents.
Winding roads with hairpin bends
Serene mountains, man, life to it lends.
Saharanpur, Sarseva, Kinnaur all were hit,
Incessant rains and snow, creating havoc bit by bit.

48 hours rain it's fury, slowly did unfold.
Trickles of rivulets, slowly gaining momentum untold.
Eroding the soil in its path, mounting worries
As Army & Air force to help did scurry.

In its wake by now the floods uprooted hotels & trees
Bringing people, the Govt, and everyone on its knees
Uttarkhand, & Kedarnath* shrines now, posing a threat to life,
As Pilgrimage was bringing more and more strife.

Know why man-made disaster, it was called?
To encroach for house and shops. So when it snowballed
Because Mandakini River banks were misused
'twas the rivers way with 'fury', man's action..abused

Now floods erupted washing away property, in its stride.
Spreading disaster, claiming lives, far and wide.
Suddenly boulders, from hills, took a tumble
Hills getting eroded, while clouds, louder did rumble
Sweeping people off their feet, panic it did spread.
Soon a drastic turn it took, thousands more were dead.

The shrines in shambles, they did lie
All around for miles, men, women and kids, did die.
Rescue by Army undertaken on a massive scale
As relatives far & wide, for their dead, shed a tear or did wail.

Survivors, in 2 days should all be back
As the Army, it's efforts in this, will never look back
Then India can concentrate for the dead, a homage,
Putting behind us the rains, deadly rage.

To our brave forces, you, A Salute Deserve,
For fighting all odds, rescuing, you never lost your nerve
Proving to all of us that for everything, you will always fight
As you did, the floods, faced by these Devotees Plight.

Special Kudos to Gauchar & Guptakshi
They did it all without a fee
Agencies that also helped in rescue work
Like the Army & Air force, responsibility didn't shirk.

It's reported, some are stranded still
At Badrinath, Dharsu* and Harsil*.
While Kedarnath is evacuated totally
so also at Mutli*, Bhatwari* and Maneri*.

Finally a Salute and homage to those valiant IAF men
Army personnel too, toiling hard, both Officers and men.
Not resting till every possible man was saved
Unfortunately Castellino's copter, fell in the glade.

Undeterred others, shouldered the cause to save,
without pomp and show or rave.
Yet, some Politicians reached there to gloat
Of fictitious Rescues, just to ensure a vote.

Those towns and shrines today, wear a Ghost town look
As this goes down as a worst disaster, in our history book.
Those Muddy river waters will take time, to again get white
Scarred and bruised for life was our DEVOTEES PLIGHT!!

- Uttarkhand = A State in North India. * Kedarnath= Holy Pilgrim centre in North India.
*Dharsu, HarsilMutli, Bhatwan, Manen small hill towns in the region.

Chapter XIII

Shrouded in Mystery

Right through Life man experiences a sense of mystery whether

he faces 'happiness, loneliness..' or witnesses something or someone

'Hanging for Life'. It's a sense of Puzzlement. Even his

'Inseparable Love' at times cannot help him. However,

in this Chapter, the reader is taken verse by verse

into a mystery that makes him/her knit their brows

trying to decipher whether what they think is right,

till finally, when truth hits they conclude

about this poet 'He belongs to an extinct clan'!

(13. 1)

Hanging For Life!!

Composed by Leo DSouza Tuesday, August 28, 2012 at 1:28am

We are from a very big family, but differ in shapes and sizes
Some are bought, other's won as prizes!
Round our necks we all wear a chain
Some long, some short, beauty to gain.

The poorer of us, of plain wire we're done
Some with Slogans, full of Fun!
The fairer sex of us has beads and bells
When we arrive . . . everyone can tell.

Some of us carry our owner's name
Though it's not ours, we are not ashamed!
Some arrest and tie us to their waist
Afraid we'll escape . . . . in their haste!!

Still, at times we hide and get left behind
Then, at owners we laugh, while teeth they grind!
Without us nowhere can they go
To Market, or Movie or a Concert show!!

We love to go on a scooter ride
But, don't like cops 'handling' us when, you jump red lights.
Going by car is always a delight
Especially when the AC keeps the Temperature right.

Quite a few of Metal, coloured like Silver and Gold
Each working for an organization, New or Old.
But from hanging there seems no respite
It's just our luck, to hang day or night.

Normally everyone is hung by the neck till dead
But it's LIFE for us in my poem it is said.
For all, this will a Mystery always be
But to this Mystery only we..Hold the Key!!

(13.2)

Can Sir??—

Composed by Leo DSouza Tuesday, February 7, 2012 at 12:07am

No one to him would compare-my fleeting thoughts would be . . . Can Sir,
Not be better? If Teresa our Geography Ma'am could bring rain dripping
In the Coniferous Forest . . . I'd ask myself . . . . Can Sir
Not move Rain clouds? . . . my mind would go flitting.

'Can Sir' . . . . I was with it Obsessed
Can Sir . . . . I added questioning everything I said or Possessed.
Every thought of mine..I'd suffix with..Can sir?
Every breathe I'd take . . . I'd whisper . . . Can Sir?
Every Step in life I took . . . would move towards . . . Can Sir?
Every Morsel I ate.. I'd inwardly swallow..Can Sir?

From my toddling days . . . he always stood strong and Tall
Always there to play with me.. Doll or Ball.
When I was little, with my flowing Curls
He'd ride me in his car..for a city whirl.

For a Teenage girl he was my 'Knight in Shining Armour'
I secretly 'pictured' and for him did clamor
I cried the day they said he'd gone home to Marry
A thought I turned around but couldn't fathom or parry.

Feelings of mine . . . . he's forgotten . . . . Can Sir?
Heartbeats of mine . . . . he can't hear . . . . Can Sir?
Teardrops trickling down my cheeks . . . . he can't see . . . Can Sir?
My heartbreak . . . he'd not realise . . . . Can sir?

Then One day at HIS usual time . . . the door Bell rang,
My heart leapt, I jumped, I rushed forward and inwardly sang
'He's Back-He's Back!.. I almost yelled but . . . . Can Sir?
It was his wife's Telegram . . . . He'd gone forever . . . . 'Twas CANCER!!

(13.3)

Fear Conquered!!
by Leo DSouza. Wednesday, August 3, 2011 at 9:36am

She looked at me with 'wondering' eyes for, I
Had not a Murmur, not a whimper not a sigh.
Gently she lay me down on her couch
Expecting me to resist or, cry out 'Ouch'

Then gently she held my head
Made me feel the couch was a bed.
Her soft voice cajoling me all the while
Took away my fears . . . mile by mile.
If and when I showed signs of pain
She stolidly stood behind me with her flowing mane.

Then delicately and deftly into my mouth went her finger,
To a 'Romantic' 'twould be,' memories that 'linger'
25 minutes of her closeness and probing eyes
Transported me from 'anxiety' to 'appreciative sighs'.
A kind of numbness into my being she brought
Why I stayed away so long . . . I Thought.

Now who she is—to tell you I just can't resist
She's none other than . . . my gentle 'Dentist'

(Composed after my 1st visit to Dr Arya's Clinic.)

(13.4)

Epitaph written when . . .

Composed By: Leo DSouza July 13, 2013 at 12:40am

I scratch my way every time
As I travel line by line
The surface I travel along is always clean
As I move however, my movements are seen.

I'm familiar with any subject under the sun
And I can duplicate them one by one.
With a cap on my head, and a transparent dress
My slim body, guys love to caress.

Holding me close, always to their heart
If I fall, Life ends for me, even before I start.
Unisex I am a companion to a girl as well as boy
To be in both's company, gives me great joy,

When you do wrong, I am red
Generally blue, even when with others I see you.
My sisters are always seen
With Executives, smartly dressed in Black and Green

I'm sure surprised; you'll find 'My Epitaph's' written when,
I'm still around—alive—as your faithful . . . Ball Pen.!

(13.5)

Happiness Loneliness . . . Bonding
Composed by Leo DSouza

She, barely 12, gathered her friends, all homeless like her,
Danced in the rain, in gay abandonment, without fear.
Carefree were they, like the droplets of rain
Uncaring in falling, spreading pleasure . . . . not pain.

He pulled from his packet, a pouch of Tobacco,
To him . . . . this was the only way.. to make hunger go.
He learned this very early, while just a teen
Abandoned by his known mother, A Father, he hadn't seen.

She wagged her tail, as into his bedding she curled
While others threw stones, this beggar for her a sheet unfurled.
Daily he saved a Chapattis, from his meager share,
To offer her, as he stroked and brushed her hair.

With her friends, she knew, it didn't matter at all
This gay abandonment, from no 'Status' they had to fall.
It didn't even matter, from where came the next meal,
Or even if it didn't . . . the pangs of hunger, they learnt not to feel

The Tobacco would bring on the sleep
A thing he enjoyed now, having long forgotten to weep.
Tomorrow, his cycle rickshaw, he'll again need to pull
Just to earn enough, maybe not even for a square meal.

After the brushing, she nuzzles under his half torn sheet,
Sharing her body warmth, sleeping at his feet.
She too knew the morning, would bring more uncertainty
Not knowing Luxuries of Morning B'fast and Tea.

How dare, they splash on them, from the Mercedes
Muck from the ditch, spoiling their only clothes . . . these.
Aren't the rich taught, for others to care?
Or are they so shameless, and on the poor, they continue to dare?

He often watched those lively kids, unrelated, yet a team
Just like his Moti, moving on her own steam.
They too had seen him from across the road,
Always seemed happy, but never of routine, bored,
So when he beckoned to them to come,
They strolled across, foreboding they had none,
If Moti trusted him, they too should have no doubt
Agreeing wholeheartedly, in one voice they let out a shout!

He told them, for a ride, his dog & the beggar he'll take,
After all its Sunday, don't they all deserve a Break?????
Under his seat, in a forgotten packet he found fifty Rupees
So Biryani at Abdul's, then down the road, in the cool cool breeze

Happiness came to each one of them today
Bonding with each other, like no other way.
Moti too wagged her tail, filled with utter joy,
She for once, wasn't made to feel a dog, but the world held sway.

(13.6)

He's a Member of an Extinct Clan!!,
Composed by Leo DSouza Sunday, August 26, 2012 at 5:02pm

He comes knocking at mid day like a daytime ghost
Carrying for you, from someone a toast.
He has to go from door to door
Climbing stairways to each and every floor.
A Tiresome job he does everyday
At times searching houses on the way.
He's familiar even with your Dog's bark
That doesn't hamper him, his bicycle to park.

He knows each one's name but doesn't show
Because of his dead pan face, you'll never know.
He's always one to vouch for you
When called upon because only he, everybody knew.
He carry's with him tidings from far
Or 'Notice' for delivery of your car.
At times he has to walk many a mile
Especially in villages, he does it with a smile.

Young Lovers since ages eagerly for him would wait
Cursing him too, if perhaps he was late.
Sadly with the advent of the net
His coming lessened, but he was there yet.
Now his visits are few and far between
He's seldom heard and rarely seen.
He is a member of a fast becoming extinct clan
I'm talking about our beloved "POSTMAN"

(15.7)

Inseparable & Loyal Love . . .
Composed by Leo DSouza Wednesday, March 21, 2012 at 11:45pm

I Fell in Love with her at 1st sight,
though' I ne'er ever dreamt that I ever might.
Her attractive looks, so smooth to the touch
Always there when I needed her . . . so much.

I've never left her . . . taken her wherever I go
In front of others . . . I'm proud 'her 'to show.
Kept close to my heart . . . she's always been
There's not a place I go she's never seen.

I envy & doubt others whenever her they touch
That's why I eagerly, her return, watch as her I clutch,
At the Movies or shopping at any of the Malls
She keeps me company like li'l girls their dolls.

She never allows me funds to Stash
Ever ready, if I want, . . . to give me CASH.
She buys my groceries, clothes and shoes
Curtains for the Hall and Sanifresh for the Loo's

Anytime whatever I think I want . . . she's there..it, to buy
Resisting her I'm desperate but can't, even if I try.
She fills my Petrol so everywhere I can freely drive
That's why for 'another', her, I'll never swipe.

In her 'honour', I can just pen a few words..like a Bard
'Cos she's my Inseparable and Loyal . . . . 'CREDIT CARD'

(13.8)

'Railjacked Parents and I"
by Leo DSouza on Tuesday, August 14, 2012 at 10:08am

I was born in a railway coach under a seat
My mother having rail jacked a trip, where she, Dad did meet.
Travelling ticketless, she was beyond shame
Hiding like others, whenever the TT came
Food was scarce on a running train
So she just had to use her brain.
'Twas then she spied Dad in a corner
Big and brown, he looked a loner!.
Using her feminine charm, she made her move
Past caring.. she didn't have to anybody, anything to prove.
They struggled thus, homeless, trying to exist
Wondering how life brought to them, this cruel twist,
At stations..people past them rushed in chaos utter
Some were going, being replaced by others
Careless people at times, their toes almost did crush
Making them huddle in a corner to avoid the rush.
Sadhwani the Sindhi family with their roti's and pickle
Mum and dad's taste buds.. they did tickle,
From the Punjabi Aunty and her daughter Jyothi
They tasted some Makka-ki-Roti.
That was the night I was born, Dad brought some milk
From the bottle of the lady in silk.
For breakfast we had left over of Toast and Jam
From Aunty Mabel and her son Sam.
From Patel, the Gujarati boys back-pack
We shared a very tasty snack.
We silently watched & listened to the co-travelers chatter all day
And learned that Mrs. Fernandez to Goa, was on her way
The Sausages she took out smelt so good
Wondering, if for some, to ask, we should.
The new TT passed and looked at us in disdain
I'm sure, like us, there were many more on this Train.
The Night brought Calm with all asleep
We could now, afford . . . outside to peep.

Early morning we heard hawkers yell Chai and Samosa
While Mr. & Mrs. Iyer took out..Idly and dosa*.
In a short while we were to reach Mumbai
That's when mother said, we're reaching the city of Joy!
As we reached Mumbai, attention to us was drawn
By the Parsees Mrs. Batliwalla and her daughter Dawn
As they got ready to detrain from the coach
Seeing us they yelled a high pitch Shriek.. . . ." COCKROACH"!!!

---

*Idly and Dosa = A South Indian Snack now famous throughout India

(13.9)

Sweet Little Things In Pinks And Blues!!—
Composed by Leo DSouza. Saturday, March 24, 2012 at 1:00am

When I was young..their shapes to me didn't matter,
Nor their outer coatings . . . did me flatter.
They fascinated me yes . . . both big and small
Never took to any . . . come Winter Spring or Fall.

As the years rolled by . . . Peer pressure made me see
Come what may . . . . at least one..there was for me.
Soon I found . . . no longer I could be aloof
I definitely needed one at all times under my roof.

In my youth, I averted them, I was told
I kept my distance and acted Bold.
I always felt they looked good when on display
With dresses of White, Blue, Pink or Grey.

Closing 30, I now knew I could now no longer Run
Escape for me there definitely . . . was none.
Soon becoming an integral part of me
Bringing me Solace . . . when none could see
My pain & Grief . . . . as I lost one by one my Family.

In the morning she came in her gown of Pink
Keeping my spirits up, so into depression I wouldn't sink.
For my Nerves & Spasms she was always there in Green
And in Yellow to care for my Spleen.

My sleep was brought back with her dressed in pale blue
My headaches went with her misty white..that's true.
But what continues to fox me and will always do
How each one knows her special role to do?
All these White, Yellow, Orange, Pink and Blue you'll guess I Bet
Are all the Medication of mine' The Tablets'!!

(13 10)

Where Goes the Jam?

Composed by: Leonard DSouza Friday, October 26, 2012 at 12:41am

I was Once a Bottle full of Jam
But, in the house, there seems, a Scam!
Two little fingers everynite, into me would dip
Tell tale signs, remaining on that beings lip!

Everytime the level, would decrease, a centimeter
Foxing the household . . . . who's the eater?
Lady Jane would look daily and frown
While the Jam level inside, would daily go down.

Was it Lilly she thought, wondering How?
Or Stan? But, he loved Jam only with his Chow!
Eddie had a sweet tooth . . . but, would he?
And Why? When he could have done it openly!

Leela our servant, she's been here last 15 years
So on that count, there's definitely, no fears!
Then who could it be . . . Why and When?
Tonight she'll lay wait to spy and then

Catch the culprit red-handed, at the job
Then teach him how . . . next time to rob!
So hiding behind the drapes, just out of sight
Prepared she was, to spend the night.

An ordeal it was, she soon realized
'Cos in the dark, the mossey's* began to tantalize
Then just when she thought, of a quick shut-eye
A sound she heard, and almost let out a sigh!

It drew closer and closer, in the dark
Then she heard a faint flick, and saw a spark.
Tip-toeing he came, flashing his torch around
But a foot from the table, slipping..he fell to the ground.

355

Head covered with a dark sock
It was a Crook. . . . she got a shock!!
'Twas then she screamed to wake up all
Beckoning them to come, assemble in the Hall.

In the midst of confusion, the crook got up and ran
Stumbling he even dropped the Pedestal fan
Eddie her husband even brought his Handy Cam
But banging into the Table, he dropped the Bottle of Jam.

Soon the Jam was all over and on the Floor
So Jane decided to 'forget' to Spy . . . about where the Jam really did go!!
Little Sammy, with a sly grin and contended look,
Silently thanked the appearance of the Crook.

---

*Mossey's = slang for mosquitoes

(13.11)

No Longer Brushed Aside.
Composed by: Leo DSouza.

(Readers requested to read through without Scrolling down, and quit guessing)

For years unknown I was dressed in an aluminum foil,
For want of ideas, to change me, no one did toil.
I would lie in wait, in drudgery, every morn,
Moving hand to hand, till all were done and gone.

None cared for my feelings, as they wet my face
As though of my own, I had no grace.
Nudging me, my assistants too, just hung around,
Reminding me, we all to a common destination, were bound.

For years I was forced and pressed, to come out,
I couldn't resist, I just had no clout.
If kids took me out by themselves, ever,
They dropped me often, being not so clever.

I was often rolled, my dress made flat,
Nothing I could do, no one too, to even spat.
My Assistants were better off I guess
Regularly new ones came, always in a new dress.

Good Days arrived, I got answered my prayers,
Now I was ogled at, and got some stares.
Elegance replaced my old drudgy look
No one now, could write me off the book.

I now could stand erect keeping my form intact,
No more 'pressing demands' were there, in fact.
Just as after me . . . . my folks could Smile
I was now determined for them, to go, that extra mile.

No longer now just brushed and put aside,
But honoured with Dignity and Pride.
Being happy now, after years, I bent down in haste,
Thanking God, for changes in me and my fraternity . . . 'The Tooth Paste'

(13.12)

By your side . . . to be always seen.
.. by Leo DSouza August 3, 2013 at 2.46 pm

I've been there for you, even before your birth,
Carrying your clothes, and for Dad a shirt.
Alone in the Hospital ward, I stand,
As awaiting you, was your family, like a band.

Anxiety I've seen, on all their faces,
Small talk, Jokes and occasional paces.
I'm forgotten, while all this happens around,
For them, to make place, I sit on the ground.

As you grew, I was always there,
Accompanying you to playgrounds and Parks, everywhere.
I went with you shopping, to a market or a mall
Whatever you fancied or bought, I carried them all.

To school, as you took your books, my chest swelled with Pride,
My joy in helping you, I did not hide.
Then when you joined the Cricket Team . . . to excel,
With me around, your confidence did swell.

But when you went to College, I felt sad,
To have me around, you felt ashamed and bad.
Your adolescent days even, you liked to be free,
Though with you, I did long to be.

I liked your office, air-conditioned and cool,
At your side, as I sat on a stool.
You made me feel so . . . upbeat,
Carrying for you a Water Bottle and food to eat.

My good looks were commented on, by one and all,
I really felt, so proud and tall.
The daily Drive home, was hectic in the rush,
Carrying 'goodies' home, I would 'blush'

It had now become my routine.
By your side, always to be seen,
But sad, coming tired, your shoulders, did sag,
Not mine of-course . . . . I was only just your Handbag!!

(13.13)

A Note from your 'Darling D'
.... by Leo DSouza July 7, 2013 at 9.07 pm

I'm always there waiting for you everyday,
Lying quietly, just as you, me lay.
I feel so alone all day, with nothing to do,
To share your Feelings & Secrets, I just wait for you.

When you and I were young, and went to School
With me around, no one could play the fool.
With me, you had to follow, the School's Rule
I was always blank, and felt used, like a tool.

We grew up together, as per the Time-Table
School life passed for us, like a fable.
With me, you'd pretend I'm an aeroplane
Flying me around, till flying, I would fall in the drain.

Then to College, off you went
I too grew, but my days, in your room I spent.
I knew about your friends, your likes and dislikes
Your Girlfriends and love for Bikes.

Getting a job, your joy, with me, you shared
mentioning how on your 1st assignment, you were scared
Even when the Lottery, you did win
Everything to me, you confided in.

I remember how, your Mum, found me once
In your room, and on you did pounce
You wondered whether, how much 'Secrets' I did to her spill
UN-assured were you, 'no mention of them', she made until.

That night, I saw you, in your worst mood ever
but, before sleeping, you hugged me, under your Cover.
I was the 1st to know, your ardent feelings about Maureen
Though her, I still hadn't seen

Every outing, date and dinner with her
you poured your heart out, and with me did confer.
I was also the 1st to know when you would propose
I accepted silently my fate, being Second place, I suppose.

When as your wife she came, you introduced her to me
We three soon were a compatible company.
You nicknamed me 'Darling D', and promised I'll always be
Your One and Only 'True Love' and faithful . . . . Your DIARY!!!

(13.14)

An Unslipping Union!!
Composed by Leo DSouza. July 18,2013 at 4.23 am

I hug you, as you get out of bed,
We're together, though not wed.
Even though I'm not really your groom,
You drag me with you, into the Powder Room.

I'm so embarrassed, inside there,
Watching you, slowly getting bare.
You wet and yourself Lather,
I'm so down, and feeling sadder.

We then move into the room, to dress,
Your weight on me, you begin to press.
I hear you phoning, saying, you're off to the Dance,
Excited am I, with visuals of us two, in a prance.

Then you shattered my dreams, with a twister,
You left me and took, my fashionable sister.
I stayed in the room, alone all night,
Wondering when, of you, I'll have a sight.

Then Tip-toes I hear, I'm all beat
Till I saw with yours, Two 'Gent 'feet!
The door begun to creek, and open an inch
You were now alone, my tension had just begun to pinch.
Elated I was, seeing, my sister you left in the Hall,
Coming back to me . . . . after all.
I knew this you would do,
Always enjoying, an unslipping union, me and you.

You gently pick me up, carrying me to the bed edge,
Between us now, I knew, there'll be no wedge!
I cling on to you . . . . like a gripper,
After all, I am your Life Companion, ... your Slipper!!

(13.15)

Who Could I Be . . . ?
by Leo DSouza. July 20, 2013 at 5.13 am

I'm very popular, and this is my story,
Born in China in 1500 B.c.
Portuguese Priests & Chinese merchants embraced me in 16th Century,
Many tales were there, of me being legendary.

Shennong a Chinese Emperor once, drinking hot water, as per his own decree
when suddenly I fell in his cup, and he discovered beautiful me.
I acted like an antidote to Poison too
All they required, was me to chew.

Gruesome Legend has it that, Bodhidharma of Buddhism
While meditating for 9 yrs, found sleep overtake him.
He cut off his eyelids in disgust
It's said I grew from here, this I do not trust.

Chinese love me even if, with them I was bitter
With me around, they felt they could think better.
Laozi their Philosopher called me, 'Froth of the liquid jade'
His teachings, into a book, did Yin Hsi, to him bade.

In 50 BC there came a book all about me
In 22AD Hua Tua in 'Shin Lun', wrote about my ability
to improve one's mentality.
And that was during the Song Dynasty.

Between 589—618 AD, I had improved my span,
I now traveled into Japan.
I emboldened myself, ventured into bricks,
As Currency then had lost its kicks!!

The Song Dynasty(960-1279)A new preparation of, I had boasted
Tried the Steam and powdering, finally roasted
Legend has it that a 'Monkey' name was added to me,
Because they threw handfuls, when they were made angry.

In 1931, the Ming Court decreed me 'Loose' as a tribute,
So I increased my production, and I began to bear fruit.
By now to 52 countries I've traveled and been,
But only Japan introduced me to a tint of Green.

They experimented with me developing Green roasted
using me, when even God's they toasted.
Vietnamese gave me names as Lotus and Jasmine
But I was never really liked by the German.

I traveled to Africa, Portugal, Turkey and Britain
My Popularity was growing, that's for certain.
In Cyprus & Greece, 'spice' was added to improve my life,
I suffered 'cuts' during the Revolutionary strife.

I came because of the British, to India,
But today China beat me to it,—even here.
Indians love me so very much, I know
But, in Sri Lanka is where I really did grow.

BY now I'm sure you must wonder who/What could I be?
While some geniuses, might have guessed already!!!
Their inner eye telling them, as I admit, my identity
That I'm really just a 'cuppa' called 'TEA'!!

(13.16)

A Dual season Friend!!.
Composed by: Leo DSouza, July 1,2013 at—2.12 am

I have just two seasons in my life,
when I'm most sought after
During which, I face all the strife
The remaining two, I'm forgotten thereafter.

I'm loved by Girls and Ladies more
I envelop them, as best I can
Boys prefer to leave me, if out they go.
so their skin gets the tan.

Young girls love me so very much,
As I'm attractive in looks and colourful too.
That's why, me, they love to hold and touch
My dresses of Stripes and pretty flowers, pink and blue.

My Grandparents, mostly in villages live
They're very simple unlike us
But equal protection they too give
Even through fields they go, without a fuss.

I have a long slender spine,
Around which my ribs twirl.
I don't grumble, if I'm shut anytime
Nor do I cry and Surl.

When I venture out with them on a Sunny day
I take the heat straight on my head,
Protecting my owner, all the way.
'becoz, of me, I'm sure, they won't be dead.

And when the sky begins to rain
I'm downloaded from the shelf and dusted down
Then willingly I go without a complain
Accompanying them, to any corner of the town.

My heads wet by the rain, but I don't catch a cold
I'm okay as long as my insides are dry
Now I'm sought by the young and old
If I could say 'No' I'm sure they would cry.

I've never ever had a Pumpkin Ride
I'm even far from the beautiful 'Cinderella'
I just give off my best, taking all in my stride
As your Poor and humble . . . 'Umbrella'

(13.17)

'A Thing . . . Like a King'
Composed by Leo DSouza. Jan 12,2013 at 12.20 am

I'm treated as though I'm a King
Even though, I'm just a thing.
A separate plastic coat and home to me is provided
On this, everyone's thoughts, are undivided.

My other colleagues, are dumped each time, with a clang!
In boiling water too, they are made to hang.
Lucky am I, daily by a Pretty Nurse, awoken wide
With a deft shake, then carried away, as she does stride.

I keep a check, on a Son or Daughter
Seeing at no time in health, they ever falter.
They shake me, suck me but, dare not chew
My High's and Low's, to them give out a clue.

Accompanying them even, when they travel
On me their dependence, is a marvel.
When little John was, one day very sick
Because of my help, they brought the Doctor quick.

I'm an integral part, of peoples lives
Seeking me out, is mostly the wives.
My 'Normalcy' often acts, like a balm
As Relief on their faces I see, then they are calm.

My New Gen too, have been born smart
Only digital figures, replacing markings on a body part.
They boast to us, that they have 'Class'
We reply, 'We for ages, have had, 'See Through Glass'!!

Sadly, we cannot wear even a smile
But, trudge through others lives, mile after mile
Our findings cannot be recorded on a meter
But, yet most sought out, by asking, 'Where's the Thermometer'!!

(13.18)

Friend or Foe . . . ?
Composed by Leo DSouza. July 24, 2013 at 02.40 am

From the time we're born you are there,
Like all children, you follow even mother everywhere.
Following Father coming home, late at night,
Walking sometimes, to his left, sometimes right.

Being a Guard, with little John and his dog,
As they run behind the garden log.
Suzi tries to shoo you away, from her doll,
'Cos she cannot understand, your presence at all.

Mum imagined you, crouching in the dark,
It turned out nothing, that was a lark.
You frightened me, one day in the forest, while I walked thru,
I remember, my friends joked, 'that I would be frightened of you'.

To learn all about you, I made a study,
Somewhere I read, they said you will be a 'buddy',
Some others said, you're just like a foe,
Habituated to creeping behind someone, more and more.

I scratched my head, thinking, to know you, what should I do?
Should I confront or blindly trust you?
I looked around, everywhere for a clue
Then in the far corner, with my friend, I spied you.

I was initially angry, 'cos I thought you were only mine,
But there you were, at the Bar, behind the Bottle of wine.
A tear came to my eye, I felt so sad,
The thought of you, deserting me, made me mad.

I decided with you, I'll settle the score
Once home, behind our locked bedroom door.
Then I met my friends, these two
Mr Physics and G.K. who, said they knew,

Promised they'll show, Your flirtatious ways, to me,
The reason how & why, everywhere you go, I see
Not just a little bit of me in you but, much, much more
After all, your scientific name all know, is . . . . 'SHADOW'"

(13.19)

Dreaming Big . . .
Composed by Leo D.Souza. July 19, 2013 at 3.02 am

I was lying against the building rail,
Ignominiously dumped, this is my tale.
Awaiting orders, to be put to use,
Sadly how-when-where, I myself, could not choose.

One day suddenly and roughly, I'm yanked up, by a crane,
Hauled up by pulleys, escape now, is in vain.
Strong Iron rods clamp down on me,
I bear all this, Oh! so silently.

Computerized matter is cut and put to size,
Sorted over and over, priority wise.
Selected views are put in place,
I'm hoping they'll lend me, honor and grace.

When all is ready, I too am so,
Being guided by a chain, I start to go.
All the feedings, I accept and ingest,
Changing my outlook, for me is quite a test.

I'm pushed along, as others come from behind,
Supervisors gaze at me, with a look so kind.
Occasionally a friend, is pulled out of line,
Keenly scanned, to see everything is fine.

When with thousand others, I am ready in fact,
I am now directed to the outward track.
Then loaded for an outbound trip, on a truck,
Bound for a 5 Star Hotel, I hope, I have that Luck!

But Lo!, I find myself at the Railway station,
where crowds are rushing, in utter confusion.
A train rolls in, packed to it's brim,
The situation to me, seemed very very grim.

I was carried into the train, pushed on a berth,
Was this my fate?, was this my Worth?
Hours later, abandoned was I
Thrown on the road, exposed to the sky!

I dreamt Big, but life narrowed, and began to taper,
After all, I was just an ordinary . . . . Newspaper!!

(13.20)

Life's Cut Out for Me!!!..
Composed by Leo DSouza. July 2, 2013 at 02.49.am

I was born for others Glory,
Giving a cutting edge to Fashion too
With cuts, I'm never Sorry,
'cos every slip of mine, becomes a fashion new.

Equally adept at Paper Craft,
I design latest hairstyles too,
And then you turn and call me,'Daft'
Saying, my style, makes a fool of you.

With my help, the hedge is so, so trim,
Pruned so proper is the Rose Bush
If I'm not sharp enough, The gardener looks grim
In pensive mood, as the wheel-barrow he does push.

Then to the Doctors I do go,
To get the bandages always cut.
With Open mouth, no teeth I show
How I wish I had them . . . . but.

In Hollywood or Bollywood I'm always there
The unwanted Scenes from Films, I remove
Dont you think that, that's fair?
Or, like me you'll be in a one track groove!

I work with everyone with equal zest,
'Cos if I fail, they're put to shame
I even work long hours, with no rest
And wish everyone, adopts the same.

The only Regret I do have, I admit,
is, I'm not tagged as 'His' or 'Hers'
Like others have always, somewhere writ
'Cos I'm just a common 'Scissors'

These could be used for the 'Flaps' for the Hard Cover, as also for the Flyers and 'Highlighters' for the Book.

What people said about My Poetry

Poetic Wonders

A book of beautifully rhymed Poems. Some very very touching! A Poet truly capable of bringing out varied emotions.. I Recommend it to all schools for Elocution Contests . . . **Audrey Coutinho D'Souza. Wife.**

This is so beautifully written Leo. U have painted a picture . . . a masterpiece in words. It's almost as if you were watching it all happen as u wrote it. I think this one needs to be published to make ppl aware" . . . **Chanella Cubbins**

On "LIFE IN MUNDANE INANIMATE THINGS"—

"Oh my gosh!!! This is so amazing, everything comes alive . . . . Leo Im at a loss of words of praise for this piece." Zoe Alvares . . . A Friend.

"This is a great piece, Leo! . . ." . . . Joy Jacob . . . Friend from Times of India Nagpur

"Oh! Cut Not Us Trees"!!

"This belongs is a middle school text book Leo!!! Lovely . . ." Chanella Cubbins...A fellow Poet.

"The Waiting Room in A Doctors Clinic"!!.

"Such a vivid description.. I could picture every patient sitting there" . . . Amelia Nazareth (Cousin)

"Its really good, things we would never think of putting into words u have put into verse well rhymed". <u>K Vallari Kumar</u> . . . My younger Sister.

"LABOUR CLASS"

'It gives such a vivid picture. We see it happening every where and for most it's become the norm . . . but to read it in verse like this in black and white, it hits you." . . . <u>Zoe Alvares</u>.

<u>Words of Appreciation From Relatives and Friends:</u>

Dear All

While thanking all my friends for their appreciative words, I have chosen a few, title wise, to include into this book of mine. It was your encouragement that made me continue.

<u>ON: Rail jacked Parents and I</u>

Chanella Cubbins: this one really had me going Leo :) beautifully mysterious right till the end.

<u>Chosen & Wanted Kids: Aug 12,2012</u>

Amelia Nazareth: Poet Laureate you've done it again! Just the theme I wanted you to write on . . .

Bart DSouza wonderfully written . . .

Chanella Cubbins: beautiful Leo. and so thoughtful too. I love the things you write about . . . . so well chosen.

<u>On: A POET FRIEND's SCORN: 11th Aug 2012</u>

Stephanie Ellis: A lovely honour you have bestowed on him.. you have given him so much importance.. takes a humble person to do that . . .

<u>ON: LIFE IN MUNDANE INANIMATE . . . Aug, 7th 2012.</u>

Chanella Cubbins love it Leo . . . simply love it!!! especially the door and his nose :)

How on earth do u manage to find the time to write so much Leo?

Joy Jacob This is a great piece, Leo!

Stephanie Ellis :fantastic out of the box example!

"An Unslipping Union"!!." A real lively imagination <u>Leonard DSouza</u>, so delicately

put . . . thanks! "<u>Beulah Butler Barradas</u>-Relative from Canada

On: The Clouds, Moon, Sky and Stars . . . Aug 6th 2012.

Kevin Lucio Pinto Brightens up a Gloomy day!!!Waiting to see all this Published in a Book of Poems Uiii)

Zoe Alvares Ooooo!!! Sun on a joy ride . . . . it really looks like that :) and the rebellious stars, haha . . . . lovely reading . . . .

<u>My Grandpa's walking Sticks: Aug 8, 2012</u>

Lost for words Leo . . . totally lost. I love the simplicity of topic and words. It's nice to read things that i can relate to—not some philosophical stuff that needs to be explained. This is real poetry to me.

Shabbir Shamsi Just wonderful . . . . **Chanella Cubbins!**

<u>On . . . and the morning after:Aug 5,2012</u>

Leo this is just another one of your most touching and beautiful poems. It is wonderful and so sad at the same time. I love the story in it . . . its a life story . . . a saga. So beautiful.It's the life story of so many people, you have captured in words. I love reading your work. it's always a story that i can close my eyes and picture it all happen right before me. it makes me smile, cry, and more . . . it's as if i can reach out and touch the things and people you write about. That's the best part of it all. **Chanella Cubbins**

Zoe Alvarez: Leo Your poem takes one into their lives . . . . you can actually feel their joy and pain with tears in your eyes. . . . .

Beulah Butler Barradas Thanks Leo . . . . you have the magic of letting others relive their school days . . . . wonderful!

A Weekly Market Place.—Aug 4, 2012

Katherine Gregory Love this one—so well written I can picture everything . . . . I loved the lines, 'While I used to Shake and Shudder, Someone would come asking for Liver'.

Chanella Cubbins this is so beautifully written Leo. u have painted a picture . . . a masterpiece in words. So simple and yet so beautiful and stirring. to anyone who has been to a market place and experienced this . . . . it is a walk down memory lane. to those who have not . . . . its a picture on their wall to marvel at.

Kevin Lucio Pinto Wow!!! Very well written Uncle!!!

Zoe Alvares Oh love this is!!!!! potatoes with eyes watched us count our notes . . . . ladyfingers with no rings . . . . Next I go to the market Im sure to remember these words :)))

Rebecca Gregory: This is awesome uncle :)

On OUR PRIME MINISTERS:

Audrey Coutinho D'Souza: Lots of research done I can see Husband Dear! :)

Beulah Butler Barradas :Leo . . . . you are well informed!

Chanella Cubbins: well informed Leo and this is so apt!!! :)

On: A Month Without you . . . 2nd July 2012

Keenan Lazarus: Leo yr words made me cry.

Bryan Nazareth Beautiful one Leo.::..they only get better just when I thought the earlier one was the best . . . its the best for the best . . .

Ruella Anne Charles Dsouza ☹ **U made me cry uncle . . . i want my papa back . . . :(**

Bruno van Eeckhout very beautifully written.

Fiona Nazareth another great one from you Leo . . . touching indeed!!!!

Cheryl MaGee Beautifully written Leo, brought tears to my eyes . . .

Louella Machado I've run out of words . . . still with my tears . . . we feel your pain..

Allan Dias Leo, Just can't find the right words to express how Beautifully you have written this . . .

Amelia Nazareth: I'm Speechless . . . coz when the heart is full words don't come easy . . . but sometimes emotions given vent to in the form of Poetry & that's what U r doing.

On: SALUTING EX-NAGPURIANS AS I REMEMBER THEM. 6ᵗʰ July, 2012

Zoe Alvares I didn't know these people Leo yet one can picture them as your narration is so vivid. Ever tried St. Paul Publication?

On: A Short Tour To The Land Above. July 25, 2012

Chanella Cubbins Leo this is awesome . . . . I love the way you have so many people fitted into it. this is real talent :) Absolutely love it. Please keep writing and I hope someday soon I see your work in print :)

Zoe Alvares Great idea to write about

On: A Note From Charlie: June 21, 2012

Cheryl MaGee This is beautiful Leo, brings back memories of all those lovely people who have passed on. God Bless you!!!

Louella Machado Wow Leo . . . . you took me down memory lane and brought tears to my eyes . . . .

Zurica Carton :This is just soooooooo beautifully put uncle :) I liked this way of yours in dealing . . . straight from the heart!!

Audrey Coutinho D'Souza I just have no words, so touching . . .

On: A Tribute to Joe Pitts June 13th 2012

Joy Jacob Well written Leo and a fitting tribute to a gentleman who sacrificed much for the CI

On: A Tribute To A Brother: From June 7th to 17th 2012

Minal Solanki: truly a poignant, touching tribute to your loving brother leo

Valerie Weller: Beautiful Tribute Leo . . . just Beautiful

ON: GLITTERING STARS: May 14, 2012

Stephanie Ellis . . . loved the star studded trail! Leo

Zoe Alvares So the stars in the sky do serve a purpose . . . very nicely put Leo!!! Love the Doris Day one best :)

On: Changing Seasons . . . May 13, 2012

Beulah Butler Barradas Please, please . . . gather all you have written and PUBLISH them!!!

Chanella Cubbins speechless Leo . . . absolutley speechless!!!! reminds me so much of days gone by . . .

On: Infatuation . . . 11 May 2012

Zoe Alvares Ah! such insight, lovely . . . . but Im sure HE also had his crushes :)

Sonia Lamba very well written uncle!!

Chanella Cubbins Leo you never cease to amaze :)

<u>On: Ode to a train driver: May 13, 2012</u>

Dunstan Gamble lovely done and said. Stephanie Ellis This one I love.

Chanella Cubbins Wow! it makes me nostalgic Leo . . . so real and true :)

On: . . . but she's not my child! May 03, 2012

Zoe Alvares Thanks Leonard DSouza, for being their voice. Please publish sooooon.

Chanella Cubbins beautiful Leo . . . this needs to be published so more people will think before they act and we will hopefully have less abused children in the world . . . Come on Leo . . . PUBLISH . . . this one is for a cause.

Ode to an Indian Farmer! April 29, 2012

Chanella Cubbins wonderful Leo. love it . . . . its so true. so many ignore the huge part these simple people play in our lives . . . we never stop to consider where we'd be without them.

Zoe Alvares The backbone of our country, overlooked and neglected. Thaks for writing about them, lovely.

On: Don't CRY MUMMY, DONT CRY!! April 24, 2012

Chanella Cubbins no words Leo . . . very very touching. and beautiful too. I dont know what else to say . . . truly lost for words

On: LOVE, BETRAYAL and Conquered LIFE April 22, 2012

Chanella Cubbins Leo this is absolutely great. So very real life!

Zoe Alvares TOPS!!!! Stephanie Ellis excellent piece

On: Summers in Nagpur Apr, 14, 2012

Audrey Coutinho D'Souza It's a cooling poem btw!

Beulah Butler Barradas Very descriptive . . . . great poem Leo!

On: The 14 Stations on the way

Chanella Cubbins beautiful Leo . . . . no words . . . . this is your best yet . . . . and it really hits home.

Audrey Coutinho D'Souza Beautiful!

Alyssa D'Souza Uncle, this is lovely, I agree, it is one of ur best yet!! :)

SWEET LITTLE THINGS IN PINKS AND BLUES!!—March 25, 2012

Chanella Cubbins hahaha you sure had me fooled again Leo . . . . wonderful! I love the way your mind works.

On Inseperable Love . . . March 21, 2012

Adrian Dmello · ha ha lol . . . . good 1 uncle . . . !!! Judith David How romantic.

Charlene D'Souza David hahaha, i thought he was going all mushy again!

On: CAN SIR???? Feb 07, 2012

Chanella Cubbins haha. good one. you had me guessing all the way to the end Leo.

On: FEAR CONQUERED: Aug 03, 2011

Wow!! I really like this one!! Leo . . . I would love to see these Poems " BOUND:" in a Book one day!!:)) **Patricia Heppolette (Poet & Ex Classmate in Australia)**

(vii)

Bianca Nazareth: **Arya Dental Clinic** is pleased. Poetry dedicated to it!!! Extraordinary!! :)

On: FULFILLMENT Oct 27, 2010

Louella Machado This is beautiful Leo! Very touching—strikes a cord in all of us . . .

Rebecca Gregory Praise God! This is such a touching poem uncle Leo, i really like it.

On: A Poet gone Blank . . . 20, Aug. 2012.

Chanella Cubbins totally awesome Leo . . . as always you have a beautifully penned poem . . . and one that rhymes too!!!! I always admire the way you rhyme so easily

ON: MOBILE PHONES . . . 21 Aug, 2012

Chanella Cubbins oh this is great Leo. I love your creativity and imagination. I would never never have thought of something like this . . . . ur able to write about anything and everything so easily!!! This deserves a standing ovation!

On: TWISTED NURSERY RHYMES IN VERSE!! 25 Aug 2012

Chanella Cubbins Leo this is a walk down memory lane with the element of surprise to it . . . this is a real masterpiece . . . . so very clever of you. you deserve a standing ovation for this one.

On: FLIGHT 264:

Kevin Lucio Pinto Wow!!! Very well written uncle . . . . Could almost imagine the sight while reading and just loved the use of the the travel jargon :-)

Chanella Cubbins lovely Leo. It is so real . . . evoked so many emotions . . . the suspense, the sadness, the anxiousness . . . and finally the relief.

On: Tribute to my Godmother . . .

Agnel V DSouza A great rhyming tribute & very aptly composed

Latisha Nazareth D'Costa Awesome work of art U.Leo

Marina Nazareth Well composed Leo—its a family picture in writing!!!

On: A Last Paintif prayer: 17 Sept 2012

Audrey Coutinho D'Souza So touching that it made me choke!!!!!!!!! With tears!!

On: The Best Age to Be . . .

Chanella Cubbins Oh so beautiful Leo . . . this is every childs and adults life for real.

On: The House is Quiet: 11th Sept,2012.

Jennifer Mathew beautiful poem uncle . . . .

Ruella Anne Charles Dsouza: Thnk u uncle . . . . dts all i cn say . . . . :)

On:Save Those Precious Drops!! ®© . . . 10ᵗʰ Sept,2012.

Chanella Cubbins so apt and so true Leo!!! wonderful. I am amazed at the way you write about such everyday things and problems and the realism of it all.

On: Oh! Cut not those trees: Sept 9,2012

Chanella Cubbins This belongs is a middle school text book Leo!!! Lovely

On: Girls deserve YES and Nod: 3ʳᵈ Sept,2012

Beulah Butler Barradas Well said Leo . . . . you are gifted!

On: Murder at Harmony. Sept 01,2012

once again I love the story Leo . . . tragic yet beautiful. I am waiting for the book :) i want to have them all on my book shelf: Chanella Cubbins

On: Bakers Knead . . . Our Dough.

i love the play on words Leo. it's wonderful the way you think. And now i'm wishing for those yummy cakes too. **Chanella Cubbins!**

On: Hanging For Life:

I swear I couldn't guess till the end..what suspense! **Amelia Nazareth**

On: My Alphabets:

Chanella Cubbins hahaha that is absolutely brilliant Leo!!!! never heard it this way before :)

The END

Friends, I Promise to be back.